Velocity Management in Logistics and Distribution

The St. Lucie Press Series on Resource Management

Titles in the Series

Velocity Management in Logistics and Distribution

Lessons from the Military to Secure the Speed of Business

Joseph L. Walden

Taylor & Francis
Taylor & Francis Group

Boca Raton   London   New York   Singapore

A CRC title, part of the Taylor & Francis imprint, a member of the
Taylor & Francis Group, the academic division of T&F Informa plc.

Published in 2006 by
CRC Press
Taylor & Francis Group
6000 Broken Sound Parkway NW, Suite 300
Boca Raton, FL 33487-2742

No claim to original U.S. Government works
Printed in the United States of America on acid-free paper
10 9 8 7 6 5 4 3 2 1

International Standard Book Number-10: 0-8493-2859-4 (Hardcover)
International Standard Book Number-13: 978-0-8493-2859-6 (Hardcover)
Library of Congress Card Number 2005040582

This book contains information obtained from authentic and highly regarded sources. Reprinted material is quoted with permission, and sources are indicated. A wide variety of references are listed. Reasonable efforts have been made to publish reliable data and information, but the author and the publisher cannot assume responsibility for the validity of all materials or for the consequences of their use.

Library of Congress Cataloging-in-Publication Data

Walden, Joseph L.
   Velocity management in logistics and distribution : lessons from the military to secure the speed of business / Joseph L. Walden.
       p. cm. -- (St. Lucie Press series on Resource management)
   Includes bibliographical references and index.
   ISBN 0-8493-2859-4 (alk. paper)
   1. Business logistics. 2. Industrial procurement--Management. 3. United States.
Army--Procurement. 4. United States. Army--Supplies and stores. 5. United States.
Army--Management. I. Title. II. Series.

   HD38.5.W343 2005
   658.7--dc22   2005040582

Taylor & Francis Group
is the Academic Division of T&F Informa plc.

Visit the Taylor & Francis Web site at
http://www.taylorandfrancis.com

and the CRC Press Web site at
http://www.crcpress.com

Dedication

This book is dedicated to my wife, Kay, and my two daughters,
Amber and Bobbi, for supporting me through the years and
for their love. Everything I do is for you.

Table of Contents

Acknowledgments

A special thanks to the folks at Richmond Events, Shane and Norma, for their support. And a special thanks to the baristas at the Starbucks on Barry Road in Kansas City for keeping me supplied with coffee as I worked on this book.

To Uncle Billy and Melinda, thank you for your friendship and support over the years and for your inspiration. I drew my leadership inspiration from you two close friends. I value your friendship—you are both very dear to me.

Barry Walker and Lonnie Keyes have provided me with friendship and moral support for over twenty years. Thank you for always being there.

Everything I know about working with people and leadership I learned from my dad, Thomas L. Walden, Sr.

Introduction

Forget logistics and you lose!

General Fred Franks

The supply chain is really an information business. The need for security for this information business is evident in the need to ensure an uninterrupted flow of supplies, goods, or services to the customer.

Karl von Clausewitz tells us, "Everything in war is simple, but the simplest thing is difficult. The difficulties accumulate and end by producing a kind of friction that is inconceivable unless one has experienced war." Friction may be external but it may also be self-induced by unclear mission orders or visions, complicated plans, vague communications, or lack of proper coordination or staff work.

An advertisement in the early 1990s for Oldsmobile proclaimed, "This is not your dad's Oldsmobile." Similarly, the supply chain of the 21st century is not your dad's logistics management system. *Velocity Management* will take you through today's supply chain and use examples from the military to demonstrate that today's supply chain is not business as usual and that this is not your dad's supply chain. In so doing, the chapters of this book guide the reader in ways to improve velocity while securing the supply chain.

What is velocity management? Many companies that I have spoken to or with over the past several years have clearly understood the need to manage the speed of supplies through the supply chain. However, velocity management is more than just the speed of supplies. Not unlike Six Sigma[1] and the Theory of Constraints,[2] velocity management is a shift in paradigms from what most of us have been taught since we entered the supply chain business years ago. The common mantra for years was, "More supplies on hand equates to better support to the customer." Velocity management as a process is discussed in great detail in Chapter 7 with examples of how the U.S. Army achieved world-class status in their supply chain processes.

The RAND Corporation, as part of a study for the Army, coined the term "velocity management" in 1994–1995. This study was briefed to then Brigadier General Tom Robinson, a member of the staff of the deputy chief of staff for logistics for the U.S. Army.

The Army of 1994 was still organized logistically for the Cold War. How many companies would remain in business if their business model was based on 50-year-old practices? Or, if they continued to treat logistics and supply chains as "business as usual"? Discounters such as Best Products, Zayre's, Arlens, and more recently, Kmart, have learned this lesson too late.

The Army over a period of about three years immediately following Desert Storm (Gulf War I), "downsized" from an Active Army[3] of 780,000 to 470,000. This "downsizing" was a result of winning Desert Storm and winning the Cold War.[4] The Army was left with a logistics infrastructure designed to support a major protracted war against the Soviet Union and the Soviet bloc countries. This logistics infrastructure was designed around the concept of mass. The more supplies that we stocked forward and in more locations, the better we could support a war. The logistics infrastructure had not evolved much over the course of the Cold War. We did move from the old 80-column card format IBM punch cards and the huge IBM computers that filled rooms while we were not in the field and when we went to the field the computers filled trailers. These trailers were very popular places in the summertime because they had to be air-conditioned to protect the big computers.

Although we moved from the big computers to desktop computers, we still used the 80-column card format. In fact, we still sometimes use the same 1950s technology 80-column card format today. And in 1995, we were still subscribing to the ideology that more is better and in addition to storage depots in Hawaii, Korea, and throughout Germany, there were 28 supply depots in the Continental United States (CONUS). However, the Army did set the stage for transformation in the logistics community prior to the start of the velocity management study and program. In 1992, the Army adopted an area of concentration or functional area for the logistics community and called the officers in this specialty area "multifunctional logisticians." This was the Army's first admission that a supply chain existed that crossed over the previously sacred functions of supply, distribution, maintenance, and procurement.

A recent book by the RAND Corporation based on their support to the Army made the Army's need for a transformation very clear on the book's first page. "For decades, the quality of Army logistics fell progressively behind best commercial practices. Army mechanics would wait on average a month for spare parts from distant supply depots in order to repair a 'down'[5] weapon system."[6] This was a byproduct of the mass-based supply system. Contrast the average time of more than a month in 1995 to the five days it took the North Korean army to provide similar resupply support to their forces in 1952 during the Korean War.

Remember, the more stuff on hand, the better we could support the needs of the soldiers. The typical metric used for the mass-based system is days of supply. The more days of supply on hand, the better the support: a philosophy of "big piles equals big support." This mass theory produced victories in World War II, the Korean War, and Desert Storm. This same mass theory produced 27,000 containers of unknown contents when Desert Storm was finished. Another byproduct of the mass theory of support was over one year's supply of ammunition, using a days-of-supply computation, in Saudi Arabia when all of the Desert Storm fighting was completed.

The underlying theory of the mass theory was that the larger the mountain of supplies, the more responsive the support system. This theory is only good if the right stuff is stocked in the right quantities. The theory of mass gave birth to the concept of "just-in-case" supplies. You know the type: "I'll stock this item just in case my customer ever needs it."

One large fallout from mountains of just-in-case stocks is the potential for loss, obsolescence, and damage. In commercial industry, a fallout of mountains of supplies could very well be excess stocks, a clogging of the reverse supply chain, or in the clothing industry a glut of last year's fashions and the inability to make room for this year's fashions. One prominent store while I was in college and through the mid-1990s was The Merry Go Round. For years, this store chain had the best line of clothes for young adults. They were ahead of their time in fashion (in fact, they were the Abercrombie & Fitch of their time). Then the inability to clear old fashion out and get new fashion into the stores resulted in the demise of the chain.

However, there are times when the large stockpiles can be beneficial. If the right items are not stocked or if there is a chance that the supply lines will be interdicted as they were in Iraq, a certain amount of just-in-case is a necessary evil. But only if the right stuff is stocked in the just-in-case inventories.

Is just-in-case a military phenomenon? Not exactly. Many commercial firms continue to stock just-in-case stuff because, "We have always done it that way." Have you ever heard that line in your company? We address that in the chapter on knowing yourself. One of the costs of just-in-case is the carrying costs for the inventory. You can justify some of those costs if the stockout would result in the loss of lives, but in everyday business, the cost of a stockout is not that critical. According to one "supply chain" expert at a Council of Logistics Management professional meeting, the cost of a new automobile is increased 25 percent by the carrying costs and holding costs of the car.

For the Army there was an alternative. Let's look at the RAND book again.

> There is an alternative to mass-based logistics that avoids its limitations. The alternative is to improve the speed and reliability of support processes so that cutters of the logistics system can receive what they need when they need it without having massive stocks in the area of operations. In short, the alternative to mass is velocity. . . . As the name "Velocity Management" implies, the initiative seeks to replace the traditional reliance on mass with the modern business concept of high-velocity processes tailored to meet evolving customer needs. This solution for the problems associated with the mass-based approach is the same for the Army logistician and for his commercial counterpart.[7]

The velocity management program solved a great number of peacetime problems for the Army but also created some wartime issues during Operation Iraqi Freedom. These issues are discussed at greater length in the chapter on velocity management and achieving speed in your supply chain.

Now that we have looked at the background that prompted the Army to look for ways to reduce mass and improve velocity, we need to look at what created similar situations in commercial supply chains.

In the 1950s and 1960s, there were distribution, materials management, transportation, supply, warehousing, and procurement. This led to the next wave of terms for what we do every day. In the 1970s, everyone became a logistician except for the procurement departments. By the 1990s, the next wave of terminology was introduced by consultants at what is now Accenture with the birth of the term "supply chain." All of a sudden, we all became supply chain managers. As we move forward in the 21st century, the next wave will be the advent of supply chain leadership.

The term logistics has its roots in the military. For that reason the basis of this book is to look at the lessons from the military and the military way of doing business to emphasize the criticality of achieving world-class logistics to the survival of a corporation.

It was not until after World War II that logistics moved from being a purely military term. George Thorpe's book, *Pure Logistics,* written in

1917, looked strictly at military logistics. Thorpe starts his classic book with, "Napoleon never used the word *logistics*. Of course he employed all the elements of Logistics necessary to war in his day, as he did the elements of Strategy and Tactics. But while he conceived of the two last-named functions as distinct divisions of labor, he did not realize (except, perhaps, when it was too late) that logistical functions comprised a third entity in war functions."[8] A great number of companies have fallen into a similar trap. They look at manufacturing and marketing/sales as distinct divisions of labor but do not realize until it is too late that supply chains are a third entity of the corporation and a necessary entity for profitability and success.

Later in his book Thorpe tells us, "Whether a nation's strategy be offensive or defensive, there are certain logistical functions, not always obvious, that should be active at all times."[9] Commercial companies are no different. Regardless of the company's strategy, there are some supply chain activities that may not be obvious but should be active at all times. A past president of the Council of Logistics Management stated this very clearly in an article in *Transportation and Distribution* magazine:[10] "Logistics done well is all but invisible."

I am often asked why I quote Sun Tzu regularly. The primary reason is that he seems to have grasped the importance of logistics and supply chains long before anyone else did. The early writings of Sun Tzu in 500 BC talked of the need to attack supplies and routes to win battles. Chapter 1 looks at supply chain security and the need to conduct risk assessments to identify vulnerable areas and weaknesses. The first part of the book (Chapters 1 to 3) covers the security aspect of supply chains. The next part of the book (Chapters 4 to 7) addresses how to achieve velocity in your supply chain. The final section (Chapters 8 and 9) looks at applying military theory, practices, and lessons learned to your supply chain. The final chapter provides a summary of the key themes and their applications to today's supply chains.

Risk Assessment/Management and Security

The first step in providing security for supply chains is to conduct a thorough risk assessment. That is the focus of Chapter 1, "Risk Assessment," and the use of information/intelligence to improve operations. The Army has a very methodical technique for analyzing and assessing risk before every training event and tactical operation. This chapter includes a detailed look at applying the Army's risk assessment program to commercial operations to mitigate risks. Included in this area is a discussion on the use of planning to identify the shortfalls and areas of weakness in a supply chain. Included in this theme is the idea of planning, developing multiple alternative scenarios, and then war-gaming these scenarios to ensure every possible contingency action is considered before implementing a plan of attack. This chapter also looks at ways of assessing the risks to the other links in the supply chains. Once these weaknesses are assessed, Chapter 1 then addresses how to plan for mitigating the risk from suppliers through collaboration.

A recent issue of *Logistics Today* magazine states, "Risk management takes a new shape in the extended supply chain. Risk management and the security of supply chains took on a new emphasis after the attacks of September 11, 2001, and the reactions of the world to security. Included in this heightened security awareness are initiatives such as C-TPAT and homeland security initiatives.

Chapter 2, "Risk Management and Supply Chain Security," first looks at the impact of events on supply chain security. Then it looks at how to establish a risk management program for your supply chain and the steps to take to improve the security of the supply chain and mitigate the risk inherent in global enterprises. One of the critical pieces for the security of the supply chain is the visibility of assets. Visibility is covered in this chapter with a look at how RFID will influence visibility and thus, security. This chapter looks at risk management methodologies and their applications to today's supply chain operations. Chapter 2 then looks at how to provide greater security to your supply chain by knowing what risks are inherent in the operation and then taking steps to mitigate the impact of the risk across the supply chain.

This chapter includes checklists and templates for risk analysis and assessment. In addition to looking at physical security of the supply chain, this chapter also looks at the requirements to provide security for information and data sources. It covers the need to provide increased security for the cash flows associated with supply chain transactions in light of the fact that the number of electronic transactions continues to increase exponentially every year.

Chapter 3, "Securing Your Supply Chain," is the final chapter of the risk assessment and security section. In military operations, security is a must. In fact, security is one of the universally accepted principles of war. To achieve effective supply chain management, security of your warehouse or distribution center is a must. Military supply chains also have to consider the possibility of the interdiction of lines of communications and attacks on transportation nodes. Failure to do so results in the inability to distribute supplies. Firms establishing an operation in a developing country have similar considerations to be successful. Establishing military supply chain operations in an undeveloped or developing country provides real examples of areas that must be considered in establishing commercial supply chain operations in a similar environment. One of the methods of securing military supply chains is the use of armed convoy escorts. This is a bit drastic for the security of commercial supply chains but the thought processes and the need for total asset visibility are not unique to the military. All supply chains have vulnerable areas that need to be assessed and secured to ensure that the company remains profitable and the customers get what they want, when they want it. This chapter addresses the ways to secure supply chains and ensure total visibility.

Supply Chain Velocity and How to Achieve It

Over 2500 years ago Sun Tzu told the King of Wu, "If you know yourself and know your enemy, you will be successful in all battles." Chapter 4, "Knowing Yourself, Your Customer, and Your Competition," looks at what Sun Tzu said about the importance of knowing yourself and your competition, the impact of this knowledge on your ability to succeed, and how that knowledge will enable success in supply chains. A well-drawn process map provides the ability to see the big picture and provides insights into the smaller details within the supply chain. This chapter looks closely at the benefits of "walking the process" and developing a detailed process map. Dr W. Edwards Deming repeatedly told audiences and clients, "If you cannot describe what you are doing as a process, then you don't know what you are doing." The development of the process map will enable the reader to "describe what you are doing as a process." The understanding from the process map will drive the improvement in the supply chain. The discussion looks closely at how the Army and commercial industry have developed techniques for "seeing yourself" and using that to improve your supply chains and customer order cycle times, and it also looks at why it is important to know your competition and your customer. Chapter 4 provides the reader with diagrams and techniques for developing understanding of the supply chain. This discussion looks at the type of flow charts that are useful in mapping the supply chain processes. It also looks at how to develop process charts and how to use them for training as well as problem solving. Included in this chapter are some applications to handle the problems discovered as a result of developing the process map. These discussions look at Six Sigma and the Theory of Constraints (TOC) as methods for bringing about change in the supply chain as a result of knowing yourself, your customer, and your competition.

Chapter 5, "Personal and Professional Development," addresses the need to keep yourself and your employees current and relevant in supply chain operations. In 2003, the U.S. Army spent over $1.9 billion on professional training beyond the initial entry training (basic combat training and advanced individual training). Toyota spent over $50 million to develop Toyota University to provide quality training for its employees. Before that, Motorola established two campuses for its Motorola University to train employees and others on professional development topics such as Six Sigma. Every year *Fortune* magazine lists the "Top 100 Places in America to Work." Every year the top firms listed provide professional training to their employees. This chapter looks at how the military and commercial supply chain firms meet the need to remain current and relevant in the supply chain business using corporate-sponsored professional development and personal professional development. In addition, this chapter looks at techniques for training teams and groups as well as individuals, and how to develop a training plan.

Chapter 6, "Leadership and Lessons for Leading 21st-Century Supply Chains to the Next Level of Excellence," should be self-explanatory. However, leadership remains a lot like love—everyone knows what it is but very few can really define it. Confusing this issue even more is the all too common mistaken view that management and leadership are the same thing. There is a great difference between the two. Although both are needed to keep a company running, the difference between a good and great supply chain or a good and great organization is the quality of the leadership. This chapter provides a discussion of leadership styles and techniques. The focus is on techniques and applications to improve the reader's style using examples from history to emphasize the key points. Too many theorists proclaim that leaders are born and not made. This chapter takes the opposite approach: leaders have to be trained and developed. People are not born with leadership skills and they certainly do not come out of the business schools with all of the necessary skills to be leaders. Included in this section on leadership are the methods for developing subordinates through mentoring and counseling. This section includes a detailed look at the attributes common to world-class leaders and how to develop these attributes in yourself and your subordinates. Chapter 6 provides the reader with a series of checklists and techniques used by the Army and world-class firms to develop leaders and the corporate culture necessary to allow leaders to grow and learn.

Just as speed, not haste, is important in conducting military operations, speed in supply chains is critical to meeting the needs of customers and may be the "order winner" that enables firms to keep their customers. Some firms have adopted the mantra of "Better, Faster, Cheaper." As the Department of Defense has learned over the past couple of years in Afghanistan, Kuwait, and Iraq, this mantra is not always the best way to support customers. Speed can take many forms in the supply chain. Chapter 7, "Speed and Velocity—How to Achieve Them," examines the areas in the supply chain that through a management of velocity can significantly improve operations. Specific examples detail methods for improving customer order cycle times. These examples show specific steps to take to improve cycle times within the supply chain. Included in this chapter are checklists and techniques for improving the velocity with which supplies and information move through the supply chain.

Military Theory, Practices, and Lessons Learned as They Apply to 21st-Century Supply Chains

Chapter 8, "The After Action Review," is a critical part of every military operation, training or real-world. One of the most successful developments over the past 20 years within the Army and the Department of Defense is the use of an After Action Review to assess how to improve operations. Corporate America has shown a great interest in the use of After Action Reviews during their periodic visits to the Army's National Training Center. This chapter provides a detailed look at the use of After Action Reviews to look at events and operations to determine what went wrong and how to improve an operation. This discussion includes an in-depth look at how the Army conducts an After Action Review and the training value of such a review. The key to the After Action Review is not in fixing blame but in assessing what went right and making sure that those actions are sustained, and what went wrong and how we can fix it. Chapter 8 looks at specific examples of how the After Action Review can be beneficial and the different techniques for conducting it, including specific guidance on how the Army conducts such a review.

Over the course of my 25 years of supply chain and military planning experience, I have seen a large number of good and bad operations. From these operations, Chapter 9, "Lessons Learned from Military Operations and the Application for Commercial Supply Chains," looks at how these key lessons from the military can be applied to today's commercial supply chains. In addition to drawing on my personal experiences, this chapter also looks at some of the lessons learned from operations in the Korean War, Viet Nam, and Operation Desert Storm. It then looks at some of the lessons learned from commercial ventures that are similar to some of these operations. From these valuable lessons, supply chain practitioners will be able to learn what pitfalls to avoid and will set the stage for achieving supply chain excellence.

In Chapter 10, "Conclusions," we tie all of the key themes from the three sections together and look at how the application of these themes to your supply chain will improve security and velocity while improving customer support and responsiveness. At the same time, the application of these themes will produce world-class results and improve the profitability of your company. This chapter looks at the interdependency of the themes and the need to master all of them to move from also-ran to world-class.

A recent article in *Inbound Logistics* magazine opened with the following comment.

> Two opposing forces are at work in the business today: the need to reduce costs and the need to improve service levels. Bolstering one almost certainly causes the other to suffer. For example, lower your inventory to reduce costs and it becomes difficult to meet varying customer demand. Increase safety stock to meet peak demands and you could wind up with a great deal of excess inventory on the books and nowhere to sell it.[11]

However, if you are subscribing to the velocity management principle of replacing mass with information to increase the speed of movement through the supply chain, you may very well be able to improve customer service and reduce costs and inventory piles at the same time. The added benefit is the reduction of excess goods on your shelf, thus providing more room to stock what the customer really wants and needs (better responsiveness to the customer's needs) and allowing you to save more money from less obsolescence and damaged or pilfered goods on your shelves.

Visibility of your supply chain provides you with more than a method of tracking goods and the ability to improve your supply chain velocity. Technologies such as Global Positioning System (GPS) devices help to improve your customer service by telling customers where the shipment is, thereby giving them a good idea of when the shipment will arrive at their receiving docks. This information improves their confidence in your ability to provide the goods and services that they need and improves their internal velocity by allowing them to plan around the projected receipt time and ensure that the maximum workers are available to offload the truck when it arrives.

> Army Logistics has undergone significant improvements in the past decade as a result of the lessons learned during Operation Desert Storm. Some of those improvements include the partial fielding of radio frequency identification devices (RFID). . . . In addition, Army Logistics has worked to reduce the "iron mountains" of materiel through better business practices and enhanced supply and distribution automation efforts.[12]

In other words, replacing the "iron mountains" so commonly associated with 20th-century military logistics with information will improve the supply chain operations and improve customer support. This book looks at ways that you can replace your piles or mountains of supplies or merchandise with information and better business practices to improve your supply chain profitability, efficiency, and effectiveness.

Notes

1. Six Sigma is the name given the process improvement program started by Motorola in the late 1980s. The goal of the Motorola program was to improve the quality of their products. Six Sigma is a measurement of variation away from the median of a process. The farther to the left of the median, the worse the quality. The farther the measurement moves to the right of the center line, the smaller the number of variations and the fewer quality issues resulting from the process. The literal measure of Six Sigma is 3.4 defects (or errors) per one million opportunities (also known as DPMO). Motorola and later General Electric, Penske, Honeywell, 3M, and others adopted the Define, Measure, Analyze, Improve, and Control (DMAIC) methodology for process improvements.
2. The Theory of Constraints (TOC) was first postulated by Dr. Elihu Goldratt in his classic book, *The Goal*. Like Six Sigma, TOC is a methodology for improving processes. For more on The Theory of Constraints, see *The Forklifts Have Nothing to Do!* published in 2003.
3. The Army of One is composed of three basic components: the Active Army or full-time soldiers, the U.S. Army Reserve, and the Army National Guard. With the onset of Operation Enduring Freedom and Operation Iraqi Freedom, the clear definitive lines between the "Active" Army and the other two components have become blurred as over 140,000 U.S. Army Reserve soldiers and Army National Guardsmen have been called to support the efforts of the global war on terrorism.
4. The fall of the Berlin Wall in 1989 followed by the collapse of the Soviet Union in 1991 marked the end of the 45-year-old Cold War.
5. A "down" weapon system is one that is not completely ready to perform the mission for which it is designed. A good example of a "down" system is your car when it fails to start because of a dead battery or a failed starter.
6. Dumond, John, et al., *Velocity Management*, RAND Corporation, Santa Monica, CA, 2001, p.1. This booklet from the RAND Corporation is a great reference regarding the detailed work that went into moving the Army from low class to world class in a short period of time.
7. Ibid., pp. 3–4.
8. Thorpe, George C., *Pure Logistics*, Franklin Hudson, Kansas City, MO, 1917, p.1.
9. Ibid., p. 68.

10. *Transportation and Distribution* is now *Logistics Today* and can be found at www.logisticstoday.com.
11. Simchi-Levi, David and Edith, "Inventory Optimization: The Last Frontier," *Inbound Logistics*, March 2004, p. 42.
12. "The New Paradigm: Bringing U.S. Army Logistics into the 21st Century," published by the Association of the U.S. Army as part of the Torchbearer National Security Report, April 2004.

About the Author

Colonel Joseph L. Walden has over 26 years of supply chain and leadership experience. He graduated from North Carolina State University in 1978 and entered the Army as a supply officer. His assignments over the past 26 years have included commander of the Distribution Management Center at the Army's National Training Center, program manager for the Army's Supply Chain Process Improvement Program that was given the Vice President's Award for Reinvention in Government, chief logistics officer and commander of the Logistics Brigade at Fort Irwin, California, and director of the Distribution Management Center for Operation Iraqi Freedom. He is a Certified Fellow in Production and Inventory Management by APICS, selected one of the "Top 20 Logistics Executives in America for 2002–2003," and was named the "2004 Supply Chain Practitioner of the Year" by *Supply and Demand Chain Executive Magazine*. Walden is a frequent speaker on supply chain issues and recently published a book on supply chains and leadership.

ASSESSING AND MANAGING RISK AND SECURITY

I

Chapter 1

Risk Assessment

If you do things the way you've always done them, you'll get the same things you've always got.

Darrell Waltrip*
Three time NASCAR Winston Cup champion

Prevention of security breaches results from a proactive, not a reactive security program. This chapter focuses on the first proactive step to securing your supply chain, risk assessment. The Army's doctrine on risk assessment is contained in *Field Manual 100-14, Risk Management*. Incorporated into risk management are two distinct phases: risk assessment and risk management/controlling risk. We start out by looking at risk assessment.

What is risk? According to the Mc2 Management Consulting Web site, risk is "a measure of uncertainty. In the business process, the uncertainty is about the achievement of organizational objectives. It may involve positive or negative consequences, although most positive risks are known as opportunities and negative risks are simply called risks.

The Army defines risk in *Field Manual 100-14, Risk Management*. According to this manual, "Risk is characterized by both the probability and severity of a potential loss that may result from hazards due to the presence of an enemy, an adversary, or some other hazardous condition. Perception of risk varies from person to person. What is risky or dangerous to one person may not be to another. Perception influences leaders' decisions."[1]

---

* Waltrip, Darrell, with Jade Guess, *DW-A Lifetime Going Around in Circles,* G.P. Putnam's Sons, New York, 2004.

This Army manual goes on to state,

> War is inherently complex, dynamic, and fluid. It is characterized
> by uncertainty, ambiguity, and friction. Uncertainty results from
> unknowns or lack of information. Ambiguity is the blurring or
> fog that makes it difficult to distinguish fact from impressions
> about a situation. . . . Friction results from change, operational
> hazards, fatigue, and fears brought on by danger. These charac-
> teristics cloud the operating environment: they create risks.[2]

In commercial supply chains and distribution operations, there exist
some of the same characteristics. There is always a bit of uncertainty in
the supply chains with threats to every link and mode of transportation.
There is friction brought about by the competing demands of increasing
customer support, reducing cycle times, and reducing costs and inventory.
There are certainly operational hazards, thus the OSHA forklift safety
certifications; there is risk created by fatigue, thus the hours-of-operations
regulations; and there is always a bit of fog that makes it difficult to
separate fact from impressions in some organizations. And anyone who
thinks that today's supply chains are not complex, dynamic, and fluid has
been away from the business for way too long. The terrorist attacks of
September 11, 2001 demonstrated to the entire world that an act of
terrorism can and will bring the world's supply chain operations to a
complete halt. This one incident should have identified some of the risks
inherent in every supply chain.

> *The tragic events of September 11, 2001 dramatically affected
> the entire world. Imagine if . . . a WMD device in a container
> within the sea cargo environment were detonated.*

Barry Brandman
Presentation on C-TPAT Requirements

Ports and sea environments were once considered safe from terrorist
attacks, yet in the Army we have always considered the need for port
security. This is but one reason why it is necessary to conduct risk
assessments and have a risk management program to provide security to
the supply chain.

How many moving parts do you have in your supply chain? Global
commerce has over 200 million cargo containers moving per year and
over 300 United States ports of entry. All of these moving parts mean
opportunities for terrorist activities. To get a glimpse of the impact of

closing a port from terrorist activity, just look at the 200-plus cargo ships backlogged in 2002 with the port closures on the West Coast due to the longshoremen's strike. The costs from these delays and port closures included the spoilage of goods and delays of critical supplies. Couple these known costs with an attack at an important airhead such as Los Angeles International Airport (LAX) or Memphis International Airport (MPS) and consider the impact on the United States and world economies. Reportedly, the U.S. economy lost approximately $2 billion a day immediately following the 9/11 attacks when all aircraft were grounded for four days. At the Army's National Training Center, on September 11, 2001, we were in the middle of assisting one brigade-sized unit (approximately 6000 soldiers and 3000 pieces of equipment) in their preparation for return to their home stations and were getting ready to receive another brigade-sized unit at the National Training Center for a month of intense realistic training in the Mojave Desert. Preparing to return to home stations is a very maintenance- and logistics-intensive period of time in which there may be as many as 6000 repair parts ordered over the course of a day. The impact of the terrorist delays on parts arriving from the East Coast meant over a week in delays in receiving the parts. This meant that soldiers, potentially needed for contingency missions, were delayed in fixing their equipment and then delayed in returning home because their aircraft were not allowed to fly. In addition, the restrictions on air flights meant that the helicopters at Fort Irwin were not allowed to fly to the aviation maintenance facility located about 45 minutes away.

Now that we have established what risk is and that it may in fact exist in our supply chains, what is risk assessment and how do we identify risks in the supply chain and in our processes?

For years, the term risk has been associated with insurance assessments and investment activities. So how does this insurance and financial term apply to the 21st-century supply chains? Today's supply chains are under constant risk in the forms of terrorism, loss, pilferage, obesity of stocks (way too much stuff on hand), natural-disaster interruptions, labor interruptions (such as the 2002 dockworkers' strike on the West Coast), commercial espionage, or obsolescence of stocks. Anything that can interrupt your ability to provide the expected level of support to your customers should be considered a risk to your operations.

The Army uses risk assessment to determine the risks to the soldiers and equipment required for an operation and the overall risk to mission accomplishment. We use a similar approach in this chapter to establish a methodology for assessing supply chain risks. The next chapter looks at how to manage risk after we have identified the potential risks to our operations.

The risks to your supply chain can take a variety of forms. The more dependent supply chains become on information technologies and cyber-technologies, the more vulnerable they will become to external risks and interruptions. Risks such as obsolescence of stocks, damaged goods, stock obesity, and pilferage are internal risks and are usually easier to identify.

The risk to cyber-technologies led to the development of the Department of Homeland Security's National Cyber Security Division (NCSD). This division was created as a result of the Presidential National Strategy to Secure Cyberspace and the Homeland Security Act of 2002. This new division provides the United States with 24/7 cyberspace analysis, alerts, and warnings coupled with information-sharing and analysis to prevent potential cyber-attacks. In addition, the NCSD analyzes vulnerabilities and identifies risks to provide protection to cyber-infrastructure.

Financial companies and resource managers have fulfilled similar functions regarding resources for decades. In 1983, the United States Army Signal Center established internal control reviews to conduct audits of all resource management functions. The purpose of these audits and reviews was to identify areas that were vulnerable to waste, fraud, or abuse and to establish controls to ensure that the vulnerable areas were safeguarded and monitored.

The purpose of risk assessment is very similar to the actions of the resource management community. The purpose of risk assessment is to identify those areas of the supply chain that are vulnerable to interruptions in support flow.

An article dated March 1, 2004, on www.insurancenetworking.com by the managing editor, Therese Rutkowski, titled "A New Look at Operational Risk," asked the question, "Who knows what the future holds?" The preface of the article stated, "Insurers are beginning to understand the necessity of taking a new, more proactive approach to assessing their own risks of loss related to people, processes, technologies, or external events."

The article goes on to say "These 'operational risks,' as defined by the Bank of International Settlement (BIS) in its proposed Besel II accord,[3] are exemplified by events and failures such as Enron and WorldCom, the power outage in the Northeast last summer (2003), the continual stream of viruses infesting the Internet, and of course, the September 11 terrorist attacks."[4] These operational risks that affect the insurance and financial industries also pose threats to supply chain processes.

Rutkowski goes on to say, "But operational risks also include everyday failures, such as employee errors, systems downtime, and the loss of key talent." Again, these are risks to your supply chain as well. How do you identify these risks? Can you do this from your office or do you have to get away from the computer and e-mail and physically walk the process? Are the risks controllable or systemic in nature and beyond your control?

The only way to define risks is to walk the process, look at what is being done, and analyze the plans for the future to see what risks are inherent in those plans.

The Royal Bank of Canada's executive vice president, Grant Hardy, is responsible for risk assessment and management for the bank. Hardy identified the risks to the Royal Bank through a system of self-assessments similar to the resource management internal control reviews discussed earlier. The goal of the Royal Bank of Canada's programs is to get these assessments to become part of the culture of the bank and encourage the employees to coordinate, oversee, and assess risk in their respective areas.

David McNamee in an unpublished paper sponsored by the New Zealand State Services states,

> A year from now is going to be somewhat different from today, and one hundred years from now will be very different indeed. If each tomorrow would be exactly like each today, there would be no need for the study of risk. . . . Risk management practices of yesterday focused largely on hazard insurance and probable risk. Risk management today focuses on the broad issues of general management. Managers put assets at risk to achieve objectives.[5]

Although McNamee was writing about the insurance industry, he is right on target for supply chains as well. Every day in the operations of supply chains, managers risk assets to get the proper quantity of the proper items to the customer. When this happens, risk occurs to the flow of the supply chain.

Before getting into the details of conducting a risk assessment, let's take a look at an example from the Army of what can happen when a proper risk assessment is not conducted. A lack of proper risk assessment is evident in the 1993 Blackhawk helicopter crash at the Wiesbaden Air Base in Germany. On the same helicopter that fateful evening was the deputy corps commander (an up-and-coming major general with great potential for continued success and advancement in the U.S. Army; the deputy corps commander is basically the chief operating officer for the 65,000-soldier U.S. Army Corps stationed in Germany), the operations officer for the corps, and the intelligence officer for the corps. All three of these important officers perished when the Blackhawk helicopter crashed on the landing approach to the air base. The loss of these three key leaders left a void in the leadership team for the Army in Germany at a critical time of deployments to Croatia, Somalia, and preparation for possible deployments to Bosnia. A proper risk assessment would have identified the potential risk of having so many key leaders on the same helicopter, even in peacetime. The conduct of a proper risk assessment would have probably placed the officers in different helicopters to prevent such a loss from occurring.

The use of the process map will assist in identifying risk areas or parts of the supply chain with the greatest vulnerability to risk. The key to such a self-assessment is to establish a climate where the workers and managers are willing to be open and honest about the operations and vulnerabilities. When the Army first started the internal control review and assessment program, the program was almost punitive in nature, which defeated the purpose of the program. If an area was deemed to be vulnerable, an annual report, in detail, was required and additional painful forms were necessary. The pain of the additional reports, questionnaires, and forms encouraged workers to not identify vulnerable areas. This was worse than no program at all because workers aware of risks did not identify them to prevent having to submit to the process required by the resource managers.

Let's take a look at how the Army assesses risk. The Army got into the risk assessment business after analyzing the breakout of the causes of casualties in armed conflicts. The Army discovered that they were experiencing more losses from accidents than from enemy fire. In fact, the number of accidental casualties increased almost 20 percent between World War II and Desert Storm. Risk management for the Army is a five-step process. These five steps are:

1. Identify the hazards.
2. Assess hazards to determine risks.
3. Develop controls and make risk decisions.
4. Implement controls.
5. Supervise and evaluate.

Obviously, the first two steps involve identifying and assessing hazards and determining their associated risks. These steps are the focus of this chapter. Chapter 2 focuses on the final three steps of managing and controlling the risks. In order to identify and properly assess the potential threats to an operation, it is necessary to discuss the planning process used by the military. A clear understanding of the planning process will enable the reader to understand when the risk assessment takes place in the process. In addition, there are some great applications of this planning process to supply chain operations.

Just what is the military's planning process? The military planning process is often called the Military Decision-Making Process.[6] This process is a detailed methodology for looking at an operation or mission and developing, comparing, and analyzing multiple courses of action or alternatives for solving the problem or accomplishing the mission.

The Military Decision-Making Process helps leaders to examine a situation and reach logical decisions. It assists the leader by allowing the leader to apply thoroughness, clarity, sound judgment, logic, and professional knowledge to reach a decision. The model is a detailed, deliberate, and sequential process when time allows. When time is critical as it sometimes is in war, as well as in making supply chain decisions, an abbreviated version of the model can be used. Some of the advantages of this model over other methodologies for problem solving are:

- It analyzes and compares multiple courses of action to identify the best possible action.
- It produces integration, coordination, and synchronization for an operation.
- The model minimizes overlooking critical aspects by looking at multiple actions and reactions.
- When followed, the Military Decision-Making Process model results in a detailed plan.
- This model provides a common framework that enables parallel planning at multiple echelons.

The Military Decision-Making Process model is a sequential model that includes, for the purpose of this discussion, the following steps:

1. Receipt of a mission
2. Mission analysis
3. Course-of-action (alternatives) development
4. Course-of-action analysis
5. Course-of-action comparison
6. Approval of the recommended alternative
7. Rehearsal
8. Execution of the mission or operation

Now let's take a closer look at each of the steps in the planning or decision-making process that have an impact on risk assessment.

The first step in the process is that of receiving a mission or task that must be accomplished for the success of the supply chain or the organization. This mission can come from anywhere, corporate headquarters or customer statements of need.

The next step in the planning process is mission analysis. Exactly what is the boss asking us to do or what is it that the customer is really asking for and what do we need to do to meet their needs? The steps in the mission analysis phase are:

1. Analyze the higher headquarters' order or the identified problem.
2. Determine the specified, implied, and essential tasks. What tasks were specified implicitly by the higher headquarters' order for us to do? What are the implied tasks that must be accomplished in order to meet the mission requirements or solve the problem that has been identified? Which tasks are essential to completion of the mission or solving the problem?
3. Review available assets to accomplish the mission or solve the problem. Do you possess the resources to successfully accomplish the mission?
4. Are there any constraints that will limit your ability to meet the requirements of the higher headquarters or the customer?
5. What are the critical facts and assumptions? For this discussion, facts are statements of known data and assets available for the mission. Assumptions replace necessary but missing or unknown facts.
6. The next step in the mission analysis is to conduct a risk assessment. What risks are you willing to take in accomplishing this mission? What are the risks to the organization if this mission is not successfully completed? This is where we get into the meat of a risk assessment. The goal of our risk assessment is to identify and find weaknesses before the competition or terrorists.

The course-of-action development phase is the next step in the Military Decision-Making Process. During this step, you have to determine the feasible alternatives to accomplish the given mission. Obviously, for every given mission one potential course of action is to do nothing and hope the problem will go away. This is not usually a viable course of action and could very well be the reason for the problem's existence. This alternative is much like the solution Jenny gave to Forrest Gump in the classic movie of the same name. Jenny's solution was, "Run, Forrest, run!" Choosing to do nothing or run from the problem or mission usually is not a feasible alternative.

The final step of the Military Decision-Making Process that has an impact on the assessment of risk is the course-of-action comparison step. During this step of the decision-making process, the emphasis is on highlighting the advantages and disadvantages for each alternative developed. This includes determining which alternative has the highest probability of success and poses the minimum risks.

Before we delve into the process of conducting a risk assessment, this is a good time to establish a common understanding of terms used by some companies in the conduct of risk assessments. Although these terms come from the insurance world, they are applicable to our look at supply chain risk assessments. The Mc2 Management Consulting Web site has an online glossary of risk assessment terms that are germane to this discussion to provide a common framework and understanding.

1. *Absolute Risk:* Pure risk without the mitigating effects of Internal Controls.
2. *Accepting Risk:* A Risk Management technique that allows management to weigh the cost of managing the risk versus the benefits of reducing the risk. Risk acceptance is a matter for the Governance Team of senior management and the Board. The amount of acceptable risk should be determined beforehand.
3. *Avoiding Risk:* A Risk Management technique of redesigning the task to deal with a different set of risks (usually lower). Not to be confused with Eliminating Risk.
4. *Containment:* The Risk Management strategy that attempts to limit the negative Consequences of a Risk Event. This strategy can include Internal Controls and Contingency Planning.
5. *Contingency Planning:* Examines one uncertainty at a time as a base case and develops a response to that uncertainty. Can also be the sum of all such plans that deal with many different uncertainties. If defined as the metaplan, certain events might trigger a particular branch or subset of the contingency plan to be executed.
6. *Control Risk:* The tendency of the Internal Control system to lose effectiveness over time and to expose, or fail to prevent exposure of, the assets under control.
7. *Data Flow Diagrams:* A graphical depiction of the major flows of data and how these flows are linked. Used in place of Flow Charting. Useful in Risk Identification and Risk Scenarios to determine the points of greatest Exposure.
8. *Eliminating Risk:* An unrealistic ideal akin to perfect Control. See Avoiding Risk.
9. *Flow Chart:* A graphical depiction of the major tasks and activities in a function and how they are linked. Useful in *Risk Identification* and *Risk Scenarios* to determine the points of greatest *Exposure*. A detailed discussion of the use of flow charts is in Chapter 4 and ties the flow-charting process in Chapter 4 to risk assessment.[7]

Risk decisions should be based upon awareness rather than mechanical habit.

U.S. Army Field Manual 100-14, page 2-1

How do you conduct a risk assessment/risk analysis of your operations? According to the Army's *Field Manual on Risk Management*, the first step in assessing risk is to identify the hazards. This manual defines hazard as

> . . . an actual or potential condition when the following can occur:
> ■ Injury, illness, or death of personnel
> ■ Damage due to or loss of equipment and property
> ■ Mission degradation.[8]

"Hazards are found in all operational environments."[9] Today's supply chains are no exceptions. Granted the daily hazard that may cause the death of personnel in 21st-century supply chains is not great, except from accidents. The hazard or risk of damage, loss of merchandise, injury to personnel, and mission degradation are everyday risks to your supply chain. Mission degradation can come in the form of the physical or emotional health of your employees, hazards to the links in the supply chain during specific operations, or risks from extended missions or extended supply chains. You are trying to establish the impact of such hazards and the probability of the risk occurring. In addition, you must determine the severity of the hazard based on your knowledge of the impact of similar past events.

A good methodology for conducting your risk assessment is found in a modification of the Six Sigma steps. Six Sigma, as employed by General Electric, 3M, and other major companies, incorporates five distinct steps to bring about quality improvements and customer service improvements. These five steps are:

1. Define
2. Measure
3. Analyze
4. Improve
5. Control

For the risk assessment, the first three steps, Define/Measure/Analyze (DMA), are important. Improve and Control are used during the management of risk and are discussed in the next chapter.

Defining the problem or situation is accomplished in the Military Decision-Making Process step of receipt of mission. This purpose of the Define phase of risk assessment is to determine exactly what is expected, what mission we are trying to accomplish, or what customer needs we are trying to meet.

The following questions should be answered as part of the Define phase of risk assessment.

1. Who is the ultimate customer or user of the product?
2. Who, if any, are the intermediate customers?
3. What are the processes necessary to meet the customer's needs/wants/desires?
4. Who are the key players/contributors?
5. Who are your suppliers?
6. Who are your suppliers' suppliers?
7. What are their sources?
8. What are their processes?
9. How do their processes affect your operations?
10. What are your information requirements?
11. Do you need to do an information systems analysis to identify potential risks? This may be your greatest source of risk.
12. Are you doing a trade-off of stockpiles of merchandise/materials for information? This will increase your information vulnerabilities.
13. Are you moving toward just-in-time? Sometimes the emphasis of just-in-time supply systems causes new risks or opportunities for risk of security breaches, thus creating the need for the C-TPAT initiatives.

The outcome of answering these questions and defining your processes and risks may very well be the production of a process map. One of the collateral benefits of a process map is that it provides a clear picture of the processes and potential risk points and vulnerable points in your processes. This picture provides a great training tool for your employees.

Once you have answered all of the questions and developed the process map/vulnerability map, the next step is to measure the severity of the risks that were identified in the Define phase.

In the Measure phase of the assessment, you need to conduct vulnerability assessments. In the Military Decision-Making Process, this would take place in the mission analysis step, as well as during the course of the action development step. These assessments may come in the form of self-assessments, similar to the Army's internal control reviews. In a self-assessment, every individual section of the organization does a self-assessment of its area to identify potentially vulnerable areas. The key to these self-assessments is to spot-check the completeness and thoroughness of the self-assessments. One solution to this is to bring in an external team to look at some of the vulnerable areas identified or those identified by similar departments at other locations.

Other ways to measure your vulnerabilities include supplier certifications, ISO 9000/9001 programs, or through the use of external consultants that conduct the entire assessment for you. The main purpose of this phase is to focus the efforts of the analysis phase of the risk assessment.

During the analysis phase (mission analysis and course-of-action comparison), the goal is to determine the impact of the identified risks on your mission accomplishment. During this phase, you will identify those risks that can impede, impact, or interrupt your ability to meet the customers' needs. The data from the Measure phase of the assessment enables you to stratify the severity of the risks and develop a plan to focus on those areas with the greatest ability to affect your operations based on the level of vulnerability, probability of occurrence, and the cost to protect against and minimize or reduce the impacts of the risks to your supply chain operations.

The use of the Military Decision-Making Process to develop a plan coupled with the first three steps of Six Sigma—Define/Measure/Analyze—provide you with a solid framework for identifying risks and the start of a plan to minimize, mitigate, or possibly even eliminate risks to your supply chain.

Chapter 2 discusses how to develop a risk management plan and the necessity of one in order to develop a plan of action to secure your supply chain, as detailed in Chapter 3.

Summary

Risk is anything that can hamper your ability to move supplies, merchandise, or materials through the supply chain and any area that is vulnerable to attack, loss, interdiction, interruptions, or delays in your supply chain and information systems. The U.S. Army conducts a risk assessment before every mission to ensure that risks to soldiers and equipment are considered and that all potential risks to mission accomplishment are identified and considered in the planning process, commonly referred to as the Military Decision-Making Process, and in the execution of a mission.

This same process has applicability to your supply chain operations. Although the risk of loss of life is not as great in supply chain operations as in military operations, there are inherent risks to today's supply chains that must be considered and planned for. These risks include incidents such as the September 11, 2001 terrorist attacks, the dockworkers' strike on the West Coast in 2002, and the blackout in the northeastern United States and Canada in the summer of 2003.

Risk Assessment

Military Decision-Making Process	Risk Assessment Steps	
	Identify hazards	Assess hazards
Mission Receipt	X	
Mission Analysis	X	X
Course of Action (COA) Development	X	X
COA Analysis	X	X
COA Comparison		
COA Approval		
Rehearsal	X	X
Execution	X	X

Figure 1.1   Risk assessment steps and the Military Decision-Making Process.

Figure 1.1 is adapted from the Army's risk assessment program. Figure 1.2 provides an example of a Risk Management/Assessment Questionnaire as shown on the Mc2 Management Consulting Web site. Figure 1.3 provides an example of a matrix from the Army's *Field Manual* for comparing risks and determining the most dangerous risks to your operations.

Questions for Thought

1. What are the risks to your supply chain?
2. How can you identify these risks and the severity of the potential impacts on your operations?
3. How can you use the Military Decision-Making Process to plan your operations and conduct a risk assessment?
4. Is Six Sigma applicable to your assessments?
5. Are the state-of-the-art technologies creating new impacts on or risks to your supply chain operations?
6. What areas cause the greatest risk to your operations?
7. What are the ways you can reduce, mitigate, or minimize your risks?
8. Can you completely eliminate risk from your operations?
9. Does cooperation with supply chain partners increase or decrease your risks?

Mc^2 Management Consulting

Risk Management Questionnaire

Date:
Name:
Title/Group:
Location/Telephone:

1. What is the Purpose/Mission/Objective of this work unit?
2. What are the primary strengths of this work unit?
3. What obstacles do you see that affect your goals and objectives?
4. If you had additional resources to help you achieve your objectives, what would they be?
5. What is the worst thing that could happen in your work unit?
6. What is the worst thing that has already happened in your work unit?
7. What are the critical interfaces (other work groups), and which give you the most concern (and why)?

"OK to reproduce, use, or modify in anyway helpful to you."

Figure 1.2   Sample risk management/assessment questionnaire.[10]

Risk Assessment Matrix						
		Probability				
Severity		Frequent A	Likely B	Occasional C	Seldom D	Unlikely E
Catastrophic	I	E	E	H	H	M
Critical	II	E	H	H	M	L
Marginal	III	H	M	M	L	L
Negligible	IV	M	L	L	L	L

E – Extremely High Risk
H – High Risk
M – Moderate Risk
L – Low Risk

Figure 1.3   Risk assessment matrix.

Extremely high: Loss of ability to accomplish the mission if hazards occur during mission. A more frequent probability of catastrophic loss (IA or IB) or frequent probability of critical loss (IIA) exists.

High: Significant degradation of mission capabilities in terms of the required mission standard, inability to accomplish all or parts of the mission, or inability to complete the mission to standard if hazards occur during the mission. Occasional to seldom probability of catastrophic loss exists. A likely to occasional probability exists of a critical loss occurring. Frequent probability of marginal losses exists.

Moderate: Expected degraded mission capabilities in terms of the required mission standard will have a reduced mission capability if hazards occur during mission. An unlikely probability of catastrophic loss exists. The probability of a catastrophic loss is seldom. Marginal losses occur with likely or occasional probability. A frequent probability of negligible losses exists.

Low: Expected losses have little or no impact on accomplishing the mission. The probability of critical loss is unlikely, while that of marginal loss is seldom or unlikely. The probability of a negligible loss is likely or less.

Book List for Introduction and Chapter One

1. Dumond, John, et al., *Velocity Management*, RAND Corporation, Santa Monica, CA, 2001.
2. Thorpe, George C., *Pure Logistics*, Franklin Hudson, Kansas City, MO, 1917.
3. *U.S. Army Field Manual 100-14, Risk Management,* Department of the Army, Washington, DC, 2000.
4. Walden, Joseph L., *The Forklifts Have Nothing to Do!*, iUniverse, Los Angeles, 2003.

Notes

1. *U.S. Army Field Manual 100-14, Risk Management,* Department of the Army, Washington, DC, 2000, p. 1-1.
2. Ibid., p. 1-2.
3. The BIS Besel Accord is very similar to the Sarbanes–Oxley reporting requirements in the United States.
4. Rutkowski, Therese, "A New Look at Operational Risks." Available at www. insurancenetworking.com/protected/article.cfm?articleid=2248, March 1, 2004.
5. McNamee, David, CIA, CISA, CFE, CGFM, "Risk Management Today, Tomorrow."
6. For a detailed discussion of the Military Decision-Making Process as it pertains to supply chain issues, see Chapter 4 of *The Forklifts Have Nothing to Do!* by Colonel Joseph Walden, CFPIM.
7. McNamee, David, www.mc2consulting.com.
8. *U.S. Army Field Manual 100-14, Risk Management,* Washington, DC, 2003, p. 2-1.
9. Ibid., p. 2-3.
10. http://www.mc2consulting.com.

Chapter 2

Risk Management and Supply Chain Security

A real knowledge of supply and movement factors must be the basis of every leader's plan; only then can he know how and when to take risks with those factors, and battles are won only by taking risks.

A.C.P. Wavell[1]

Risk management is fundamental in developing competent and confident leaders and employees. Is risk management important to your company? Absolutely. The failure to effectively assess and manage risk may very well make your operations too costly after the fact. It is better to assess and develop a program to mitigate or minimize the risk in your operations before embarking on the operation. In Chapter 1, we looked at risk assessment. Once the assessment is complete, it is time to focus on how to manage the risk or hazards identified in the assessment. This chapter addresses developing an effective risk management program.

Are all of the threats to your supply chain external? Your assessments during the risk assessment process should have identified all of the internal and external threats to your supply chain. This question brings back the story of Brian Bosworth, the Oklahoma Sooner and Los Angeles Raider linebacker, in *Sports Illustrated* in the late 1980s. In an interview with *SI*, he told of his days working in an automobile manufacturing plant during his summers in college. During this interview, Brian Bosworth spoke of the times he and his friends tried to intentionally mess up the cars they were being paid to build. Part of your risk management plan has to look at the management of risks from inside the supply chain. This is the easiest part to control and the area that can quickly disenfranchise customers.

> *Be prepared to do things differently than you did the rest of your career.*

William H. Lyerly, Jr.
Director, Office of WMD Operations and Incident Management,
Department of Homeland Defense

The Army's *Field Manual* on risk management provides the following principles for establishing a risk management framework.[2]

■ "Integrating risk management into mission planning, preparation, and execution." In supply chain operations, the planning, preparation, and execution of operations must consider risk management and the hazards/risks identified in the risk assessment. This is necessary in order to minimize or mitigate the impacts created by these risks to the successful support of our customers—both internal and external.
■ "Making risk decisions at the appropriate level in the chain of command." Leaders and managers at all levels must be willing to make risk decisions that affect their operations after carefully considering the facts and the potential severity of the risk. The potential severity of the risk determines the level at which the decision should be made. For example, as the theater support commander at the Army's National Training Center, if the risk assessment determined that the risk associated with an operation was moderate, I allowed the battalion commanders to make the decision. They always made sure that I was aware of the decision and the rationale for the moderate risk decision. And they had the confidence that they had my support, which then gave them the confidence to make the decision without fear of retribution. However, if the mission involved using helicopters, the call was reserved at my level if the subordinate commander deemed the risk high. This was done not because I did not trust the subordinate commanders but to allow me to provide better top cover for them in case something did indeed go wrong. Any operation deemed to be a high risk required careful consideration before allowing the mission to go on in a training environment. Obviously, in a wartime

situation the assessment and analysis would still be performed but there is a willingness to take greater risk based on the specific situations.

■ "Accepting no unnecessary risk." Leaders and managers at their respective levels, regardless of the type of operation, have to "compare and balance risks against mission expectations and accept risk only if the benefits outweigh the potential costs or losses."[3] In supply chains, or any other operation, there is no difference. The reason people are placed in management or leadership positions is to make decisions on risk based on the potential payoffs. In a gambling casino, the greater the odds (or risk) to a number on the roll of the dice or on the roulette table, the greater the payoff if that number shows up.

In commercial operations, the same is true, if you are willing to take risks after careful consideration and analysis, you will probably reach greater heights of excellence and quality in your operations. However, remember that there is always a great risk in doing nothing. That risk is that the competition will meet your customers' needs rather than you and you will be out of business. Take a look at Figure 2.1. It could be any

Figure 2.1   A prominent distribution center that chose the option of doing nothing rather than take some risks to improve operations.

> **Risk Management Assists the Leader or Manager in:**
> (adapted from US Army Field Manual 100-14, *Risk Management,* Figure 1-2)
>
> ---
>
> • Conserving resources while avoiding unnecessary risk
> • Deciding on the approval of an alternative
> • "Identifying feasible and effective control measures where specific standards do not exist" (FM 100-14, Figure 1-2)
>
> **Risk Management Does Not:**
>
> • Take away the leader's/manager's initiative or decision-making ability
> • Eliminate risk or establish a climate of zero defects (we have all been through that too many times!)
> • Allow the leader/manager to violate any laws

Figure 2.2   Risk management.

operation in the world, but the significance of this facility is that they had a chance to improve their operations with only a low level of risk and chose not to. Now they are no longer in business.

The Use of Risk Management

One of the uses of risk management within the Army that has applicability to commercial operations is training using realistic conditions while ensuring the avoidance of unnecessary risks during critical training exercises (see Figure 2.2). Another key area that affects risk management is the skill level, experience, and expertise of the leaders and managers that are involved in an operation or training event. Obviously, the higher the experience and expertise levels of the trainers, the better prepared they are to identify risks inherent to the operations.

> Risk management does not convey authority to violate the law . . . or deliberately disobey local, state, or national laws. It does not justify ignoring regulatory restrictions and applicable standards. Neither does it justify bypassing risk controls required by law, such as life safety and fire protection codes, physical security, transport and disposal of hazardous materials and waste, or storage of classified material.[4]

Completing a risk assessment does not provide you with a license to cut corners or take shortcuts. An example is the OSHA regulations for forklift operators. You may conduct a risk assessment and determine that because of the aisle widths, pallet weights, fork truck driver experience, and so on, the OSHA rules do not apply to you and use your assessment to justify not certifying your operations. This is not the purpose of the assessment and risk management program. In addition, you certainly will not convince an OSHA inspector that your assessment provided you the excuse not to properly certify your drivers.

One of the ways the military controls risk as part of the risk management plan is through the use of what is known as the Intelligence Preparation of the Battlefield. This process links risk management to security and planning. According to paragraph 1-1 of the draft *Field Manual 2-01.3, Intelligence Preparation of the Battlefield,*

> Intelligence Preparation of the Battlefield is a systematic, continuous process of analyzing the threat and environment in a specific geographic area. It is designed to support staff estimates and the military decision making process. Applying the intelligence preparation of the battlefield process helps the commander apply and maximize his combat power at critical points in time and space on the battlefield.

A risk assessment and risk management plan for a supply chain or any other operation is also a continuous process of looking at the competition, the customer desires and needs, and the internal environment. This process helps a company's leaders and managers to maximize support to the customer, internal and external, with the minimal amount of risk to the operations.

Intelligence preparation of the battlefield and, yes, sometimes the corporate environment is not unlike a battlefield of sorts, includes the following steps.

1. *Define the battlefield environment.* What are the significant characteristics of your supply chain environment? What are the limits and constraints on your operations as identified by your risk assessment?
2. *Describe the battlefield effects.* What are the effects that affect your operations? In the military we analyze the effects of terrain, weather, history, assets available to us and to the enemy, and the available information or intelligence. From a commercial perspective, that would be the operational terrain, the effects of weather on your operations (the year-round weather conditions and location combined to make Memphis the location of choice for the Federal Express hub), the history of operations (the outcomes of similar operations), and the marketing research or sales history for a similar item or service.

3. *Evaluate the Threat.* Identify and assess the threats or risks to your operations. What are the capabilities of the competition to better meet the consumers' requests or wants? What are your high-value targets? A high-value target is where you will get the greatest return on your investment. Do you need to conduct more marketing research to ensure that you have considered all possible threats to your operations?

4. *Determine threat courses of action.* What are the competition's alternatives and potential actions in response to your new product or service? What can the competition do to counter your offering to better serve the customer? Are there any key situations or events that will tip the competition's intentions? How will the consumer or customer react to the new offering? Will a new incentive upset old customers? All of these questions must be considered in developing the plan to mitigate the potential risk from the actions of the competition and the customers.

The use of intelligence preparation of the battlefield provides military commanders with information about the enemy and the operational environment, and how these factors may affect an operation. Using the same concept will provide supply chain leaders with similar information on their operations. In addition, this process can also serve as the starting point for situational awareness and seeing yourself as discussed in Chapter 4. Additional benefits from applying this process to your operations include better knowledge of the competition. Sun Tzu tells us that if you know yourself and know your competition you will be successful, have a better understanding of your business environment, and have a framework for visualizing your operations into the future.

There are a number of questions that this process should address and answer in order to effectively mitigate or minimize risk.

1. What do we know about the competition and the customer? What are the competition's core competencies? What does the customer really want? How can the competition better meet the needs of the customer now?

2. What can the competition no longer do? Why did they lose that capability? Why did they stop providing that service or product? You may find out that the competition stopped offering that service because it was not profitable. If so, why was it no longer profitable? Do you have a way to provide the customer the service more efficiently and effectively and still make a profit?

3. What can the competition do? In addition, what can they do in reaction to your new product, service, or process?

4. What are you going to do about it? How can you position yourself above them in the eyes of the customer?
5. Do you need to consider any additional facts or make assumptions? If you are going to make assumptions about the capabilities of your operations or the competition's, you need to make sure that the facts are relevant to the operation. You also need to make sure that your assumptions are valid and necessary. For an assumption to be valid and necessary, you have to ask the question, "If I do not consider this will it affect the outcome?"
6. Are you reacting to the actions of the competition or are you the leader in the field? Is this causing the competition to develop reactionary plans to counter your new products or services? It is always better to cause the reaction than to be the one reacting.
7. Do you need to develop a procedural manual for the new service or process? Manuals and Standard Operating Procedures (SOPs) help to mitigate risks by providing operators with standard procedures and a reference that provides standards for the operation.
8. Is there an impact on your profits? What is the impact of this operation on the bottom line for your company, section, or division? Is there an impact on the image of the corporation? If the impact will be negative, this is not a good alternative course of action. What is the risk to the bottom line or the reputation and is the value gained worth the risk?

The answers to these questions provide the basis for the risk management plan. The Army uses the form shown in Figure 2.3 to capture all of this information on one page for a quick decision on the severity of the risk and to form the basis for the risk management plan.

How do you protect against risk? In the next section we look at several areas of risk that may affect your operations including cyber-risks, information technology risks, risks from pilferage, and risks to your supply chain operations from terrorists.

We start with cyber- and information-technology risks to supply chain operations. The first example of a risk to your operations is computer viruses. These have started appearing at an alarming rate over the past couple of years and can have an enormous impact on your ability to communicate with your customers. The move toward more automated systems and less face-to-face communication exacerbates this problem.

Recently a virus/worm attacked the computer systems at Fort Leavenworth, Kansas. This worm came in a seemingly innocent e-mail to one of the employees in the Army's Command and General Staff College. By the time this worm was found, almost every computer and all of the servers were infected. The result was a shutdown of the entire information

A. Mission or Task:			B. Date/Time Group Begin: End:		C. Date Prepared:
D. Prepared By: (Rank, Last Name, Duty Position)					
E. Task	F. Identify Hazards	G. Assess Hazards	H. Develop Controls	I. Determine Residual Risk	J. Implement Controls ("How To")

K. Determine overall mission/task risk level after controls are implemented (circle one)

LOW (L)   MODERATE (M)   HIGH (H)   EXTREMELY HIGH (E)

Figure 2.3 The Military Decision-Making Process and risk management (from *Field Manual 100-14, Risk Management,* Figure 2-1, p. 2-1).

systems for the college during a critical time in the academic year. The outage lasted on and off for several days.

Just before my departure from Kuwait in April 2003, a virus attacked our servers at Camp Arifjan, Kuwait. E-mail service was down for three days. My office mail was forwarded from Fort Irwin, California, to the Arifjan system during the last weeks of my tour in Kuwait. This was a measure taken to make sure I was up to speed when I returned to my command at the National Training Center. All automatically forwarded mail was removed from my Fort Irwin mailbox by the system, when the mail was not accessible in Kuwait because of the virus shutdown; all of those messages were lost. Can you afford to have your systems down for three days?

What is your backup plan? My loss of information was a mild irritant, but what would it do to your business to lose three days of orders?

The introduction of the Strategic Studies Institute book, *The Information Revolution and National Security*, states,

> The Chinese symbols for "crisis" mean both danger and opportunity. This might also be true of revolutions, including the information revolution.

The information revolution is a phenomenon that defies simple characterization. Its origins lie in the not-so-distant past—the British code breakers at Bletchley Park during World War II created "Colossus," the world's first working computer.[5]

The opportunities gained from this revolution are endless, however, so are the dangers and the increased needs for information security. The U.S. military has long worked under the premise of "who needs to know" or only on a "need-to-know basis." Corporations need to adopt this same mindset. This does not mean keeping necessary information from the workers, but it does mean that information that is sensitive in nature should be protected and secured.

This information revolution created today's most powerful business tool, the Internet. The Internet has moved well beyond the "secure, nuclear-proof communications system for the military"[6] to a business necessity and the source of a host of opportunities and dangers. Without the Internet, the threat of computer viruses would be minimal, but the speed of business would be greatly affected. "While the United States is the world's superpower in information technology, driven primarily by the corporate sector, our dependence upon information systems creates enormous vulnerabilities."[7] If you do not believe that we are tied to our computer systems, how often has your e-mail server gone down? What was your response? In some offices I have been in the response has been, "The Net is down. How can I get any work done?" Or how often have you heard, "I sent you an e-mail. How come you have not responded?" when you know you never received that mail.

How dangerous and susceptible to viruses are you? Edmund Glabus of the Aegis Research Corporation explains, "The virus allows one to leapfrog across geography—it is easier to inject a computer virus across oceans than any other kinds of viruses. . . . It is difficult to coordinate responses to information warfare attacks, especially from viruses, and this may allow an enemy to exploit the U.S. reliance on information superiority and just-in-time logistics."[8] Viruses may well be the informational equivalent of a weapon of mass destruction when you consider the potential economic impact they can and do have on commercial industry. If for no other reason, consider the amount of money your company spends annually to protect against computer viruses.

What about cyber-terrorism? In a 2000 presentation and article titled "The Cyberterrorist Threat," U.S. Air Force Lieutenant Colonel Gregory Rattray explained cyber-terrorism.

It is the destruction or disruption of information and systems. The idea of mass disruption in particular is getting lots of play in public. It might be possible to cause train wrecks with underlying switching technology, but one would need lots of data. Crashing the stock market is the classic case of what you would do to disrupt the United States, and we do see stock markets disrupted by information problems. It would be difficult for us to recover from would-be data corruption of stock market databases, such as the disruption of clearing and settlement of trades, which would raise questions about every trade and create long-term complications. There are also some gray areas like attacks on the media, disrupting CNN, and attacking computer portals.[9]

How do you protect your information? The military uses classified systems, sophisticated virus protection programs, and telephone systems that provide security for conversations. Obviously from the above situations, these do not always protect against cyber-threats. How secure is your data? Even the giant Microsoft had some of its proprietary code published on the Internet. One of the best-kept secrets in the world is the exact formula for Coca-Cola. Imagine the impacts on business and profits if the formula for Coke were released on the Internet or the secret recipe of Kentucky Fried Chicken were released to the public. This ties into operational security, which is discussed in detail in the next chapter. How do you secure your data against attack, virus, code theft, or loss? One risk management technique is information synchronization. Cyber-security is the largest mission of the Secret Service and the fastest-growing area of crime.

Another risk to your information and communications is the proliferation of cellular telephones, camera cell phones, miniature recording devices, and pen-size disks.

The foreword to the Army War College's Strategic Studies Institute book, *The Information Revolution and National Security*, states, "The current era has seen more rapid and extensive change than any time in human history. The profusion of information and the explosion of information technology is the driver, reshaping all aspects of social, political, cultural, and economic life."[10] This explosion of information technology, very prevalent in supply chains, creates opportunities for breaches of security. Look at Figures 2.4 through 2.6, recently distributed by the Department of Defense on the new risks of technologies. These new technologies, coupled with other devices such as miniature digital recorders in a pen or camera phones, enable employees to capture more information than fit on my first three computers combined, on a device that fits into their pocket. This makes the theft easy and security of information extremely difficult. In addition to their portability, their small

Security Risks With New Technology

Mass Storage

Miniaturization

Imaging Technology

Wireless Technology Advances

Bottom Line

- Don't assume the device is legal in the facility
- Contact the Security Office if you have any questions
- Inquire about technical details of proposed purchases before ordering items

Figure 2.4   Department of Defense slide #1.

Security Risks With New Technology

New Technology poses new threats to security, not limited to Computer Security
Next Generation Devices, new devices and miniaturization

Thumb Drive

- Key Chain Size
- Requires no external power
- Flash RAM
- 8MB – 512 MB
- $15 - $900
- IBM version (and others) need no driver
- Limits RAM

Figure 2.5   Department of Defense slide #2.

size makes it easier for an employee who is legally transferring data to lose the small device.

These new devices and cellular telephones provide what the military calls "open source information." For the military, "open source" information is a valuable way to piece together what the enemy or potential enemy is doing. Open source information is just that; it comes from unclassified and open sources. In commercial industry, the Internet has made so much of what was previously not open source information into open source.

Figure 2.6 Department of Defense slide #3.

How do you protect your information? Equally important is how current is the open source information that you are using to make your decisions. When the "outdated" maps did not reveal the location of the Chinese Embassy in Belgrade, Yugoslavia, in 1999, the result was the accidental U.S. bombing of the embassy and an international incident. However, the Internet was current enough to show the exact location of the Chinese Embassy. Make sure if you are basing an important decision on open source information that the information is accurate and up to date, otherwise your decision may be as flawed as the decision to bomb the Chinese Embassy and may lead to big problems for your company.

> *Businesses are finding new ways to organize themselves to carry out risk assessment and management and to provide critical and timely services. There is much for the military to learn from the business community about flexible organization, and the private sector can learn a great deal from the military about things like redundancy of critical systems.*[11]

Another important area of risk that has to be considered a severe risk opportunity is the threat of terrorist attacks on your supply chain. The hardest area to protect against is bioterrorism attacks on food supplies. Since September 11, 2001, there has been a great move to protect against this threat to foods coming from outside the United States. The threat or risk from food supplies comes from lack of proper handling as well as terrorism. Look at the food poisoning incident in Pennsylvania in 2003.

The green onions at a Chi Chi's in Pennsylvania were fertilized with human feces unbeknownst to the procurement offices or the operators of the restaurant. The result was a large outbreak of food poisoning. Another example of not conducting a good risk analysis is the case of salmonella poisoning after a truck previously used for eggs was used to transport an ice cream premix. This incident infected 250,000 people. Both of these incidents occurred because of carelessness but provide an example of how easy it is to import bioterrorism to your supply chain. Do you know where your raw materials or food supplies come from?

The incident of only one case of foot and mouth disease in the United States is estimated to have an impact of $60 billion on the economy. Economic terrorism/bioterrorism tools only have to give the perception of the threat. With a credible threat, there is no need for an actual bioterrorism weapon. The cost to Great Britain was over four million animals destroyed and the dismissal of the Minister of Agriculture and Farming due to a loss of confidence in the ministry. Again this was not an act of terrorism but it does show how easy it is to infect a link in the supply chain and create havoc on the ability to give your consumers confidence in your operations. A good risk management plan will enable you to overcome such an event. Look at the plan put in place by McNeil Laboratories and Johnson & Johnson in 1984 after the cyanide-contaminated Tylenol. Would you prefer to have the consumer confidence that Johnson & Johnson received or be the Minister of Agriculture and Farming? The choice is yours and a good risk management plan will be the deciding factor.

Although technology should not be the driver of your risk management plan, emerging technologies create both risks and opportunities to counter risks. Look at the sophistication of the Wal-Mart point-of-sale/logistics system. This system is so sophisticated that it can tell where there is a spike in the sale of cough syrup in one particular store. This information passed to the Centers for Disease Control (CDC) allows the CDC to analyze the information and determine if the spike is from an act of terrorism or simply a reaction to nature.

Look at the risk of pilferage from your activities. The March 2004 *WERCsheet* addressed this topic. *WERCsheet* is a publication of the Warehousing Education and Research Council. Reducing shrinkage is risk management. "The first step to reducing inventory shrinkage is understanding the underlying causes of the problem." According to *WERCsheet*, some of the contributors to shrinkage include the following.

■ "Inaccurate receipts." This can be solved by automating the counting process. Too often shrinkage occurs because of miscounting by the receiving teams.

■ "Inaccurate counts during the physical inventory." This can be solved as we did at the National Training Center by putting a third shift on with the responsibility of conducting cycle counts. The third shift was not interrupted by the constant stream of customers or receipts and usually, with the exception of high-priority walk-throughs, worked uninterrupted, and became more accurate in cycle counts. In fact, over a six-month period, inventory accuracy rose from 84 percent to 99 percent by using this third shift of counters. In addition to their counting responsibilities, the third shift was used for location maintenance, housekeeping duties, and pulling requisitions for the next day's issues.

■ "Not recording or accounting for damaged product that is scrapped or disposed of." Again the use of the third shift, the move from semi-annual wall-to-wall inventories to cycle counting, and the careful review of all inventory adjustments helped us to identify this problem and quickly rectify it at the National Training Center.

■ "Inaccurate prices in the system." The Army with the help of the RAND Corporation tackled this problem several years ago. RAND published a book, *Pricing Policies,* in 2001 that discusses this problem in detail. Basically what the Army discovered was that there were prices that changed every single month and when an order was processed, dictated what price was charged to the customer for the item. Think about that for a moment. You place an order for an item through a Web site or catalogue, you pay for the item with a check, and the check clears the bank for an amount much larger than you recorded in your checkbook. In some cases in the Army the difference was as much as $10,000. Try to balance your checkbook with those curves thrown at you. After the RAND study was complete, the Army fixed the pricing problems by limiting the price changes and fixing the information systems so that the customer paid only what was reflected as the cost of the item on the day of the requisition and not on the day of receipt.

■ "System inaccuracies in the receiving/shipping process." The best way to identify these inaccuracies is to walk the process and use the techniques in Chapter 4 on "Knowing Yourself."

Why is shrinkage from pilferage increasing? According to the March 2004 *WERCsheet* from the Warehousing Education and Research Council there are three main reasons.

1. The Internet has "increased the ability to turn stolen goods into cold cash."

2. "Redirected law enforcement resources." The focus on the war on terrorism has taken away assets normally used for detecting and arresting corporate pilferage.
3. "Lenient criminal penalties." According to the WERC research, the punishments for those who are caught are not enough of a deterrent to prevent future incidents of pilferage.

You need to do a thorough risk assessment or audit of your security systems. The military constantly monitors loss-prevention systems. Regular tests of alarm systems and monitoring devices will assist in reducing pilferage. Do not wait for a major occurrence of pilferage from your operations before you take action. Several years ago a distribution center in Germany lost a large number of night-vision devices from their distribution center. It took several weeks to notice that the items were indeed lost. Why and how? The alarm systems were not fully functional, so when an often-used door was found open, no one was alerted. The other and probably the major contributing cause that enabled this to go on undetected was the housekeeping of the warehouse in which these particular items were stored. Because the managers of the center did not enforce standards of organization and housekeeping, these night-vision devices (critical to the Army's ability to see at night and potentially deadly in the hands of the wrong people) were placed on a mobile cart and moved around this particular warehouse for several months prior to their disappearance. Part of your risk management program has to include the setting and enforcement of standards to prevent such pilferage.

How does risk management affect you? Every link in the supply chain is a potential security target. Does your company have a response plan? Risk management also includes natural disasters and their impact on the supply chain. There is a Federal Response plan for such disasters, natural or technological.

What is a catastrophic incident to your supply chain? Only if it hits CNN? The proliferation of news services and the Internet makes it easier to get information out. But any incident that hampers your corporate image, reputation, or ability to support your customer is a potentially catastrophic event that needs to have a risk management plan and a risk assessment. Look at the anthrax scare in Washington, DC. The discovery of anthrax at the post office received the news coverage. What was not covered was that this closure of the post office branch almost bankrupted the local electric company because of the nondelivery of mail to that region. The closure of the post office branch meant that there were no deliveries to the post office boxes in the branch. This meant no cash flow from the customers and therefore a shortage of cash to pay suppliers and employees.

Other potential risks that need to be addressed in the risk management plan include the impacts from the recently enacted hours-of-service rules for truck drivers. Although one prominent food management executive commented in March 2004 that the new rules were a "non event in our world. In the first 3 months of the new rules, only one truck has had to stop to keep from exceeding the Hours of Service rules. And, that truck was in the middle of Wyoming." This may be a rare exception but as time passes the hours-of-service rules will affect your supply chain operations. In Chapter 7, "Speed and Velocity—How to Achieve Them," we look at some of the ways to counter the effects on velocity from the implementation of these rules.

Is collaboration a risk to your operations? Is it a benefit to your operations? Only a careful assessment and analysis will reveal the answer to these questions. The keys to mitigating risks associated with collaboration are the following.

1. Make sure everyone involved understands the goals and the objectives of the different trading partners that are involved in the collaborative efforts.
2. Openly share information between trading partners.
3. Periodically review transportation opportunities. Are the partner constraints costing you business or opportunities to maximize truck loads or time-definite deliveries?
4. Adopt an open approach to communications with your trading partners.
5. If you find out that the partners are using your information to compete with other companies or your competition, get out of the collaborative partnership immediately.

Conclusions

The former Speaker of the House, Tip O'Neil, once said that all politics are local. Politics may be local but all supply chains are global and because of that the risks inherent in their operations increase and therefore the need for a risk management plan and the need for security increase. The next chapter looks at developing a supply chain security program.

Risk management looks at consequence management. A quality risk management program focuses on the consequences that may result from the risks and hazards identified in the risk assessment and the effects of the action. Focusing on the action or risk itself and not the effects and how to counter them is analogous to treating the symptom and not the disease.

As we show in the next chapter, there is a direct relationship between security and risk management. Even a good risk management program can have loopholes if all possible risks are not thoroughly considered. A good example of this is the security in 1996 in Atlanta, Georgia, for the Olympics. Every "possible" precaution had been taken to ensure that a terrorist attack did not disrupt the pageantry and events of the Olympics. And yet, one disgruntled bubba was successful in attacking the Centennial Park and forever marring the games. How difficult is it to identify a one-person cell? Perhaps the threat to your organization is not from the outside, from a computer virus or hacker. Your risk may very well be a one-person cell of a single disgruntled employee. Can that happen to you?

Look at the U.S. Army in Kuwait immediately after the start of Operation Iraqi Freedom. In a base camp in Kuwait a sergeant threw a grenade into a tent of sleeping soldiers to protest the war. The result was several dead and wounded soldiers and a unit with a wounded morale. At Fort Lewis, Washington, a disgruntled National Guard soldier was arrested in February 2004 for trying to sell information to the insurgent leaders in Iraq. As security conscious as the Army is, these types of incidents can occur. How security conscious is your company and could one employee with a computer virus on a "thumb drive" take out your communications and information systems?

You have to manage risks, not react to them. The only way to manage risk is to first assess your vulnerabilities. Once these vulnerabilities are identified, you can then establish a program to manage and mitigate the risks. Failure comes from becoming risk averse or not properly identifying your risks.

There is a potential trade-off between security issues and velocity. According to John Ramsey of the Computer Emergency Response Team Coordination Center, "Little academic work is being done in the area of the speed of business. Just-in-time logistics in business is everywhere. At the Chrysler plant in South America, parts arrive just two hours ahead of when they are needed. Wal-Mart has no stockroom; each store instead has a satellite dish which enables it to order resupply as needed." Now this is no surprise to anyone in the supply chain business for more than a couple of weeks. But the implication here is that these moves that happen just-in-time provide opportunities to make trade-offs between security and velocity. Interruptions can take the form of a natural disaster, a terrorist attack, or a breakdown in the electric grid. Part of your risk management program has to address this issue.

In Chapter 1 we looked at the Military Decision-Making Process in relation to risk assessment. The following chart (Figure 2.7) shows the complete decision-making process and the risk management steps. This chart provides you with a guideline for when to do risk assessment and when you should move from the assessment to risk management.

Military Decision-Making Process	Risk Management Steps				
	Step 1 Identify Hazards	Step 2 Assess Hazards	Step 3 Develop Controls and Make Risk Decision	Step 4 Implement Controls	Step 5 Supervise and Evaluate
Mission Receipt	X				
Mission Analysis	X	X			
COA Development	X	X	X		
COA Analysis	X	X	X		
COA Comparison			X		
COA Approval			X		
Orders Production				X	
Rehearsal[1]	X	X	X	X	X
Execution and[1] Assessment	X	X	X	X	X

[1]All boxes are marked to emphasize the continued use of the risk management process throughout the mission

Figure 2.7 Example of risk management form.

Discussion Questions

1. Does Radio Frequency Identification (RFID) have a place in risk management plans and security? Most definitely! In Chapter 7, we look at the impact of RFID in increasing velocity and visibility in your supply chain. RFID has a role in security of containers. An RFID-enabled seal provides security and visibility of the container. This enables the tracking of the container through the entire supply chain and will immediately send a signal if there is tampering with the seal.
2. Explain the relationship between risk assessment and risk management.
3. What are the risks to your operations?
4. Are your greatest risks internal or external?
5. Is there a risk inherent in your collaborative efforts?
6. What is the risk to your operations from the hours-of-service rules? Is there a risk or is it as the one executive said, a "nonevent"?

Book List for Chapter Two

1. Wavell, A.C.P., *Speaking Generally,* Cambridge Press, London, 1946.
2. *U.S. Army Field Manual 100-14, Risk Management,* Washington, DC, 2000.
3. *The Information Revolution and National Security*, ed. Thomas E. Copeland, Strategic Studies Institute, Carlisle Barracks, PA, 2000.
4. Brauner, Marygail, et al., *Pricing Policies*, RAND, Santa Monica, CA, 2000.

Notes

1. Wavell, A.C.P., *Speaking Generally,* Cambridge Press, London, 1946, pp. 78–79.
2. *U.S. Army Field Manual 100-14, Risk Management,* Washington, DC, 2000, p. 1-3.
3. Ibid., p. 1-3.
4. Ibid., p. 1-7.
5. *The Information Revolution and National Security*, ed. Thomas E. Copeland, Strategic Studies Institute, Carlisle Barracks, PA, 2000, p. 1.
6. Ibid., p. 2.
7. Ibid., p. 3.
8. Ibid., pp. 83–84.
9. Ibid., p. 89.
10. Ibid., p. v.
11. Ibid., p. 7.

Chapter 3

Securing Your Supply Chain

We have proved to our management that good security is good business.

Ann Lister
Texas Instruments[1]

Why do you need to provide security to your supply chain? If you completed the risk assessment discussed in Chapter 1, you realize the number of risks that are inherent in your supply chain operations. You must protect the supply chain from the inside and from external risks. You must protect the entire supply chain. To borrow a term from the U.S. military, you have to protect your supply chain from the "factory to the foxhole," in other words, from the first delivery of raw materials until the product is delivered to the ultimate customer. Your supply chain concept requires end-to-end security and visibility to ensure that your products get where they are intended to be, when they were promised to the customer, and in the condition promised. Rita Mihalek told a group of senior executives at the 2003 Logistics and Supply Chain Forum, "No marketing, sales, purchasing, or delivery efforts mean anything to the customer if the products are held up by security at the border and can't get delivered on time."

Another reason for the requirement for security is to prevent chaos or mass disruption to the supply chain. Even the threat of disruption is enough to cause some degree of chaos and equates to a terrorist success; the threat of attack is enough to win and have impacts. Look at the British Air cancellations in 2003/2004 during the December 2003 holiday periods and again, like Air France, during the Super Bowl weekend 2004 as a result of "credible information sources."

Bob Galvin, the former CEO of Motorola, has been quoted several times as saying, "There is a new truth: quality improvement is not just an institutional assignment; it is a daily personal priority obligation." The newer truth is that supply chain security is now a daily personal priority obligation for every person in your supply chain or business. The first line of defense for supply chain security is your people. Quality is based on the actions of people. Quality is a personal obligation and a personal responsibility. In today's world, security is also a personal obligation and a personal responsibility.

In a post-9/11 world, security has become a vital link in global supply chains. As governments tighten borders and launch stricter container-inspection initiatives, security compliance is becoming more important than ever to importers that need to keep their products flowing without interruption.

This is especially true for J.C. Penney, the department store chain owned by the Plano, Texas-based J.C. Penney Corporation. With shipments arriving from nearly 60 countries, the retailer potentially faces delays and disruption at ports around the globe. But through the U.S. Bureau of Customs and Border Protection's Customs-Trade Partnership Against Terrorism (C-TPAT) program and the company's own initiative to keep foreign suppliers in line with U.S. security regulations, J.C. Penney keeps its shelves well stocked. J.C. Penney formed a team to work these security issues. The team immediately got the project underway, sending preliminary questionnaires to foreign suppliers in January 2002. This preceded by four months the Customs and Border Protection release of the official C-TPAT guidelines.

The J.C. Penney survey was designed to evaluate existing security levels and identify facilities that would not meet the anticipated standards. Examples of the questions that were in the initial survey included the following.

- Are containers inspected for damage and contamination before loading?
- Are delivery trucks and containers monitored by the factory during loading?
- Do security guards work around the clock, or does the factory have a monitored alarm system?

A factory had to be able to answer yes to 15 out of a total of 22 questions to be rated acceptable. "Our QC people developed the questionnaire based on feedback we got from Customs, from the industry, and from the factories," a J.C. Penney executive explained. "We're looking at the overall aspect of the security of the factory; we're not just focusing on one thing." If they don't have security cameras, then they should have security guards in place. Some countries, such as those in Central America, are high-pilferage areas where even prior to 9/11 the factories were using private security firms to escort containers to the port.

But pilferage, although a legitimate security issue, had to be nudged a rung or two down the ladder in terms of importance. "We wanted to start focusing not so much on what the employee could take out, but what the employee could bring in and put in a container—a potential terrorist weapon," J.C. Penney officials stated.[2]

In his seminal work on logistics in the Vietnam War, General Joseph Heiser stated, "Logistic security, including the physical protection of logistic personnel, installation, facilities and equipment was one of the more critical aspects of the logistic effort in Vietnam. . . . Ambushes, sapper and rocket attacks, and pilferage caused logistic commanders to be constantly aware of strict security measures. There was no 'secure' rear area."[3] With the advent of cyber-terrorism, the threat of terrorism, the proliferation of computer viruses, and the constant risks at the world's ports coupled with the increased reliance on information technology systems, there is no longer a "secure rear area" in today's supply chains. This makes the need for security operations more important today than ever before in the history of the world.

The February 2, 2004, *USA Today* editorial page contained an editorial titled, "US Fails to Close Security Gaps Exposed by 9/11." In this editorial the author stated,

> Last week's revelations that the U.S. Government bungled numerous chances to detect the 9/11 hijackers before they entered the USA painted a chilling portrait of U.S. borders vulnerable to terrorist entry. From doctored passports to immigration violations that agents failed to spot, Americans were put at high risk by a system that relied on trust more than scrutinizing foreign visitors. . . . Yet, progress has been slowed by a government in denial about its vulnerabilities.

This demonstrates the need for a careful and thorough risk assessment and the use of the After Action Review discussed in detail in Chapter 8 to properly assess areas that are vulnerable and need improvement.

Logistics is too important to leave to the logisticians and supply chain managers, and operations are too important to leave to the operations folks. Everyone has to be talking to one another in order to effectively support the customer. In addition, communications is key to security and risk management, especially in the planning phase.

One of the tried and true principles of war is surprise. The element of surprise has an impact on the need for security. Why security has to be in place and why intelligence is important and why you should carefully analyze that intelligence is evident in the actions of the Japanese on one critical day in 1941. On one day (December 7, 1941), the Japanese Army and Navy attacked the United States in Hawaii at Pearl Harbor, Schofield Barracks, Wheeler Field, Hickham Field, and Kaneohe Bay; British Malaya; Thailand; Singapore; Hong Kong; Guam; and the Philippines, all without anyone in the United States or Great Britain realizing that it was coming, even though the signs were there.

Another example of the need for security to prevent against surprise came to this generation on September 11, 2001. Although the pieces to the puzzle were there, the analysis of the data was incomplete, leaving the puzzle unsolved and the nation insecure. Do not allow the same to happen to your supply chain. Collect your data, analyze it, and put the pieces together to form the picture. This is a very essential part of the risk assessment and risk management needed to provide security to your supply chains.

As early as 1981, Philip Kronenberg warned us of the need to increase security measures in his book, *Planning U.S. Security: Defense Policy in the Eighties*. In the foreword he states,

> There are increasingly complex challenges to free world values and institutions and, thus, to US national security interests and objectives. To be optimally prepared to meet these challenges rationally, the United States must have a coherent national security planning process that reflects a future-oriented concept of US interest and objectives, permitting us to orchestrate all elements of the nation's power in behalf of those objectives.[4]

The same is true for your organization. You need to have clearly stated interests and objectives along with the planning process to meet your challenges. Without these, your company will not be able to "orchestrate" the sections/divisions/subsidiaries of the company to meet those objectives and secure the future of the company and your supply chain.

Before getting into the details of securing your supply chain, here is an example of security operations in action. During the buildup to Operation Iraqi Freedom, supplies arrived at the Kuwaiti ports of Ash Shu'aybah and Ash Shuwaykh, as well as the Kuwait City International Airport. Security at the airport was very tight for obvious reasons. The Kuwaiti government controlled the security at the port of Ash Shu'aybah very well. However, security concerns were one of the reasons that the storage and distribution of Meals, Ready to Eat (MREs) was eventually moved from the Ash Shuwaykh port to a more secure facility in Kuwait City. In addition to port security, there was a need to provide security for soldiers, convoys, and supplies. The Theater Distribution Center security included restricted access with armed guard forces at the entrance and exit, as well as a guard force on the perimeter to ensure personal security for the workers at the distribution center and for the critical supplies coming into and out of the center. Other examples of security operations in Kuwait include armed guards checking every vehicle coming into and leaving military bases, armed escorts for all convoys, and a requirement for military in commercial vehicles to travel in armed convoys of at least two vehicles per convoy.

Logistics is the foundation of combat power. The wider aspect of Security is also important, that of the need to conceal one's intentions from the enemy, lest by his interpretation of them he divines the overall plan.

Joint Doctrine Capstone and Keystone Primer

Just as logistics is the foundation of combat power, logistics and supply chains are the foundations of industry. Protecting and securing supply chains are just as critical to the success of a company as they are to the success of a military operation. Great leaders throughout time have grasped this concept. Alexander the Great took a personal interest in the logistics of his armies. Sun Tzu mentioned the need to protect supply lines in 500 BC. I am often asked why there is a need for 21st-century supply chain leaders to study the 2500-year-old writings of Sun Tzu. In the January 2004 edition of *Inbound Logistics*, Secretary of Homeland Defense Tom Ridge was quoted as saying, "To cripple our economy without firing a shot, that's just counter productive, that's a terrorist's dream, and that should be our nightmare."[5] Sun Tzu tells us, "To defeat the enemy without conflict is the ultimate in skill." Obviously, from Secretary Ridge's comment, our enemies have studied Sun Tzu and want to cripple our economy without firing a shot. If they have studied that part of Sun Tzu, then they have studied the rest of Sun Tzu and know the importance of supply chains to the United States and the world's economy. This means that your supply chain is in constant danger and requires a good plan for securing it. Napoleon neglected the importance of logistics in his attack on Moscow and paid a very steep price for that neglect. The purpose of this chapter is to discuss the need for security for supply chains and the increased need to protect electronic means of transmitting data and information.

The United States Army defines security in *Field Manual 101-5-1, Operational Terms and Graphics*: "1. Measures taken by a military unit, an activity or installation to protect itself against all acts designed to, or that may, impair its effectiveness. 2. A condition that results from the establishment and maintenance of protective measures that ensure a state of inviolability from hostile acts or influences."[6] Supply chain security and the security of the speed of business strive to protect the supply chain "against all acts designed to, or that may impair" the effectiveness of the supply chain to get goods and services from the suppliers to the ultimate customers. This includes the establishment of measures to prevent against "hostile acts or influences" that may affect the ability to meet the customers' needs or prevent loss of materials or merchandise.

Velocity management is based on replacing the old archaic piles of supplies with information while improving support and responsiveness to the customer. More and more business is now conducted on the Internet. All of Dell's business-to-consumer business is Internet-capable. One Theory of Constraints speaker told an audience at a recent APICS International Conference and Symposium, "If you are not doing business on the Internet, within five years you will not be doing business." With a greater reliance on concepts such as just-in-time and the electronic transfer of information through the supply chain coupled with the heightened awareness and concerns as a result of September 11, 2001, the need to secure the supply chain is greater than at any time in the history of logistics.

A decrease in inventory and the reliance on just-in-time can place the supply chain at a greater risk from the customer's point of view. Consider the impacts of the 2002 dock strike in California when over 200 ships were backlogged and floating off the coast. A reliance on just-in-time meant that my wife's 20th anniversary present was not delivered in time for our anniversary. Just as a major toy discounter learned a few years earlier with Christmas deliveries, I learned a hard lesson in just-in-time and ended up buying multiple anniversary presents.

Another emerging area that dictates securing the supply chain is the use of real-time information. This practice means an increased need to secure the information links in the supply chain to assure the uninterrupted flow of information on which to base decisions. Look at this statement from a captured Al Qaeda document on their intents:

> Martyrdom or self-sacrifice operations are those performed by one or more people against enemies far outstripping them in number and equipment. The form this usually takes nowadays is to wire up one's body, or a vehicle or suitcase with explosives,

and then to enter into a conglomeration of the enemy, or in their *vital places,* and to detonate in an appropriate place there in order to cause the maximum losses in the *enemy ranks.*

Their "enemy ranks" and "vital places" are not just military targets. Their targets include such vital places as the demonstrated targets of the Pentagon and the World Trade Center, as well as other "high payoff targets." This may well include supply chain activities. This is why security is so important in today's world. To emphasize this need for security, take a look at some of the recent headlines in papers around the country.

- The *New York Times* reported, "At Least 70,000 Terrorist Suspects on Watch List—US Believes an Unknown Number of Operatives are Already Inside the Country."
- The *Washington Post* had a headline, "U.S. Fears Use of Belt Bombs." This article discussed the suicide bombers that have plagued the Israeli–Palestinian conflict and the potential for their use in the United States.
- The *Washington Times* reported in January 2004, "U.S. Suspects Moles at Baghdad Headquarters." This article discussed the suspicion that insiders were providing information to insurgents in Iraq. The "coincidence" or timing of some attacks suggested that someone working in the headquarters of the Coalition Forces was passing information on visitors and meetings to the guerrilla fighters. Some of the attacks, such as the attack on the Rashid Hotel in October 2003 where Deputy Secretary of Defense Paul Wolfowitz was staying, appeared to be more than mere coincidences. This article also stated that guerrilla fighters seemed to know the times and routes of low-flying military aircraft.
- "New Wave of Computer Viruses Signals Rivalry among Hackers."[7] In this article from the *Wall Street Journal,* March 2004, Riva Richmond explains that there is a "new deluge of malicious computer code" that is "pitting virus against virus." These new viruses, in addition to attacking your information systems, appear to be attacking each other, thereby causing more damage to your systems. In a similar but unrelated story in March 2004, The *Journal* reported that executives from a Japanese software company will forgo part of their pay because of a leak of customer data from their computers.[8] An attack and theft at the TRICARE West offices in December 2001 meant the leak or loss of personal medical information and social security numbers for over 500,000 military members, family members, and retirees. Can you afford to have that much customer data stolen or leaked?

Just what is security? The Department of Defense defines security as:

> 1. Measures taken by a military unit, activity, or installation to protect itself against all acts designed to, or which may, impair its effectiveness. 2. A condition that results from the establishment and maintenance of protective measures that ensure a state of inviolability from hostile acts or influences. 3. With respect to classified matter, the condition that prevents unauthorized persons from having access to official information that is safeguarded in the interests of national security.[9]

This leads to the concept of security classifications. The Joint Chiefs of Staff Joint Electronic Library defines security classifications as: "A category to which national security information and material is assigned to denote the degree of damage that unauthorized disclosure would cause to national defense or foreign relations of the United States and to denote the degree of protection required."[10]

How does this fit into your supply chain operations? Do you consider the security of information and material important to your supply chain operations? Without accurate and timely information, material will not move through the supply chain. If we are not moving material and information, we will quickly be out of business in today's economy where the customer wants it now and wants to be able to know exactly where the order is in the system. Providing security for information and material has now become a "front burner" issue.

One more definition is needed to set the stage for a quality discussion of security. The Joint Electronic Library defines security countermeasures as: "Those protective activities required to prevent espionage, sabotage, theft, or unauthorized use of classified or controlled information, systems, or material of the Department of Defense."[11] As we delve into supply chain security, the application of these definitions to supply chains becomes very clear.

> *Security operations* are those operations undertaken by a commander to provide early and accurate warning of enemy operations, to provide the force being protected with time and maneuver space within which to react to the enemy, and to develop the situation to allow the commander to effectively use the protected force. The ultimate goal of security operations is to protect the force from surprise and reduce the unknowns in any situation. A commander may conduct security operations to the front, flanks, or rear of his force. The main difference between security operations and reconnaissance operations is

that security operations orient on the force or facility being protected, while reconnaissance is enemy and terrain oriented. Security operations are shaping operations.[12]

Let's convert this definition into commercial supply chain language. What is a security operation for supply chains? How does it differ from the military definition? Security operations for business and supply chains are those operations undertaken by leaders and managers to prevent interruptions of support or loss of merchandise/materials as a result of the risk assessment and risk management plan. The purpose of commercial security operations is to provide the company with time to react to threats to operations from internal or external threats, or competitors. In addition, these security operations protect the company or the supply chain from surprises that may affect the ability to support the customer. A commercial reconnaissance could be as simple as a guard force and security cameras or as elaborate as tracking devices and item-level Radio Frequency Identification (RFID) tags or Global Positioning Satellite (GPS) tracking systems.

A more detailed view of security operations is contained in paragraph 12-1 of the Army's *Field Manual* on tactics. This doctrinal manual defines five forms of security.

There are five forms of security operations:

1. *Screen* is a form of security operations that primarily provides early warning to the protected force.
2. *Guard* is a form of security operations whose primary task is to protect the main body by fighting to gain time while also observing and reporting information and preventing enemy ground observation of and direct fire against the main body. Units conducting a guard mission cannot operate independently because they rely upon fires and combat support assets of the main body.
3. *Cover* is a form of security operations whose primary task is to protect the main body by fighting to gain time while also observing and reporting information and preventing enemy ground observation of and direct fire against the main body.
4. *Area security* is a form of security operations conducted to protect friendly forces, installations, routes, and actions within a specific area.
5. *Local security* consists of low-level security operations conducted near a unit to prevent surprise by the enemy.[13]

Now we need to civilianize these terms to make them more applicable to commercial security operations.

1. *Screening Operations* are external guard forces, security cameras inside and outside, or detection devices such as those seen in retail establishments to prevent theft of merchandise. You have these devices or screening operations at the front doors of your operations if you are involved in retail distribution or retail sales, but how many of you have them at the back doors? Is your only risk of loss at the front door or do you have a risk of loss from inside?
2. *Guard Operations* are almost self-explanatory in the commercial world. And although not as elaborate as those seen in support of combat operations, the use of a guard force to provide security for your facilities falls into this category. Other forms of guard devices include security alarms and intrusion devices. In some cases, you may need to provide an armed guard for the movement of your supplies just as the Army and the Marines did for convoy operations in support of Operation Iraqi Freedom. The threat to the movement of your supplies or merchandise may not be as severe as the threat faced by the soldiers and marines on the roads of Kuwait and Iraq, but there are still incidents of hijacking of trucks in the United States.
3. *Covering Operations* in commercial supply chains consist of reaction forces or ready reaction units such as those found at large commercial industrial complexes or campuses. These units or forces react or respond to reports from the screening and guard operations. Activities in this category could also include local law enforcement and fire protection assets that augment internal assets. Although these local assets may not be part of your corporation, they are indeed part of the covering operations that provide security to your operations.
4. *Area Security Operations* include protective fences or barriers, such as those seen at most large activities, and controlled access entrances. These operations are designed to keep "the enemy" out of your operations and are usually monitored on a 24/7 basis. In most businesses, area security operations usually augment the guard operations and the covering operations.
5. *Local Security Operations* include such items as motion detectors, sophisticated light beam systems, and cage security for control of sensitive items.

Paragraph 12-5 of *U.S. Army Field Manual 3-90, Tactics,* states, "Successful security operations depend on properly applying five fundamentals: Provide early and accurate warning; Provide reaction time and maneuver space; Orient on the force or facility to be secured; Perform continuous reconnaissance; Maintain enemy contact." A successful commercial security operation should strive to do the same for its customer or client: the corporation, supply chain, or distribution center. You may not be concerned with the same type of enemy or level of threat as a military operation, but any activity, organization, or individual that presents a threat to your supply chain or to your inventory is an enemy of your supply chain.

Supply Chain Security

Supply chain security must protect the path from the supplier to the customer. This link of value-added activities from the raw materials to the finished goods or services must be protected against any form of interruption while continuing to focus on meeting the needs of the customers. The keys to a viable and successful supply chain are the very areas that make it the most vulnerable to attacks or interruptions. Those are the agility and flexibility of the supply chain and the dependence of 21st-century supply chains and other businesses on information technology.

According to the *U.S. Army Field Manual, 3-0, Operations,*

> The National Security Strategy of the United States defines how this country intends on meeting the challenges in the complex and dynamic global environment. The National Security Strategy establishes broad strategic guidance for advancing US interests through the instruments of national power. . . . the National Military Strategy, derived from national security policy, forms the basis for all operations in war and military operations other than war.[14]

Your company security strategy and your supply chain security strategy are the instruments that describe how you will operate in every possible environment. Your supply chain strategy is derived from your long-range plans for the future of the company and is one of the ways that senior leadership of the company ensures the longevity of the firm.

The latest initiatives for supply chain security are tied to homeland security measures and efforts. The most visible of these include the Customs-Trade Partnership Against Terrorism, better known as C-TPAT. C-TPAT is a good example of securing the supply chain before an incident occurs. In an article in the January 2004 *WERCSheet,* Dr. Hua Lee stated that "similar to quality initiatives," security initiatives "cannot be after the fact built into the system."[15] Just as quality has to be built into the product from the beginning, so must security initiatives. Why? "It is estimated that an attack on a U.S. port could lead to the collapse of the U.S. economy within 20 days."[16]

The *WERCSheet* article went on to say, "It seems that almost weekly, there's a new regulation that warehouses must adhere to in an effort to keep the supply chain secure."

Indeed, the U.S. Customs requirements that all containers headed to the United States be preceded by a full manifest of what's inside are still a thorny issue. Many companies and trading partners have complained that the requirements are too burdensome and hurt their bottom line. But the price is necessary when you look at the potential cost to the U.S. economy and the resultant impact on the world economy.

Exactly what is the Customs-Trade Partnership Against Terrorism? And why do we have it? "Terrorists are well aware of the opportunity that global supply chains present to deliver a devastating attack on the U.S. It's up to both the government and U.S. importers to protect us all."[17]

Robert C. Bonner, commissioner of the U.S. Bureau of Customs and Border Protection (CBP), has a recurring nightmare: a dirty bomb explosion in a major city like Chicago delivered in an ocean container. Bonner says that the CBP has determined such an event would kill or injure thousands of people, close every U.S. seaport for at least one week, create a backlog of container traffic that would take at least three months to clear, cost the U.S. economy $58 billion, and result in years of chronic security disruptions. "Such an event is simply unacceptable," says Bonner. "The government and the trade community have a shared responsibility to prevent such an incident."[18]

Pfizer's Corporate Security Manager Richard E. Widup, Jr. says that C-TPAT was a boost for Pfizer's security programs. "C-TPAT has helped us move our programs along faster because it got our top management focused on the need for better supply-chain security," he says. William S. Ansley, vice president of trade management services for UPS Supply Chain Solutions, points out that C-level executives do not spend money on highly theoretical supply chain security risks just because they want to be good citizens. "CEOs want to gain tangible benefits for participating and avoid costly consequences if they don't," according to Mr. Ansley. "CBP is now articulating the values of C-TPAT, so high-level executives understand the economic benefits."[19] As of January 2004, there were over 4600 participants in C-TPAT. "C-TPAT has become a new benchmark standard for import supply chains," according to Richard Bank, a partner in the Washington, DC, law firm of Thompson Coburn.

One C-TPAT initiative is a "Smart Box," a secure seal and a device inside the container that provides shipping location, and tells if the shipment has been tampered with. Army operations for containers have used a tamper-proof seal for many years to prevent unauthorized opening of equipment containers. This C-TPAT initiative will provide greater confidence to dockworkers that the containers have not been tampered with. According to the Customs and Border Protection Agency Commissioner Robert Bonner,

> The best factory and loading dock security, and the best supply chain security is of little value if the box is not secure—if a terrorist can simply break open a container in transit and conceal a terrorist weapon, including, potentially, a weapon of mass destruction.[20]
>
> In the post-September 11 era, our border, our zone of security, must extend to the loading dock of a foreign manufacturer that exports goods to the United States. Our border is the foreign airport where people board airplanes to the United States or ship air cargo to the United States. It is a foreign seaport where a container is loaded for the United States. If we are to have a smart border, our zone of security must extend to all those places.[21]

The C-TPAT provides a screening force operation against terrorism. Is this important given today's world situation? Absolutely! The impact of a disruption to the American economy is predicted to cost as much as $2 billion a day if a major port is the subject of a terrorist attack. The need to prevent such an attack is the reason for the establishment of the C-TPAT. The establishment of the C-TPAT is a result of the vulnerability assessment conducted by the Department of Homeland Security.

Vulnerability Assessment

After a commander has obtained a threat analysis, he proceeds to complete the analysis by conducting the vulnerability and criticality assessments. This process considers a mission review and analysis of the installation, base, unit, or port in relation to the terrorist threat. The review should assess the cost of anti-terrorism measures in terms of lost or reduced mission effectiveness. It should then assess the level of acceptable risk to facilities and personnel given the estimated erosion of mission effectiveness. Often the best operational method and routine may be the worst to counter potential terrorist activities.[22]

The risk assessment and the development of the risk management plan were discussed in Chapters 1 and 2. These two actions form the basis for the development of a security plan.

Now let's take a look at some of the areas that need security plans based on potential risks to the supply chain that these areas pose.

Information Security

On January 26, 2004, Rowan Scarborough in an article in the *Washington Times* reported, "U.S. Suspects Iraqi Moles at Baghdad Headquarters." The article detailed the concerns of some U.S. officials that there may be more than mere coincidence regarding some of the attacks on U.S. compounds, convoys, and aircraft. There appeared to be too many incidents of terrorists appearing to know exactly where high-ranking officials such as the deputy secretary of defense were and the subsequent explosion attacks in the same location. In October 2003, Deputy Secretary Paul Wolfowitz was visiting Baghdad and stayed at the Rashid Hotel. There was a rocket attack on the floor below the Deputy Secretary. Mr. Wolfowitz escaped unharmed but one of the military police officers assigned to protect Mr. Wolfowitz did not. There have been other incidents of low-flying helicopters and "classified" convoys that have been attacked.

When there are too many coincidental occurrences such as these, there is a good indication that there may be a need for greater security for information networks and information sources. Another example of potential breach of information security occurred on February 12, 2004. On that day, General John Abizaid, the commander of all U.S. military personnel in the Middle East, was visiting an Iraqi civil defense post with the commander of the 82nd Airborne Division when a rocket and bomb attack ensued. Another mere coincidence? Perhaps not. According to Robert Burns of the Associated Press, "A defense official in Washington, speaking on condition of anonymity, said it was likely that the insurgents had been tipped off to the presence of the senior general."

To secure your information sources and networks you have to be constantly aware of who is saying what and when. In the military, there is a program known as Operational Security or OPSEC.

One of the greatest areas requiring information security is e-mail. Not only is e-mail a constant distraction in the office for many office workers, but it is also one area that poses a great risk to your information security program. Once you hit the send key on your e-mail, it may be around forever and available to almost anyone. Consider the Iran–Contra hearings during the 1990s, long before most people knew what e-mail was. During the Congressional hearings regarding the "scandal," LTC Oliver North found out about the ability of systems to maintain e-mail and information that was thought to be "erased." This same technology about ten years later surfaced in the investigations of Enron. The audit trail of e-mails helped to bring down the Enron house of cards.

E-mail messages are very similar to bullets fired from a rifle or artillery cannon. Just like a round fired downrange on a target range, you know where the e-mail is aimed, but you have no control of the e-mail once you hit the send key. You have no idea where the information may end up after your intended receiver reads and forwards the e-mail. Several years ago, I sent an e-mail to my boss with the subject line and the first and last lines of the e-mail, "Please do not forward." However, my boss forwarded the e-mail to several officers. These officers forwarded the e-mail with their questions, and before it was over this e-mail was forwarded several times around the Army. Within a week, I was explaining the information and my analysis of the information to several general officers. None of the information was classified or even sensitive and was available to anyone in the Army but the analysis of the data made one particular installation look bad. Unfortunately, this installation had not noticed the bad trends in customer support and logistics process times identified by the data. I even received several abusive e-mails from some senior officers telling me to mind my own business. One particular general told the world (well, not literally) that I was not in a position to make such an analysis. When I confronted him about the analysis and my background and experience in the area, he agreed that I did indeed have the right and experience to make the analysis and that in fact the analysis looked to be correct.

The moral of the story is that if you do not want your words miscon-strued or taken out of context, put them in writing but not in an e-mail. If the information that you are passing in an e-mail is sensitive to the nature of your business, do not put it in an e-mail. The rule of thumb with e-mail is if you do not want everyone to know something, do not put it in an e-mail. You may very well end up seeing your message on the front page of a major newspaper. Information operations and market-ing operations both have the same goal: to shape the thoughts of the intended audience. The key with security of information is to ensure that you are doing the shaping.

Cyber-Terrorism

In an article titled "Safeguarding against Cyberterrorism,"[23] Jennifer Lang-ford wrote, "Securing cyberspace is a difficult strategic challenge that requires coordinated and focused effort from our entire society—the federal government, state and local governments, the private sector and the American People."

Cyber-attacks are increasing in volume, intensity, and sophistication. Usually cyber-attacks are on high-payoff targets. We now define high-payoff targets.

The Institute for Security Technologies Studies has identified the following likely attacks on our nation's information systems.

1. Deface electronic information sites in the United States and allied countries and spread disinformation and propaganda.
2. Deny service to legitimate computer users in the United States and allied countries through denial-of-service attacks, the use of worms and viruses, and the exploitation of inherent computer security vulnerabilities.
3. Commit unauthorized intrusions into systems and networks belonging to the United States and allied countries, potentially resulting in critical infrastructure outages and corruption of vital data.

The four programs to promote awareness, training, and competence in information systems security are:

1. Promoting awareness of the importance of system security
2. Fostering training and education programs
3. Improving Federal security training programs
4. Promoting professional cyber-security certifications

The February 12, 2004, edition of the *Leavenworth Lamp*[24] reported, "DoD drops Internet vote citing security concerns." The article from the American Forces Press Service stated,

> The department has decided not to use the SERVE (Secure Electronic Registration and Voting Experiment) program in the November elections because of our inability to ensure the legitimacy of the votes. . . . The cancellation follows a report by four of the ten computer security experts asked to test the system. Those four concluded the system did not ensure the legitimacy of the votes. The report they issued said there were a number of ways that computer hackers could crack into the system.

This is another example of the need to protect information systems. A hack into this system could conceivably swing the entire presidential election or cause the nation's electoral systems to become infected by a virus. The implications of either of those events on the future of America could be disastrous.

What happens when information security is breached? How do you react? What do you do? The first step is to have preventive security measures to prevent the breach of your information systems. Although this is becoming harder with each passing year, here are some ways to protect your information systems and the information within the system.

- *E-Mail Encryption*—Software and hardware are available to encrypt your e-mail and your data transfers to protect against interception of the information.
- *Back Up Data on a Regular Basis*—If you do not perform regular backups of your system, you may very well find yourself with no data at all if your system is hacked or a virus attacks your servers. A good security plan will include standard operating procedures for routine backups. Make sure that if you have to restore your data you are using the most current backup. This sounds so simple but you would be surprised the number of times that I have seen Army supply activities use an old backup and lose valuable customer data.
- *Passwords and Protected Areas*—Every system has the capability to protect the system using passwords. I am always amazed at the number of companies that do not use passwords for protection of information. One company that I have worked with set their cash registers to require a password before every transaction. A bit severe perhaps, but based on their risk assessment, this was necessary and has prevented future losses.
- *Server Protection*—Before joining the Army, I worked at the Amoco Oil Credit Card Center in Raleigh, North Carolina, in the mid-1970s. All of the computer processing of credit card payments was on a set of computers that filled one half of the first floor of the center. Entrance to the building was controlled by use of an employee identification badge (a company ahead of its time) and the access to the computer room was controlled using a password keypad. Only those who had a need to access the computers had the access code. Security of computer servers was much easier during the "old days" of large servers and tape drives. Now a server can be a desktop-size computer and access has to be more controlled than it was in the days of the large-reel tape-machine computers.
- *Disaster Recovery Plan*—Do you have backup plans to process your data on a computer system at an alternate location? When I was with the 19th Corps Materiel Management Center in Germany, we were required to have a backup plan and had to practice the plan on a regular basis. When was the last time you tested your backup plan to make sure you can continue operations with

minimal interruptions to your supply chain? A backup that is never tested is of no value.

■ *Test Security of the System*—How often do you perform an audit of your security system? The Army has regular tests of security systems to make sure they are doing what they are supposed to do. If you do not test your security systems, how do you know if they work?

Today's consumers expect their product when they want it and that is usually the day before they ordered it. Your information systems have to be responsive to the customers' needs. To achieve end-to-end supply chain security, information must flow seamlessly across integrated systems.

Information Collaboration

Does the sharing of your information with supply chain partners increase the risk to your supply chain? There may be an increased risk and security requirement. You have to know who your partners are and develop a sense of trust. A lack of trust between supply chain partners is evident in the grocery industry. This lack of trust creates inaccurate data resulting in an excess of supplies because of the lack of synchronization of data in the supply chain. One grocery firm even went as far as saying, "We became very efficient at being inefficient." Wegman's, a northeastern United States grocery chain, started a program to synchronize data within the supply chain. Wegman's moved from 12 suppliers incorporating data synchronization to 200 suppliers using data synchronization between 2002 and 2004. The results of this data synchronization effort were over $1 million in savings for every $1 billion in merchandise sold. In addition, this initiative enabled Wegman's to get merchandise to the store two weeks faster with a two to four percent reduction in stockouts and a reduction of five to ten percent in handling times for inbound stocks. The success of this data synchronization and collaboration effort was the trust developed between Wegman's and their suppliers.

Another symbiotic relationship with data sharing occurs in the operations of DSC Logistics in Colonial Heights, Virginia. DSC collaborates with Phillip Morris in Richmond to provide third-party logistics support. This partnership allows the sharing of information on the shipments of tobacco products coming from the Richmond plant to the Colonial Heights facility. Using GPS tracking and Advanced Shipping Notification, DSC knows when to expect a shipment and also knows if the shipment is not where it should be, or if it has been hijacked or simply stuck in traffic. The sharing of this information allows both DSC and Phillip Morris to enhance the security of their shipments.

The advent of Internet-based technologies to provide real-time communications increases the need for security of information and information systems. Any time there is a connection or transfer of data or information with access for all supply chain partners, there is a potential security issue. The use of end-to-end systems and back-end systems integration increases your security needs.

The Latest Threat to Your Information Systems and Proprietary Data

With the increase in the number of Internet-capable cellular telephones to pass information, there is an increase in the opportunities to "capture" sensitive information. In the military, the proliferation of cell phones on the battlefield and the passing of information over the Internet poses a great risk. One of the most sensitive areas is the passing of information on unit moves or worse, on the injury or death of a soldier. The downside is that families have access to information before all the facts are known.

Here is an example of information reaching the public before all of the facts are known or before the Army is ready to release the information. There was a fatal mortar accident in March of 2002 at the National Training Center. The training accident left three soldiers dead downrange at the National Training Center at Fort Irwin, California. Before the MedEvac helicopters were back at Fort Irwin's Hospital, the National Public Radio and several local stations were already broadcasting news of the accident and the loss of lives based on cell phone calls from the field to families back in Kansas.

Another area of risk to information is the passing of information via e-mail. An example of this was seen in the blocking of most of the Internet and all civilian e-mail providers prior to the beginning of Operation Iraqi Freedom. This was done to prevent soldiers from passing potentially sensitive information to families and friends before the invasion. This is another example of Operations Security.

The March 24, 2004 edition of the *Wall Street Journal* contained an article on page D-1, "America's Funniest Phone Videos." This article by Walter Mossberg announced the newest threat to security, the video cell phone. "Gyms, schools, and some companies sensitive about security have banned the camera phones. The video models will only add to the controversy and discomfort over hiding a camera in a common device people don't normally associate with photography." We have already mentioned the security risk of cell phones and camera phones to transmit sensitive data, now with the new video phones you can take up to 15 seconds of video and broadcast it to whomever you please over unsecure means that anyone can intercept. This will make security and risk management even more important as this technology is improved and becomes more accessible.

In a similar article on the front page of the *Kansas City Star* on February 14, 2004, Matt Campbell wrote, "In a flash, camphones can intrude." In this article, Campbell detailed how the use of camphones could easily provide a breach of security, and allow for the undetected capture and transmission of proprietary information, security data, or simply a breach of privacy. The American Association for Nude Recreation has banned the use of camphones at any of their resorts or camps. However, they are not the only ones. The United States Air Force has banned all portable telephones from secure areas to prevent the "accidental" transmission of classified data. During Operation Iraqi Freedom, all cellular phones were banned from the briefing areas. The logistics command center went as far as prohibiting their use in the adjoining areas during classified briefings. The goal was to prevent the "accidental" passing of classified information or even bits of information that could be pieced together into a classified picture.

Here are some questions to ask your trading partners and suppliers to ensure that your operations and your information will not be compromised.

1. How long have they been in business? How long have they been in *this* business? Some companies change core competencies and may have been in business a long time but in the supply business for only a few years.
2. How many customers do they service or collaborate with?
3. Who are they? What do you know about the company?
4. What companies do they collaborate with?
5. What other contracts does your partner have?
6. Is the company financially stable?
7. What do you know about the leadership and senior management personnel and their leadership philosophies? How do they treat their employees?
8. What is the history of the company?
9. What is their security program?
10. Do they have a history of loss or security breaches?
11. What is their security response program, assuming they have one?
12. How do they hire and screen or bond employees?
13. What technology, if any, do they use for tracking of shipments?
14. Do they use or are they planning to use RFID?
15. Do they have a history of hijacking or internal losses?

16. What is the employee morale and your partner's standards for screening employees?
17. Do they have an SOP for handling losses?
18. Do they perform routine and unannounced security audits?
19. Do you have access to their data? Who else has access? Here is an example of data loss. In December 2001 the TRICARE West Region Service Center in Phoenix had their computers stolen. These computers contained over 200,000 files with social security numbers for every soldier, retiree, and family member serviced by this region. The impact? Every active duty soldier and retiree had to contact the credit agencies and place a fraud victim alert on their credit files to prevent credit/identity theft.
20. Are they C-TPAT compliant?
21. Do they have written security standards? If so, how often are they checked or audited?
22. Do their systems have system integrity? Are there controls in place for their processes?
23. What are the financial impacts of the collaboration? Do their suppliers have the ability to secure supplies from their own dock to your partner's dock?
24. Security partners: what is in it for me to collaborate with you?
25. Is there a marketing advantage to collaborate with this supplier?

The Impact of RFID on Security and Visibility

One of the questions dealt with the use of RFID. Can RFID increase your security? Because of lack of visibility, there is an average of ten weeks of inventory in the consumer packaged goods supply chains. Radio frequency identification technologies are an answer to this visibility and security problem. RFID started as a tracking and security initiative and has spread into other supply chain uses. For example, every Rolex has an RFID chip embedded in the watch. This helps insurance companies recover stolen watches. Bookstores have employed the use of random RFID tags for several years to prevent theft. The Army employs active RFID tags on every container leaving the two major distribution centers. The addition of the information and ability to track containers of supplies throughout the supply chain increases the confidence of the customer that his or her supplies and equipment are inbound. This increased confidence on the part of the soldier reduces redundant orders for the same supplies and thus assists in unclogging the supply chain and reducing the number of containers of supplies shipped. This also reduces the amount of stuff that needs security protection in the pipeline or supply chain.

Recently, Gillette moved into RFID usage to provide greater visibility and control over the sale of its Mach III razors. Gillette produced 1.3 billion Mach III blades in 2003. Of those, they could only track and account for 750 million. A 58-percent accountability rate is not very good and definitely not very profitable. Therefore, Gillette decided to spend $0.17 on RFID tags for each of the packages of blades. They purchased 500 million tags. This initiative enabled the company to track the blades and where the blades were being sold. They were able to identify five sources of shrinkage in their supply chain. One example of the shrinkage they discovered was a shipment of blades destined for Boston that were being sold by a discount store in New York City.

In another well-publicized application of RFID tags to consumer products, Proctor & Gamble believes that they will save 50 percent on their inventory costs because of the increase in visibility as a result of the use of RFID tags on all of their products. However, there are some inherent problems at this point with wholesale use of radio frequency identification tags in the supply chain. The most prominent of these include:

1. The lack of a common standard. Until a standard is accepted throughout all supply chains, this will continue to be a potential problem and create potentially incompatible systems.
2. The cost of the tags. Wal-Mart executives and leaders from the Department of Defense are still predicting a 5-cent tag, but the largest implementation to date, Gillette, cost approximately 17 cents per tag. At that cost, the manufacturer lost money to get into the market.
3. Systems integration and the need to maintain a separate system for items going to Wal-Mart and the Department of Defense and those for other customers. For the smaller companies, this poses the greatest threat to the profitability of the company. Most companies will still have to maintain dual systems until the widespread acceptance of RFID technologies. How long will that be? Look at how long it took for barcodes and the universal product codes to catch on.
4. Privacy. When Benneton, the British clothing retailer, announced a plan to put tags in their labels, the public outcry of invasion of privacy squashed the idea. As long as there is a misunderstanding of the technology by the public, this concern will remain. And, as long as "watchdog" companies do not understand the technology and the capabilities and shortfalls of the passive RFID tags and put out bogus information, this concern over privacy will continue to grow and spread.

Another benefit of the RFID tag from the security viewpoint is improving visibility, one of the benefits the Army received from its large active tags. For example, the Limited only gets about half of what it produces to their stores. This creates a good case for the use of RFID tags, but when you look at the items that the Limited brands cover, who really wants an RFID tag in their bras or panties?

The airlines could adopt the use of RFID tags for their baggage operations to improve the flow of baggage through busy terminals. In addition, the added visibility and reduced handling would speed passengers through the terminals. This would make for happier passengers who would more than likely become frequent flyers of that airline. After all, how many hours have you spent waiting for bags in an airport? An added benefit would be the tracking of lost bags or a reduction in the number of bags lost because the bar code on the tag was not readable.

Bioterrorism Security

Since the anthrax discoveries in DC and Florida in 2001, as of March 2005, there have been over 20,000 false alarms that have stopped work at postal and other facilities. As an example, at Fort Irwin, California, the Emergency Response Team was called in to investigate a "suspicious powder" in one of the bachelor enlisted quarters. After a full-blown scare at the installation, it was discovered that the powder was in fact corn starch that had leaked out of a container taken from the kitchen.

There is a new form of terrorism that has food industry professionals very concerned. They have worried about pilferage, spoilage, and damage throughout the history of the food industry. In fact, the food industry already faces over $1.6 billion per year in damaged goods from shipping. Now they have a new threat to the industry.

We mentioned earlier the threat of bioterrorism and how easy it could be to get a contaminated product into restaurants. Because of the concerns over bioterrorism, importers of food-related products are under scrutiny regarding compliance with the Food and Drug Administration (FDA) rules implemented under the Public Health Security and Bioterrorism Preparedness and Response Act of 2002 (Bioterrorism Act). As of December 12, 2003, importers of food and food-related items have to register every domestic and foreign facility that touches their food supply chain, including plants, warehouses, and distribution points. These importers also have to notify the FDA in advance of importing any food-related shipments so the FDA can do a risk assessment to determine if there is any threat to the food supplies. Fortunately the longshoremen are on the lookout for suspect shipments coming into the ports. According to Beth Rooney, Port Authority of New York and New Jersey, "Our longshoremen are the port's first line of defense. If anybody can make a judgment about suspicious cargo, it's these guys."[25]

Port Security

Logistics Management ran a special supplement in their October 2003 edition titled "Covering the Waterfront: Port Security Since 9.11." This article points out the problems in providing port security.

> Essential to the problem and its elusive solution is the fact that ports, with their extensive landside and waterside exposure, represent a very large and very variegated vulnerable target. No two ports are alike in terms of topography and types of inbound and outbound traffic.
>
> Unlike government or military installations, ports are working commercial enterprises dependant on the hourly coming and going of vessels, vehicles, and personnel for their economic existence.[26]

Although there is a lot of truth in the preceding paragraphs, the author of the article does not appear to have an understanding of the amount of logistics movement involved in a military installation. So, let's look at how the military installations do security and how those precautions, if not already in place, can affect your security operations for your supply chain positively. For this example, we look at the security procedures from the time a shipment leaves a military supply depot until it arrives at a unit location in the field at the Army's National Training Center. Every vehicle leaving a distribution center bound for the National Training Center is checked and then a distribution center official places a security seal on the truck's cargo doors. A GPS tracking system allows the customers at the National Training Center and the central distribution center personnel to track the vehicle from the originating distribution center to the distribution center at Fort Irwin, California. The truck receives an inspection upon arrival at the front gate of Fort Irwin and an automated information system interrogator records the time of arrival at the front gate. If the seal reveals tampering, the military police are immediately notified and the truck must be cleared by the military police before entering the installation. After the truck is cleared at the front gate, the driver is directed to the appropriate distribution center where the loading dock is a controlled access area for unloading. Granted, the level of threat at the National Training Center is not as great as at the Port of Los Angeles, but the constant movement of trucks and commercial vendors in and out of the area do present a continued risk.

Security against Theft

Security of supply chains is not limited to security against outside threats. Theft continues to be a large source of losses for many distribution centers. Theft of supplies is not a large problem in military supply chains. However, it does exist. In the case of military supply chains, the "theft" is not for personal gain inasmuch as most of the military supplies are not usable on non-military equipment. There are not a lot of applications for tank pads or treads in the commercial world, nor are there a lot of applications for the M1 Abrams Tank engine outside of the military. So, most of the "thefts" in the military supply chain occur when a soldier sees the part he or she needs in another unit's customer bin and decides it "must have been put in the wrong bin since that is the part I ordered." I watched this occur at the National Training Center on a regular basis. After a 14-day training exercise in the rough desert terrain of the National Training Center (located in the middle of the Mojave Desert in California), a large number of vehicles need maintenance before the equipment is loaded on trains and retrograded back to the unit's home installation. During this intense maintenance period of approximately 7 to 14 days, many soldiers will "shop" the customer bins for the parts "that were obviously put in the wrong bin." The impact of this on the unit that really did receive that part is that they lose time in repairing the equipment and have to reorder the part.

In commercial supply chains there continues to be pilferage from the receiving docks and shelves. Why does this continue to plague supply operations? All too often, there is a feeling that "it will not happen here." Another contributor to this problem is that employees see it as a low-risk action. This attitude, coupled with a lax security system, leads to increased opportunities for theft.

With the advent of the Internet economy and online auctions, certain items can be easily "fenced" or sold to unsuspecting consumers. The pilferage of items leaves the company in a potential stockout situation. The potential for a stockout leads to the loss of a sale and potentially the loss of a customer. After all, if you do not have the item on the shelf, it is really hard to sell it. This is the reason that Gillette moved early into the use of RFID. With over 1 billion Mach III razors produced in 2003, only approximately 750,000 could be accounted for by the time they were supposed to reach the stores.

The use of guard operations and screening operations in the form of security cameras is an effective guard against internal theft. Can you stop it all? Probably not. Dishonest workers will find a way around the system, but prevention through background checks and unannounced security checks will help prevent the majority of internal theft. Do you do a background check before promoting or hiring an employee? The U.S.

Army does a background check on every officer that is selected for promotion before announcing the results of a promotion board. Why? To make sure that the employee has not done something that will compromise his or her ability to lead or may indicate a security risk.

Remember that not all theft is simply taking the items from the retail establishment or distribution center. One local cellular telephone company in Kansas discovered that one of its "prized" employees was cutting deals with the employee's friends and upgrading their cellular phones for them at cut rates. Remember that the dishonest employee will find a way if you are not taking precautions based on your risk assessment.

Do you need to be as secure as a casino? Every casino has cameras focused on every vulnerable area in the casino to prevent cheating and theft, or simply to let folks know that someone is watching and thereby deter theft or cheating. Your operations probably do not need the level of security of a casino, but the casinos set a good example of security operations. In addition to the cameras, every employee must go through a thorough background investigation. Security background checks are becoming more popular in today's world. Like the casinos, the military does a background check on all employees. According to an article in the *Wall Street Journal*, February 24, 2004, "Security clearances for employees have become a hot commodity among companies bidding for sensitive government home-land-security and military contracts." This has led to a "423,000 person, 12 month backlog of people seeking clearance."[27]

Operational Security

One of the best ways to prevent the loss of information or compromising your operations is to implement an Operational Security Program.

> The U.S. Army has a long history of successful operation's security from the Revolutionary War's Yorktown campaign to Operation Desert Storm. Current Operations Security (OPSEC) methodology originated during the Vietnam War. The Purple Dragon Team under the U.S. Pacific Command, viewed friendly combat operations from the enemy's perspective. The team used systems analysis to determine what critical information the enemy could learn about friendly operations.[28]

The Army sets forth the definition of Operations Security in *Army Regulation 530-1, Operations Security*:

> Operations security maintains essential secrecy, which is the condition achieved by the denial of critical information to

adversaries. Adversaries in possession of critical information can prevent friendly mission accomplishment. Thus, essential secrecy is a necessary prerequisite for effective operations. Essential secrecy depends on the combination of two approaches to protection:

1. Security programs to deny adversaries classified information.
2. Operations security to deny adversaries critical information, which is always sensitive and often unclassified.[29]

There are five parts to a successful operations security program:

1. Identification of critical information
2. Analysis of threats
3. Analysis of vulnerabilities
4. Assessment of risks
5. Application of appropriate measures

When making the conversion from military terms to commercial supply chain terms, these steps would look like this.

1. What is important to the operation and success of our company? Amazon.com has a proprietary system for their distribution centers and they are not willing to share this system or even allow "outsiders" to tour their distribution centers as a measure to protect this system that obviously gives them a competitive advantage. The key with critical information is that all of the information does not necessarily have to be released together. In the Army, we constantly remind our soldiers that information security and operations security can be like a jigsaw puzzle. Another analogy is the old *Concentration* game show. You do not need to see the entire picture at one time to understand what is there. A piece of unclassified information here and another piece from somewhere else and you have the complete "classified" picture or information without ever seeing the classified documents. A large source of this type of information is the infamous "undisclosed source" or the "senior defense official who refused to be identified."
2. Analysis of threats. What will be the reactions of the competition to this action? If this information leaks out, will it affect our new product development or offering to the customer? Can the competition beat us to the market on this initiative if this information leaks out?

3. Where are we vulnerable to the competition? Where are we vulnerable to a quick change in the desires of the customer? The fashion industry is a classic example of this. The shelf life of a new fashion design is limited and sales could be ruined if the new fashion gets to the market under a competition's label before yours gets on the shelf or rack.

4. Assessment of risks. This was discussed in great detail in Chapters 1 and 2. Again, the key is that a little information lapse here and a little lapse somewhere else may very well allow the competition to get a jump on an offering before we can get it to market.

5. What are the appropriate measures to prevent leaks and disclosure of information? Many companies require a nondisclosure agreement from their employees that may cover the company for a period of time after the employee terminates the relationship with the company. Several companies that I have worked with have required a nondisclosure statement before allowing me into their facility.

Operations security is analogous to employing Emerson's five wise men. If you can fill in the who, what, when, why, and where of an operation or prevent the competition from filling in the blanks, your operations security is working. The key with operations security is that if you can get the answers to four of the questions, you can complete the puzzle and determine what may be coming down the way. In addition, if you can get the answers to four of the questions, so can your competition.

Is operations security important to your operation? Do you have a process or patent that gives you an advantage over the competition? If so, the answer is yes. Is there a reason why the original Coke formula is kept secret or why Colonel Sanders' original Kentucky Fried Chicken recipe is not published in every cookbook in America? These are classic examples of corporate operational security. Is the Windows® software code important to Microsoft?

Although it has been a few years since Walt Disney started work on Disney World in Florida, he mastered the techniques of operational security. Instead of sending in corporate lawyers to buy up the 27,000 acres of Florida wetlands, now known as the Reedy Creek Development or better known as Walt Disney World, Walt Disney sent in an army of buyers at different times with no idea that they were working together. If the corporate lawyers had gone in to buy 27,000-plus acres, someone would have realized something big was going to happen and the price of the land would have been astronomical. By using operations security, Walt was able to buy the land without tipping his hand and was able to get the land at a very reasonable price. This is just one example of operations security.

Another more recent example of operational security in practice is President George W. Bush's trip to visit soldiers over Thanksgiving 2003 in Iraq or Prince Charles' trip in February 2004 to visit British soldiers in Basra. Both of these incidents went off without a hitch because of the operational security measures and the restriction on reporting the incident until after the two dignitaries were out of hostile airspace.

A more recent example of bad operational security comes from the pages of the *Wall Street Journal*. In an article on page one of the June 14, 2004 issue, Michael Phillips details the story of Steve-O, a 14-year-old Iraqi who did not want to fight against the Coalition Forces and was tired of being beaten by his father.[30] This teenager went to the American soldiers of the Third Armored Cavalry Regiment. He offered his information to them on the insurgents in his hometown of Husaybah, Iraq, near the Syrian Border. The amazing thing about this story is that the facts surrounding the surrender and assistance from Steve-O were supposedly classified to protect the young informant. Through a series of interviews, Mr. Phillips pieced together a very clear picture of what happened, when, and how it happened into this front-page story. He even pieced together detailed information about Steve-O's background and his family. Now this young informant is in constant danger, his "adopted family" in the Third Armored Cavalry Regiment redeployed to Fort Carson, Colorado, and everyone knows who he is and the value of the information he passed on. This is why operational security is necessary to prevent bits of information from being pieced together to form a clear picture of what should be kept classified or at a minimum, held close.

Another benefit of good operational security is the ability to gather information from enemies or competitors and piece together their intentions. In an article titled "Washington Briefing 2004—Enemies at the Gate," in the January 2004 edition of *Inbound Logistics*, Lisa H. Harrington wrote,

> Since Christmas Eve, 2003, about a dozen flights into the United States from abroad have been grounded or delayed over security-related fears. British Airways, in particular, cancelled several flights between London and Dulles International Airport outside of Washington, DC, over such concerns.
>
> Perhaps these new security measures we hear about on the news are the most visible realities of heightened alert in America 2004—procedures such as fingerprinting foreign visitors, eavesdropping for terrorist chatter and canceling or delaying flights.... Security, in fact, is the driving force behind regulatory changes that are reshaping both commerce and how U.S.-based companies and enterprises manage their inbound supply chains.[31]

Lessons in Security

Before wrapping up this chapter on security, let's take a look at some lessons in security from history. During World War II, because of the U-boat threats in the English Channel, the United States had to reevaluate their original idea of providing resupply from Great Britain. The success of the antisubmarine campaign in the Atlantic Ocean made it possible to actually supply the forces more quickly from the United States than Great Britain. However, for security reasons the United States logisticians designed a system of loading ships by commodity. The goal was one commodity per ship leaving out of New York harbor, to minimize risk to the cargo destined for Europe.

During the ramp-up to D-Day, June 4, 1944, one prominent officer was overheard discussing logistics problems associated with the invasion. After having too much to drink one night, he was supposedly overheard telling some folks that these problems would be over by the next week.[32] Imagine the impact this information would have had if the wrong people heard that conversation. Another example of operations security during the buildup to D-Day is seen in the leaking of information that General George S. Patton was building an army at Calais. This information, when coupled with the German intelligence on Patton, led the German Army to assume that the invasion would come from Calais and not at Normandy. Sometimes operations security measures purposely provide a false picture of reality.

According to General Heiser, during the Vietnam War, "personnel and equipment authorizations for logistic organizations were inadequate for the additional mission of security."[33] To counter this security problem, there were frequent inventories, the use of identification badges, and limited access areas, not unlike what most of us do every day in our operations 40 years later. In addition, convoy commanders had to address the security issue for every convoy, a lesson that should have been learned for Operation Iraqi Freedom and the 507th Maintenance Company.

One of the most visible and enduring lessons from the Vietnam War was to be flexible and be able to adapt to the changing world environment. The U.S. Army did not to a large extent adapt their doctrine and tactics to meet the situation in Vietnam. The U.S. Army continued to rely on large-force tactics and units against a smaller, more adaptable enemy. Today's U.S. Army is adapting their force structure and tactics to fight a thinking and adaptable enemy. You need to do the same thing. Twenty-first century supply chains need to be able to quickly adapt to "thinking, adaptable" customers and their changing desires and needs.

Conclusions

One of the goals of velocity management is to measure and reduce cycle times in the supply chain. The same goal is applicable to security. Security is necessary to prevent delays and interruptions to your supply chain, thus causing increases to cycle times. With the concepts of better, faster, and cheaper creating a new focus on the customer, it is important to remember that the cost of securing the supply chain is minimal compared to the cost of a terrorist attack or other interruptions to your ability to support your customers. These risks to your supply chain come from your risk assessment and risk management plans, as discussed in the previous chapters.

There is a link between the quality of your security programs and the quality and frequency of your personnel training. There is a link between security and velocity. With an increased emphasis on the speed to get supplies and goods to the customer, there is a greater reliance on information systems. This greater reliance on information systems and information synchronization creates more opportunities for risk within the supply chain. Sun Tzu reminds us that speed is the essence of warfare and speed is the essence of supply chains. Do not let security issues slow your supply chain. Just as a lack of speed in warfare is deadly to the forces on the battlefield, a lack of speed in supply chains may prove deadly to the corporation.

Just as logistics is too important to leave to logisticians and supply chain managers, operations are too important to leave to the operators. Supply chain managers and leaders have to work closely with the operations departments to ensure the security of the supply chain operations. Everyone has to be talking to one another in order to effectively support the customer. Do not control your communications so tightly that internal customers cannot communicate with each other, but protect your communications and information from the competition.

The military theorist Karl Von Clausewitz stated in his book, *On War*, that "in war . . . things happen differently from what we expected, and look differently when near from what they did at a distance." Another way of putting this is, "All things change when you go from the abstract to the concrete." Make sure your security plans work as well in practice as they did in the conceptual phase.

Discussion Questions

1. What is your security plan? Who in your organization is responsible for developing the plan?
2. Does your plan address all of the threats to your supply chain?

3. How would you answer the list of questions on your supply chain partners? How would they answer the same questions about you? (See questions in previous section of this chapter titled "The Latest Threat to Your Information Systems and Proprietary Data.")
4. Does your facility design enhance security?

Book List for Chapter Three

1. Axelrod, Alan, *Nothing to Fear—Lessons in Leadership from FDR*, Penguin, New York, 2003.
2. *Army Regulation 530-1, Operations Security*, Headquarters, Department of the Army, 1995.
3. *Field Manual 3-19.30, Physical Security*, U.S. Army, Washington, DC.
4. *Field Manual 3-0, Operations*, U.S. Army, Fort Leavenworth, KS, 2001.
5. *Field Manual 3-90, Tactics*, U.S. Army, Fort Leavenworth, KS, 2002.
6. *Field Manual 101-5-1, Operational Terms and Graphics*, U.S. Army, Washington, DC, 1997.
7. *Planning U.S. Security: Defense Policy in the Eighties*, ed. Philip S. Kronenberg, Pergamon, Elmsford, NY, 1981.
8. Heiser, Joseph, *Logistic Support*, Department of the Army, Washington, DC, 1974.

Notes

1. Foster, Thomas A., "Taking the Risk Out of Your Supply Chain," *Global Logistics and Supply Chain Strategies,* January 2004, p. 30.
2. "Secure from the Start," John Shanahan, associate editor, Logistics Management, http://www.manufacturing.net/lm/index.asp?layout=articlePrint&articleID=CA380534.
3. Heiser, Joseph, *Logistic Support,* Department of the Army, Washington, DC, 1974, p. 34.
4. *Planning U.S. Security: Defense Policy in the Eighties,* ed. Philip S. Kronenberg, Pergamon Press, Elmsford, NY, 1981, Foreword.
5. Harrington, Lisa H., "Washington Briefing 2004, Enemies at the Gate," *Inbound Logistics,* January 2004, p. 176.
6. *Field Manual 101-5-1, Operational Terms and Graphics,* United States Army, Washington, DC, 1997, p. 1-144.
7. Richmond, Riva, "New Wave of Computer Viruses Signals Rivalry among Hackers," The *Wall Street Journal,* March 2, 2004, p. B3.
8. The *Wall Street Journal,* "Business Briefs," March 1, 2004, p. A8.
9. http://www.dtic.mil/doctrine/jel/doddict/data/s/04733.html.
10. http://www.dtic.mil/doctrine/jel/doddict/data/s/04738.html.
11. http://www.dtic.mil/doctrine/jel/doddict/data/s/04740.html.

12. *Field Manual 3-90, Tactics*, U.S. Army, Fort Leavenworth, KS, 2002, p. 12-1.
13. Ibid., Chapter 12, p. 12-1.
14. *Field Manual 3-0, Operations*, U.S. Army, Fort Leavenworth, KS, 2001, paragraph 1-30.
15. *WERCSheet*, "Supply Chain Security Without Tears," Warehousing Education and Research Council, January 2004, p. 10.
16. Ibid., p. 10.
17. Foster, Thomas A., "Taking the Risk Out of Your Supply Chain," *Global Logistics and Supply Chain Strategies*, January 2004, p. 30.
18. Ibid., p. 30.
19. Ibid., p. 32.
20. *Inbound Logistics*, January 2004, p. 176.
21. *Inbound Logistics*, January 2004, p. 178.
22. *Field Manual 3-19.30, Physical Security*, U.S. Army, Washington, DC, appendix K.
23. "Protecting Our Homeland"—a supplement to the *Leavenworth Lamp*, March 4, 2004, Liberty Publishing Group, 2003.
24. The *Leavenworth Lamp* is the weekly newspaper of Fort Leavenworth, Kansas.
25. Quinn, John Paul, "Port Security Since 9.11," *Logistics Management*, October 2003, p. S60.
26. Ibid., p. S60.
27. Fields, Gary, "Security Vetting of Employees Is Highly Prized," The *Wall Street Journal*, February 24, 2004, p. b1.
28. *Army Regulation 530-1, Operations Security,* Headquarters, Department of the Army, 1995, Appendix D-1.
29. Ibid., paragraph 1-5.
30. Phillips, Michael, "Iraqi Teen Turned in His Father, Faces Dangerous Future," The *Wall Street Journal,* June 14, 2004, p. 1.
31. Harrington, p. 176.
32. Axelrod, Alan, *Nothing to Fear—Lessons in Leadership from FDR,* Penguin, New York, 2003, p. 16.
33. Heiser, p. 35.

SUPPLY CHAIN VELOCITY AND HOW TO ACHIEVE IT

II

Section 1 looked at how to secure your supply chain against internal and external threats identified in the risk assessment and risk analysis. Now it is time to look at ways to increase the velocity of your secured supply chain operations.

Chapter 4 looks at ways of seeing yourself, your customer, and the competition in order to identify areas that are not adding value to the supply chain or improving customer support operations. Included in this discussion is a look at the development of the process map and applications of Six Sigma methodologies to improve operations.

One of the shortcomings identified for many companies through this process is a need to create a better professional development and personnel training program. Chapter 5 provides an example of a professional development program and information on establishing a viable program for you and your employees. Included in this discussion is a look at how some top companies have employed professional development programs to produce a more highly motivated and productive workforce.

The bedrock of any successful company is the quality of the leadership at the helm. Chapter 6 looks at the qualities of world-class leadership and provides examples of leadership in action—both good and bad—and the impacts that this leadership has had on companies and organizations. Leadership is a learned trait that all too often is identified in the processes from Chapter 4 but overlooked in creating the professional development programs from Chapter 5. Chapter 6 addresses how to better develop your subordinates into leaders.

Chapter 7 is the culmination of this section and looks at how to tie the previous chapters together to achieve greater velocity in your supply chain. Greater velocity results in shorter customer-order cycle times. These shorter cycle times, when coupled with perfect order fulfillment, produce greater customer satisfaction while reducing the cash-to-cash cycle, thereby affecting the bottom line for the company. The goal of any successful supply chain is to reduce non-value-added processes and add velocity to the supply chain. Chapter 7 provides techniques and tips for supercharging your supply chain velocity.

Chapter 4

Corporate Awareness and Velocity

Know your enemy and yourself and in one hundred battles you will be successful.

Sun Tzu
The Art of War, 500 B.C.

You must be able to see yourself from the customers' eyes and from the competition's eyes. How do they see you? The commander of the Operations Group[1] at the National Training Center addresses every unit that comes there to train. One of his bits of guidance is that they should be able to see themselves in order to gain a better understanding of their ability to do their missions. The goal of every leader and manager in a supply chain should be the same. The better the leader or manager is at seeing himself or herself, the better he or she can direct and lead the organization in accomplishing the mission. Knowing yourself is not enough. To be successful in the supply chain, you have to know your competition and your customer. This chapter looks at why it is important to know yourself, how to gain this knowledge, and how to apply it to improve the supply chain.

Knowing yourself is the cornerstone to programs such as Six Sigma. The first step of the process of Six Sigma, regardless of the subscribed methodology, is Define.[2] This includes defining what your core processes and competencies are, what your customer expects from you, and what you and the competition can or will do to meet the needs of the customer. Before you can meet the customer's needs, you have to be able to define what it is you do, what you do better than anyone else, and how that enables you to meet the needs of the customer. Defining the situation is a form of seeing yourself. One of the Army's methods to assist soldiers and leaders to see themselves is the After Action Review.

The Army's After Action Review process is one way to "see yourself" or to be able to know yourself. The Army has a training circular[3] that serves as a guide for leaders at all levels on how to "plan, prepare, and conduct" an After Action Review. The After Action Review is a structured process that facilitates seeing yourself. We delve deeper into the After Action Review and how to conduct one in Chapter 8.

When defining the situation it is important to decompose all areas into manageable pieces or parts. The concept of breaking the problem into usable pieces was first explained to me in graduate school at the Florida Institute of Technology in Melbourne, Florida. My calculus instructor, Jim Carbone, was an engineer for Dictaphone. Jim had the ability to write with his right hand, explain the problem, and erase it with his left hand all at the same time. After my first graduate school experience in taking a calculus exam, I had a long talk with Jim explaining my concern that my exam score would not accurately reflect my knowledge of the subject. In retrospect, it probably reflected my understanding very well. The guidance that Jim Carbone gave me was to take the complicated problems and break them into workable sections rather than trying to solve the entire problem as one long formula and series of symbols. This same approach is necessary to the concept of seeing yourself and understanding your supply chain processes or business processes. One of the best ways of depicting all of these workable parts of your process is to map each one of them and then use the individual parts to form a complete process flow chart or process map.

The use of a process map provides several benefits to your operations. The greatest benefit comes from the graphic picture the process flow chart provides for your processes from end to end. Another benefit is the ability to use the flow chart for instructional purposes for new employees and refresher training for current employees. A corollary benefit comes when it is time to apply for the Malcolm Baldrige National Quality Award or ISO 9000 certification or recertification. The process maps you prepare as you are defining your processes will assist in the certification process.

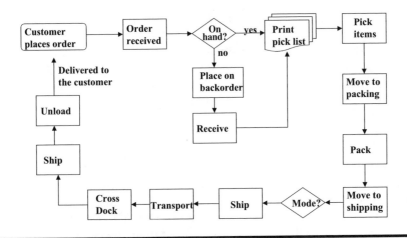

Figure 4.1 Sample process map for order fulfillment process.

Just what is process mapping and how do you develop a process map? A process map is a flow chart of your processes (see Figure 4.1). The process map will show every process, action, delay, and activity associated with your process. Process mapping is not an easy task but one that is well worth the effort. The purpose of the process map is to assist you in understanding your supply chain processes and the flows of inventory and information within your supply chain. The process map will assist you in identifying your weaknesses and provide a baseline for measuring your improvements.

What do you map? To create a meaningful process map you need to identify the sources of supply: raw materials, finished goods, or components; the modes of shipments; the information sources and flows; the retrograde of materials and goods; inputs from third-party providers; distribution centers involved in postponement, cross-docking operations, and any other activity that occurs in the process from the raw material to the final customer. Figure 4.1 is a simple process map. Every one of the steps on this process map could and probably will have a separate process map as you get into more detail.

As you map your processes as a way to see and know yourself, look at the concept of a perfect order. This could be defined as the product arrives on time to the receiver and buyer, is delivered complete, is billed correctly, and meets the needs of the buyer and receiver. What is important about the process-mapping concept is what you learn about your processes.

Once the process map is complete, it is time to start placing time stamps on the processes to determine where items sit, wait, rest, or simply identify where there is no value added to the process. The Army went through this process in 1995 at the start of the velocity management program. With the assistance of the RAND Corporation's Arroyo Center in Santa Monica, California, the order and customer fulfillment process was mapped and associated times placed on the map. The process map was a result of physically walking the process from the time a customer ordered a repair part for a piece of Army equipment until the part was actually received and ready to be applied to the broken piece of equipment.

After completing the process map, the next step is to measure and apply times to the process map or time mapping. Proctor & Gamble completed their time mapping upon completion of the process mapping. Their first time-mapping exercise looked at the time lapse from the sourcing of raw material to the cash receipt. Their discovery was a lapse of 41 weeks with a value-added time of only 90 minutes. The Army made similar discoveries when they time mapped their repair parts distribution system. Although readiness rates and the time a piece of equipment was not available for use because of mechanical failure did not look bad on paper, the Army discovered it took a total of up to 122 days to get parts from Pennsylvania to North Carolina.

For the Army, the process map revealed few surprises. Where the real surprises came was when the Army and the RAND Corporation started applying available data to come up with the time the processes took at each activity on the process map. The average time for a soldier to get a part was over 22 days. When the Army measured out to the 95 percent level, the total cycle times for some installations were as high as 122 days. As if that were not bad enough, to the surprise of many senior leaders in the Army, the time to pass the requisition electronically through the system was almost exactly one-half of the total processing time. Imagine taking as long to pass electrons through the information system as it took to physically move the supplies from the distribution centers to the customers.

Boise Office Supplies also did a complete process map of their processes. For Boise Office Supplies, customer knowledge is key. To get an integrated view of all of their customer interactions they look at the orders, the returns, customer questions, customer issues, and the services that their customers need and ask for. This approach is very similar to the first four steps in the Six Sigma process from the Motorola methodology.

The first step of the Motorola approach is to "identify the product you make or the service you provide."[4] In order to do this you have to be able to know the start and stop points of your operations. Knowing these is the first step in building a process map. The next step in the Motorola methodology is to "identify your customers and determine what's important to them."[5] This information is important to building your process map because you need to know if the processes that you currently have in place meet the needs of the customers and if the processes and activities add value to what you are offering the customer. This is similar to the time-mapping information that Proctor & Gamble uncovered, thus revealing a lot of non-value-added time in their raw material processes. When identifying your customers for your process maps it is important to remember that depending on where you are in the supply chain, you may have customers internal to your company as well as external customers. You may very well supply parts to the final assembly of the product and parts to external customers in the form of repair and replacement parts. Remember the words of Sun Tzu at this stage of the process map. It is just as important to know your customer and his or her processes as it is to know yourself and your processes.

As you develop the process map and start asking questions as part of the time mapping, remember to look for non-value-added activities. Also, look for activities that may cause defects to your product or service. Motorola defines a defect as "any action or inaction that causes customer dissatisfaction."[6] The other side is, if the customer does not care about a potential defect, then it really is not a defect. A defect is in the eyes of the customer. Any activity that produces potential customer dissatisfaction needs to be looked at carefully and either discarded or reengineered.

The next step in the Motorola methodology is "identify what you need to provide the product/service that satisfies the customers."[7] This will become evident as you walk the process and listen to the voice of the customer. If your processes do not meet the needs of the customer, you are doing the wrong processes.

Step 4 in the Motorola process is to "define the process for doing the work."[8] Once you have identified the customers, the needs of the customers, and walked the process to determine how you meet the customers' needs, you have compiled the necessary information to develop your process map. Motorola calls this version of the process map the "as-is process map." They call it the as-is map because you now know how you are doing business. From this as-is map you can start identifying how to improve the process and remove any non-value-added activities or fix activities that may be causing defects to your product.

It is only by seeing yourself that you can analyze your processes. Take a look at this analysis of the distribution processes in place in Kuwait to process supplies coming into the country to support Operation Iraqi Freedom (OIF).

Here is an example of being able to see yourself. Every briefing and every discussion of Operation Iraqi Freedom always includes a discussion of the logistics problems. One such meeting included the opinions and perspectives of several essential combat leaders. These leaders based their perspectives on the quality of the logistics systems in Operation Iraqi Freedom, appropriately, on where they were on the battlefield. Two of these important leaders expressed concern over the inability of the logistics system to support their operations. Interestingly enough, both felt that the systems they controlled were adequate and the systems above them were woefully inadequate.

Other opinions on the quality of the logistics system supporting Operation Iraqi Freedom range from a company commander at one end of the supply chain who reported that he did not receive any repair parts from the time he "crossed the berm" (when his unit left Kuwait) until sometime in July. At the other end of the supply chain, the Association of the United States Army magazine, *ARMY,* quoted a senior logistician as saying that velocity management worked well in supporting the operation. Reporters embedded in tactical units reported on a regular basis that food was in very short supply, soldiers have reported surviving on packages from home and "pogey-bait," yet *Jane's Defense Weekly* reported recently that the inability to distribute food was not as big a problem as initially reported.

Where does the truth lie, what was the logistics structure for supporting OIF, and how do we fix the system to make it more responsive to the soldier? A recent book on supply chain management suggests that regardless of how well you think you are doing in supporting your customers, if they are not happy then you are not doing as well as you think you are.

Let us start by looking at the flow of supplies into the theater. Items for all four services, the Army and Air Force Exchange System (AAFES), the U.S. Embassy, and the Defense Intelligence Service arrived incountry at the Kuwait City International Airport on Air Force 463L pallets[9] with Radio Frequency (RF) tags. These shipments originally came from Dover, Delaware but after a winter snowstorm left the Dover facility in ruins, the shipments came from Charleston, South Carolina. Initially, the pallets arrived at the Theater Distribution Center (TDC) with supplies for all four services on the same pallet.

Figure 4.2 shows a simplified flow of supplies into the theater. After arrival at Kuwait City Airport, the aircraft were unloaded and the pallets were transported to the holding area at Camp Wolf (less than a mile from the tarmac). This met the Air Force metric for clearing the tarmac. This also employed a convoy of security-cleared trucks dedicated to this mission. Because these trucks and their drivers were cleared to enter the airport area, they were on a "permanent" assignment to the tarmac-clearing mission. At Camp Wolf, the pallets were again downloaded and staged in rows by their date of arrival. This allowed the staging area detachment to adhere to a first-in, first-out metric. A better solution would have been to sort them by major customer identifier or, at a minimum, by service component. However, the metric was first-in, first-out and that dictated the date sortation lanes.

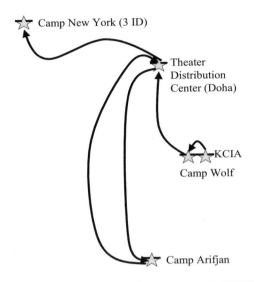

Camp New York (3 ID)

Theater
Distribution
Center (Doha)

KCIA
Camp Wolf

Camp Arifjan

Figure 4.2   The flow of supplies in Kuwait.

Figure 4.3   The Theater Distribution Center receiving area on March 8, 2003. (photo by Troy Kok)

The next leg of the movement was from Camp Wolf to the Theater Distribution Center (Figure 4.3). A set number of contracted trucks worked this mission. Like the cleared trucks and drivers for the tarmac-clearing mission, dedicated cleared trucks and drivers ran the convoys from Camp Wolf on the airport grounds to the distribution center. The limited number

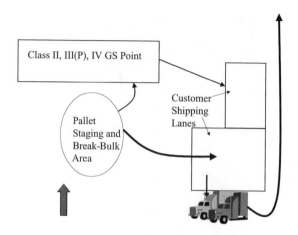

Figure 4.4 The flow of supplies in the Theater Distribution Center.

of trucks for this mission resulted from stringent security measures for admission onto the airport grounds. The staging area crew loaded these trucks and dispatched them to deliver the pallets to the Theater Distribution Center. The security clearances required that these trucks be used for the loop from the staging area to the distribution center and back to the staging area. The only backhaul they did was empty 463L pallets and cargo nets for retrograde back to the U.S. depots and an occasional outbound air cargo load heading to Qatar or Afghanistan.

Once the supplies arrived at the Theater Distribution Center (DC), a series of operations began. On those rare occasions that "pure" pallets (for the purpose of this discussion, a "pure" pallet is an Air Force pallet that contains supplies or equipment for only one major consignee, for example, Third Infantry Division, 101st Airborne Division, 82nd Airborne Division, U.S. Marines) arrived at the distribution center, the staff could cross-dock the pallets to outbound trucks. This was more of a miracle than a planned occurrence, although the DC was originally envisioned to be a cross-docking facility. If the pallet was packed for multiple consignees, the DC staff sorted the boxes on the pallets, repalletized the supplies, and moved them to the proper customer-shipping lane.

The Theater Distribution Center staff established a shipping lane for every major support unit (see Figure 4.4). That is, there was a lane for every Army Division Support Battalion, the Navy, the Marine Corps, the Air Force, the Camp Doha Supply Warehouse, the General Supply and Direct Supply Distribution Centers, the United States Embassy, the Defense Intelligence Agency, and Army–Air Force Exchange Service (AAFES).

During the peak periods at the Theater Distribution Center, the number of outbound trucks reached 190. The number of inbound trucks averaged more than 100 per day. (This is the equivalent of approximately 800 standard warehouse pallets.) The outbound trucks carried supplies directly to the customer units in Iraq and Kuwait (some of the local customers picked up from the DC to reduce the wait times), to the AAFES distribution center at Camp Doha (only a few minutes away), and to the Direct Support and General Support Distribution Activities at Camp Doha and Camp Arifjan. Some of the supplies were retrograded to the Kuwait City International Airport for shipment to Afghanistan and Qatar. The variety of supplies coming into the Theater Distribution Center ran the gamut from blood for the Medical Command to parts for the U.S.S. Constellation to F-16 engines.

The Theater Distribution Center served as a convoy consolidation point for outbound cargo. Therefore, supplies sent to the other distribution centers usually came back to the Theater Distribution Center in boxes marked for customer units. Items that fell into this category were touched as many as six times incountry before the customer unit ever saw the item. Every time an item is touched, the chances of being lost or placed in the wrong lane increases. The chances of being placed in the wrong lane were increased by the language barriers between the American soldiers and the Bangladeshi forklift drivers.

A further complication resulted from the RF tags (see Figure 4.5) on the Air Force pallets losing their identity upon arrival at the Theater Distribution Center. This created great frustration for the folks tracking supplies into the theater using the data from the RF tags. This gave the illusion that items arrived incountry and then disappeared. In some cases, this may have been true. In most cases, the truth is that the item arrived incountry on a mixed pallet, was sorted into the proper lane, and shipped to the designated location in Kuwait or sent forward into Iraq in a consolidated shipment. However, because of the inability to write detailed individual tags for every part, units were not able to track critical supplies once they arrived in the Theater Distribution Center. This produced several major fallouts. The first was that the unit could no longer track the item and, assuming it was lost, ordered another of the same item. The second effect was the inability of the theater to assure customers that what they needed was indeed incountry. The third effect was a considerable amount of frustration regarding the unidentified cargo. The solution to the loss of visibility and tracking may lie in the ongoing efforts of the RFID Center in Cambridge, Massachusetts. An RF tag for every part would provide constant visibility of items even after removing the massive pallet RF tag.

One prominent leader went on record as saying that the biggest problem with the logistics system was the Theater Distribution Center. The fact that the Army had never established a theater distribution center in an active theater before meant there would be problems. The fact that

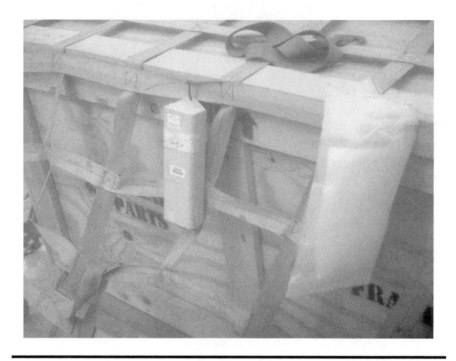

Figure 4.5   Radio frequency tag attached to an Air Force 463-L pallet.

the DC was not properly manned contributed to this problem. The fact that the DC was too far from the supply points (collocating the Theater Distribution Center with Camp Arifjan would probably have been a better decision in hindsight) contributed to the problem. The fact that there were not enough trucks in the theater to meet the distribution needs contributed to the problem. Prior planning for the design and functions of the DC was a problem. The lack of a distribution capability in the Army contributed to the problem.

Was the Theater Distribution Center the problem? No, it was a symptom of the problem. Although the Theater Distribution Center operated with borrowed military manpower for the first two weeks, they did a good job of clearing the inbound lanes on a daily basis. In fact, Figure 4.6 shows the Theater Distribution Center on March 16, 2003.

The Road Ahead—How Do We Improve?

How do we fix these problems for the future? We have already addressed the asset visibility aspect, so let us look at each of the other contributing factors individually.

Figure 4.6 The Theater Distribution Center on March 16, 2003, looking back at the point where the photo in Figure 4.3 was taken just eight days earlier.

Does this mean that the distribution system for Operation Iraqi Freedom was a failure? From the foxhole looking back (the perspective of the soldier should always be the most important), the answer has to be yes. Regardless of all the successes of getting supplies, equipment, and soldiers to the theater, the inability to effectively get the supplies forward has to be addressed and fixed.

How does this apply to your supply chain? By walking the process and mapping out every step in the process, the Army was able to identify the root cause of the distribution problems and not just the symptoms that so many people had already reported to the press. It is only through being able to see yourself and knowing your processes that you can identify the real issues and establish a plan for change and improvement.

Another example of knowing yourself is evident in the many studies of Dell Computers. The Dell model of cash-to-cash and minimal inventories receives more than its fair share of publicity. However, the Dell model is nothing new but it is a fancy twist on older models of operations. It is a combination of MRP, just-in-time, and the Toyota City model mixed with European billing standards (end of accounting period plus 55 days to settle supplier accounts). After looking at their processes, Dell claims an obsolete/excess rate of 0.5 percent. However, if they really have the more than 500 turns as reported by supply chain evangelist Mike Gray, then 0.5 percent is too high. There should be no excess or obsolete parts.

Another part of the Dell model, like the Motorola methodology, focuses on the customer. The Dell goal is to provide the best customer experience. To accomplish this, they use the metrics of order to target. The goal is 7 days or less. However, when the Supply Chain Research Institute ordered an "uncustomized" laptop in 2003, the delivery took over 14 days. No one contacted the Supply Chain Research Institute to see if Dell met their metric or not. A computer not delivered as promised does not meet their metric. Another Dell metric for their processes is "Quality of Experience." Because no one ever contacted the Supply Chain Research Institute via mail, e-mail, or telephone, how do they measure this metric? If you are going to publish metrics that measure parts of your process map, make sure the metrics are accurately tracked.

Like the Motorola definition, Dell defines quality as being in the eyes of the customer. Dell looks at their customer experience as a matter of responsiveness and simplicity. After completing the process maps within the Department of Defense, some people were amazed at the number of logistics automation systems working within the Defense Department. Compare the more than 600 logistics systems identified with the simplicity of the Dell model.

Another methodology for seeing yourself is through the use of the "Theory of Constraints." The Theory of Constraints (TOC) was developed by Dr. Elihu Goldratt. Dr. Goldratt developed the application of the Theory of Constraints in his business novels, *The Goal, It's Not Luck,* and *The Critical Chain.* The Theory of Constraints provides a methodology for defining every system as a chain. In his book *The Theory of Constraints,*[10] Dr. Goldratt lists the following steps in applying the theory.

1. Identify the system's constraints.
2. Decide how to exploit the system's constraints.
3. Subordinate everything else to the above decision.
4. Elevate the system's constraints.
5. If a constraint has been broken, go back to step one, but do not allow inertia to cause a system constraint.

Obviously, the only way you can identify the system's constraints is to walk the process. This is not one of those tasks that you can do from the comfort of your office or from the computer screen.

Let's take a look at some examples of seeing yourself from the Army's National Training Center. The environment of the National Training Center is harsh. It is cold and windy in the winter; windy and dusty in the spring and fall; and very hot, dusty, and windy in the summer. Equipment that is not properly maintained will not survive the 28-day training program for Army units. More important, equipment not properly maintained will not be ready for use by the unit if they have to deploy immediately following a training exercise. For this reason, knowing your maintenance posture and how to track your systems is very important. The majority of units that train at the National Training Center do not know what maintenance right looks like when they arrive at the training center. Through a series of maintenance classes, briefings, and hands-on experience, the leaders of the units get a grip on what right looks like and are able to then use that knowledge to see how well they are doing in maintaining equipment.

Another way that leaders get the chance to see themselves while at the National Training Center is by reviewing the day's operations. After every operation or planning session, time is taken to look at what the operation plan was, what happened, and what could be done to do the operation better. The training exercises at the National Training Center, under as close to realistic training situations as possible, enable all soldiers to know exactly how well they were trained before they came to the training center and then reflect back on how far they have progressed during the training period.

Applications of Seeing Yourself and Knowing Yourself

One of the latest buzzwords in business is transformation. Knowing yourself is necessary to develop a transformation plan. The U.S. Army is going through a major transformation to remain relevant and ready for any potential action. Successful transformation of your organization starts with knowing yourself and your organization. This may lead to an attitude of "break all the rules." Dr. Robert Kriegle may have stated this best when he wrote his books, *If It Ain't Broke, Break It!* and *Sacred Cows Make the Best Burgers*. You have to move to a new level of thinking. This leads to knowing who does what at each level of the organization. The only way to know this is to walk the processes often and talk to the employees. Just as in the Motorola Six Sigma methodology, to know where you are going with the transformation, you have to develop an as-is process map.

Knowing yourself includes knowing your strategy and using your as-is process map to determine where to make changes in your strategy. Look at Cabela's strategy. "At Cabela's we build our reputation as the World's Foremost Outfitter by putting the customer first and backing everything we offer with our world famous 100% Satisfaction Guarantee." How does Cabela's know if they are providing the customer with this quality of support? They do this by making sure each of their employees knows about the products they are selling. They learned this through seeing themselves through the eyes of the customer. To move forward, not only do you need to see yourself from the inside looking out, but you also need to be able to see yourself from the perspective of the customer.

Look at the different strategies in place in Las Vegas, Nevada. At first glance, it would seem that the strategy is to attract customers to the casinos. Although this is true, the different casinos have different strategies to do this. Circus-Circus looks at attracting a family customer with the circus shows and Circus Dome amusement park, whereas the Bellagio does not want children at all and caters to the higher-end clientele.

The Theater Support Command at the National Training Center has a primary mission of providing logistics support to the training center and Fort Irwin. However, while seeing themselves, the members of the Theater Support Command envisioned a strategy of taking the organization one step further. Instead of just doing the installation support, the Theater Support Command realized that they had the talent and the capability to train units on logistics and maintenance procedures not normally covered in the training plans of the training center. The goal of this new strategy was to produce better-trained and more capable soldiers, ready to conduct support missions more efficiently and more effectively.

Successful, continuous, process-improvement programs require seeing yourself and developing an as-is process map. The goal of a continuous process-improvement program should be to orient all efforts toward delighting customers and removing waste or non-value-added processes. This is accomplished while using data and scientific reasoning to guide and evaluate improvement efforts, and to hold the gains from past improvements.

No stranger to process mapping or seeing one's self, Dr. W. Edwards Deming established his 14 points for quality. Dr. Deming's first point states, "Create constancy of purpose toward improvement of product and service with the aim to become competitive and to stay in business and to provide jobs."[11] The only way that you can create a constancy of purpose is to establish standard procedures. The only way you can establish standard procedures is to know what your procedures are. The only way to know what your procedures are is to walk the process and develop a process map.

As you develop the process map and search to determine if a process is value adding or not, you must ask why. "The 'why's' lead to the 'hows'. . . . These 'hows,' in turn, suggest possible routes towards improvement. Some of these routes are 'workarounds' rather than a long-term solution, but even workarounds are helpful until the long-term solutions arrive."[12] Asking why and then looking at the "hows" is a form of root cause analysis. Root cause analysis is another way of saying that you are attempting to see yourself. In so doing, you must provide a definition for a non-value-added process. Dr. Deming once said, "If you cannot describe what you are doing as a process, you don't know what you are doing." The only way to know how to define what you are doing as a process is to walk the process, develop the process map, and then conduct root cause analysis to find out why a process is non-value-added.

Is process mapping new? Does mapping the process really work? Look at the following examples from World War II. After mapping the processes for logistics support, the following improvements in support were made possible.[13]

1. The loading times for a ship in the United States were reduced by over 20 percent between April 1944 and August 1945.
2. The number of warehouse refusals was reduced from 5.7 percent to 1.2 percent between July 1944 and August 1945.
3. The unavailability of stocks (stockouts) was lowered by over 22 percent between November 1944 and August 1945.
4. By standardizing shipping schedules for West Coast ports, there was a reduction of $460 million in material from the supply chain.
5. Standardizing the supply procedures eliminated over 30 million copies of documents previously used to maintain accountability of material.
6. By standardizing the recording procedures for issuing and accounting for individual clothing and equipment, the necessity to maintain over 11,200,000 copies of documents was eliminated.
7. Mapping the processes and establishing standard procedures for laundry handling resulted in the elimination of 36,700,000 clerical operations.
8. Establishing standard operating procedures for supply operations eliminated the requirement to process over 125,000 forms.

Here is another example of improving processes and saving money from walking the process and seeing the activities involved in the process. The cost of returning unserviceable engines at the National Training Center created a short-term financial crisis based on the cash-to-cash cycle for returns. The Distribution Management Center immediately provided credits to customers and then had to wait for the national system to reimburse them for the credits. One such returned engine that "did not work from the very start," was opened up for analysis and rebuilt at the National Maintenance Center and had a maintenance manual from the returning unit inside the engine itself. To prevent future embarrassments and financial losses, the Distribution Management Center walked their processes and the processes of the customer units.

By walking the process, the Distribution Management Center was able to identify unserviceable engines that might result in no credits from the national system. In fact, one customer unit turned in an engine for a tank that was supposedly new and "did not work." This process walk and analysis revealed that not only did the engine perform as promised but because the crew did not follow procedures properly, the engine actually had to cool down for over 20 hours before being removed from the tank.

Time and Knowing Yourself

Know how your time is spent. How do you allocate time? Everybody has 24 hours in their day; this is the one true equality in the world. We are all allocated the same amount of time. It is necessary to know how you spend your time to know where you can improve your own personal operations.

Knowing yourself includes knowing how you spend your time. How much time do you spend in meetings? Could passing out the information and getting out of the office be a better use of that time? As a brigade commander, I held a total of three staff meetings in 26 months. One was to greet the staff upon assuming command and tell them my way of operating. The second staff meeting was to explain to all of the staff an upcoming reorganization and shifting of responsibilities. I wanted to make sure that all of the staff understood the "whats" and "whys" of the reorganization. The third staff meeting was to thank the staff for their support over the course of the command. By doing away with the staff meetings, I gave my staff an additional hour or two every week. During this time, no deadline was missed and all information was successfully disseminated.

On the other side of the coin, how much time have you wasted waiting for a meeting to start because the host was not good at managing his or her calendar? I worked for one boss where I could almost bet with assurance that my meeting with him would be delayed at least 30 minutes because of his inability to manage his calendar. One boss took great pleasure in showing his power by arriving 10 minutes late to every meeting, and another boss would keep everybody waiting until everyone was present. On one occasion this caused over 60 senior officers to wait for over an hour for one person to show up before the boss would start the meeting. My solution was to lock the door to the conference room at the exact start time and let the folks that were late wait until after the meeting to get the information rather than make a whole roomful of people wait for one person.

Perspective and Seeing Yourself

During the Kennedy administration, a team from the Department of State and the Department of Defense went to Vietnam to assess the situation. When the team returned and outbriefed the president and the National Security Council, President Kennedy is reported to have asked the team if they all visited the same country because their reports were so different from one another based on their views and perspectives. How you see things is based on your views and perspectives.

If you are sitting on a lakeshore and observe a ripple or a wake coming toward the shore, you do not know whether that ripple or wake was caused by someone throwing something into the middle of the lake or by a passing boat. If it was a boat, what size was the boat, how fast was it going, and which direction was it going? The same perspectives are true when reviewing programs and policies. If you only see things from one viewpoint (or as we say in the military, from your foxhole) you do not know the big picture.

In March 2004, a rock drill[14] (actually a belated After Action Review) was conducted at Fort Lee, Virginia, to look at the logistics operations that supported Operation Iraqi Freedom and how to improve the support to the future rotations in Iraq and Kuwait. The first problem with this review was that it was conducted almost one full year after the start of hostilities and the entry of coalition forces into Iraq. This means that it was well over a year since the buildup started. This buildup included moving almost 300,000 soldiers, marines, and civilians into the theater of operations and moving the equivalent of over 150 Wal-Mart Superstores into Kuwait to support the operations. Because so much time had passed, many of the thoughts and what had prompted some of the decisions were not fully remembered. In addition, not all of the key players were involved in the March 2004 After Action Review.

The perspectives of the participants were reflected in the comments and would be reminiscent of the previously mentioned incident with President Kennedy. For the participants on the receiving end of the actions from some of the decisions, all that they knew was the impact on them and their operations. For the decision makers, all that they knew or remembered was the decision made. One participant said, "There were no problems with food distribution." Because of the length of time, all of the really bad events and the really good events were remembered, but what took place in the middle was mostly forgotten. In the case of food distribution, there were multiple problems with suspected contamination of Meals, Ready to Eat (MREs); the distribution of bottled water; and constant emergency resupply of MREs from Qatar to replace out-of-stock warehouses.

The folks on the receiving end of the supply chain remembered all of the bad things such as constant communications to get supplies or the shortage of trucks to move supplies but were remiss in remembering the successes of the supply chain operations. The year-long bitterness affected their ability to impartially look at the system and make recommendations. Some of the items forgotten were the pallets of document protectors, picture frames, practice hand grenades, cargo parachutes, camp stoves, and electric pencil sharpeners that were ordered with the same priority as the Abrams tank engines and other repair parts that contributed to the "constipation" of the supply chain. These items took up space on critically few airplanes and trucks and delayed the processing of the really critical repair parts so desperately needed by the soldiers in the fight.

The inability at all levels to see the whole picture and not just one particular piece of the pie, and the passing of time that dimmed the memories of many of the participants, is much like the story of the blind men and the elephant or the outbrief on the trip to Vietnam. It is critical to the success of a process walk or process review to do the review as close to the action as possible, maintain a "big picture" or systems perspective, and remain as objective as possible to solve the problems and not place the blame on the next link in the supply chain.

Benchmarking

There is one more way to see yourself and see your competition that must be addressed to make this chapter complete. That form of seeing yourself is benchmarking. In the textbook, *Operations Management,* Russell and Taylor define benchmarking as "finding the best-in-class product or process, measuring one's performance against it, and making recommendations for improvements based on the results."[15] There are two real forms of benchmarking. You can benchmark your products against the competition, something that the consumers will definitely do. In this form of benchmarking you look strictly at the product attributes and qualities in comparison to the products of your competitors. Marketing research is a form of product benchmarking.

The other common form of benchmarking is when you compare your processes against those of the best-in-class or world-class companies. In this case, your products may be very different but you are looking at processes such as distribution, storage, information processing, or sourcing. The purpose of this form of benchmarking is to establish where you stand in comparison to those companies that do that process better than anyone else does. Once you have established the gap between where you are and where the best-in-class is, you can then develop your plan for improvement or adoption of best-in-class techniques.

Summary and Conclusions

Seeing yourself or knowing yourself comes from a full understanding of your supply chain operations. This comes from walking the process. This walk is a physical walk and not a "walk" from your desk and computer screen. The process walk and the root cause analysis of identified problems produce a detailed process map. This process may also produce the need for some cause-and-effect analysis or cost analysis to determine if a process or activity is value added. Experience shows that in doing the analysis, the need to ask why up to five times will assist in the root cause analysis, and cause-and-effect analysis necessary to prepare a detailed process map.

General Mills walked their processes and found out that $60 million or ten percent of their annual transportation budget was tied up in the backhaul of products from grocery retailers. Nestlé had to walk their processes to identify their annual costs for line haul, unloading, and fuel. In so doing they identified some backhaul lanes that were not profitable for them or their customers.

Here is an example of knowing yourself from the Army's recently published *Torchbearer National Security Report*. "The present Army distribution system lacks the flexibility, situational awareness, communications capacity, and unity of effort needed to effectively respond to the needs of a joint and expeditionary Army. The distribution requirements must be identified and resourced concurrently with the changes made to the combat force structure and to the doctrine." Without a careful and thorough look inward, you cannot identify such shortcomings. If you cannot identify the shortcomings in your operation, there is no way you can identify a course of action or plan to improve the operations.

This same report states, "Ultimately, the distribution system must provide reliable and predictable support that gains the confidence of both warfighters and logisticians." Your supply chain has to do the same thing. It has to provide a level of support that gains the confidence of your employees, your supply chain partners, and ultimately, your customers. Without this confidence, you will not be able to succeed.

Does your perspective influence your decisions or do you try to see what caused the wave on the lake or the ripple in the pond? What can you learn about yourself from your body language and physical reactions? What are you learning about your competition or your customers? In an essay titled, "A Matter of Black and White," in Daisy Wademan's book, *Remember Who You Are—Life Stories That Inspire the Heart and Mind,* Dr. Thomas McCraw wrote, "Yet it is imperative for you as a leader to understand where you—and by extension, your ideas—come from. You are a product of your time, your background, your parents, and your prejudices, and you must understand how each element from your past shaped your thinking in order to make the best decisions in your future."[16]

Benchmarking is a way of seeing yourself. Does your benchmarking have to be against like competitors? Not necessarily. Look at Southwest Airlines. They went to NASCAR to look at the pit stop mentality to apply to turning planes around at the gate. Was that a successful benchmark? Obviously it was; look at the continued success of Southwest in getting folks off the plane, new passengers on the plane, and the plane back in the air where they make their money. The U.S. Army went to commercial industry to look at best business practices to compare and benchmark against for improving supply chain operations.

Seeing yourself or conducting a personal accounting of your actions is an honest assessment of where you are (or where your company is), your shortcomings, your weaknesses, and serves as the basis for an action plan to improve in those areas. Just as risk assessment and risk management plans formed the basis for the security plan, the ability to see yourself serves as the basis for your professional development plan.

Questions for Thought

1. What are your processes and can you identify what you do as a process?
2. How many non-value-added activities do you have in your processes?
3. When was the last time your company did a "bottoms-up review" of your processes to look for areas of improvement?
4. What are your company's sacred cows that are draining resources and not providing what the customer really needs?
5. How could you apply the Theory of Constraints or Six Sigma to improving your operations?

Book List for Chapter Four

1. Wademan, Daisy, *Remember Who You Are—Life Stories That Inspire the Heart and Mind,* Harvard Business School Press, Cambridge, MA, 2004.
2. *Logistics in World War II, Final Report of the Army Service Forces,* Center of Military History, Washington, DC, 1948.
3. Roberts, Harry V. and Sergesketter, Bernard F., *Quality Is Personal,* Free Press, New York, 1993.
4. Goldratt, Elihu, *The Theory of Constraints,* North River, Great Barrington, MA, 1990.
5. *Utilizing the Six Steps to Six Sigma Participant Guide,* Motorola University, 1997.

6. *Training Circular 25-20, A LEADER'S GUIDE TO AFTER-ACTION REVIEWS*, U.S. Army, Fort Leavenworth, KS, September 1993.

7. Russell, Roberta S. and Taylor, Bernard W., *Operations Management,* 4th edition, Prentice Hall, Upper Saddle River, NJ, 2003.

Notes

1. A former brigade commander commands the Operations Group at the National Training Center. The mission of the Operations Group is to train all commanders and leaders at all levels in realistic combat scenarios in the harsh terrain of the Mojave Desert. The Commander of the Operations Group is a future general officer who serves as the senior trainer for the brigade units at the National Training Center. The policy of the Department of the Army is that every battalion commander (usually 400 to 1000 soldiers) and every brigade commander (2500 to 4500 soldiers) must have at least one 28-day training exercise at the National Training Center during their two-year command.

2. Six Sigma has several variations in the application of the methodology to improve operations and improve the quality of a process while reducing variability. Motorola was the "first to market" with Six Sigma. Implemented to improve the quality of the Motorola products, Six Sigma was introduced in the early 1990s as a manufacturing concept. Motorola has six steps in their quest for quality as set forth in the Motorola University course, "The Six Steps to Six Sigma." The first step of the Motorola approach is to define the problem, the customer, and what the customer wants or needs and how that need can be met. The most popular variation of the Six Sigma concept is the version used by General Electric, 3M, and Honeywell, among others. The General Electric approach uses five steps to Six Sigma. These five steps are Define/Measure/Analyze/Improve/Control. Chapters 1 and 2 looked at the application of the DMAIC methodology for assessing and managing risk.

3. *Training Circular 25-20, A LEADER'S GUIDE TO AFTER-ACTION REVIEWS*, U.S. Army, Fort Leavenworth, KS, September 1993. An Army training circular provides information to the field Army before it can be incorporated in the doctrinal publications. This particular circular provides guidance and tips for leaders to conduct an After Action Review.

4. *Utilizing the Six Steps to Six Sigma Participant Guide*, Motorola University, 1997, p. 1-2.

5. Ibid., p. 2-1.

6. Ibid., p. 2-4.

7. Ibid., p. 3-1.

8. Ibid., p. 4-1.

9. An Air Force 463L pallet is specially designed for loading military cargo planes. Depending on the configuration of the Air Force pallet, there could be as many as eight standard warehouse pallets stacked on the pallet.

10. Goldratt, Elihu, *The Theory of Constraints*, North River, Great Barrington, MA, 1990.
11. Roberts, Harry V. and Sergesketter, Bernard F., *Quality Is Personal,* Free Press, New York, 1993, p. 15.
12. Ibid., p. 39.
13. *Logistics in World War II, Final Report of the Army Service Forces*, Center of Military History, Washington, DC, 1948, p. 181.
14. A rock drill is a map exercise used by the Army to walk through a process or operation prior to completing an operation plan. Prior to Operation Iraqi Freedom, the logistics community participated in three major rock drills to make sure the staff considered every aspect of logistics support and to ensure that nothing was overlooked.
15. Russell, Roberta S. and Taylor, Bernard W., *Operations Management,* 4th edition, Prentice Hall, Upper Saddle River, NJ, 2003, p. 109.
16. McCraw, Thomas K., "A Matter of Black and White," in: *Remember Who You Are,* Daisy Wademan, Harvard Business School Press, Cambridge, MA, 2004, pp. 56–57.

Chapter 5

Personal and Professional Development

Logistics is the hottest career out there. Talk to a logistics professional and see what the excitement is about.

June S. Youngs
Vice President of Logistics Hasbro[1]

To be a genuinely successful professional in the logistics field you have to continually hone your skills and stay abreast of all the things that are going on. . . . I don't think you can really call yourself a professional unless you continuously hone your skills.

Bob Shaunnessey
Executive Director of the
Warehousing Education Research Council[2]

Erwin Rommel is reported to have said, "The best form of welfare for the troops is first-class training."

Why are there so many quotes to start this chapter? Because one of the best ways to secure your supply chain is to provide training and education for your personnel. Providing quality training will help with retention of good people, retaining good people will help create stability in your operations, and stability in the operations will help protect and secure your supply chain.

Professional development and training is important for everyone in your supply chain. Corporations have spent millions of dollars to ensure that employees are properly trained and millions more to ensure that their employees remain current in their jobs. As mentioned in the introduction, the United States Army spent almost $2 billion on professional education for officers and noncommissioned officers in fiscal year 2003. And that figure was smaller than originally planned because of the interruptions to the professional development courses due to Operation Iraqi Freedom.

All leaders should consider one of their principal responsibilities to be the professional development of their subordinates. A leader without interest in or knowledge of the intellectual content of his or her profession is a leader in appearance only.

To illustrate the normal professional development of an Army officer, I outline the courses that I have taken as part of my formal professional development program. I also outline the courses that I have taken on my own to ensure that I remained proficient and current in my profession. This is one example of a professional development program.

My initial professional development was in the form of the Quartermaster Officers' Basic Course and the General Troop Support Materiel Management follow-on course. These courses focused mainly on how to be an officer and a leader and were designed to prepare me for my first assignment in the Army. Luckily for me, that first assignment was in Hawaii.

My professional development in Hawaii consisted of being assigned to a couple of staff jobs and an important assignment as a platoon leader for what at the time was called the Main Supply Platoon. This platoon of 125 soldiers was responsible for operating a general supplies warehouse, a cold storage warehouse for food for all Army units in Hawaii, and the operation of two fuel points (gas stations). What was important about this assignment was that I was fortunate enough to get to work with some excellent noncommissioned officers with a plethora of experience and knowledge. These soldiers (Sergeant First Class Tom Barton, Sergeant First Class Eddie Williams, Sergeant First Class Leroy Kelly, and Master Sergeant Mike Lambaria) taught me how to be a leader and showed me what I needed to know to lead soldiers.

The next step in my professional development was the Quartermaster Officer Advanced Course, designed to teach officers how to be company commanders of a supply company. This course was followed by an assignment to the Army's Signal School as the Chief Supply Officer for Fort Gordon, Georgia. With a whole four years in the Army I was expected to know all about supply operations for a major installation. This required me to start my personal professional development program to supplement my tactical logistics experience. About the time that I was starting to get a handle on the supply operations, I became the chief logistics officer for a signal brigade (over 6000 soldiers). About the time I was really starting to feel comfortable in that job, I was selected to command a signal company of 550 soldiers; this is somewhat analogous to the proverbial fish out of water, a supply officer leading a signal unit. Luckily, once again I had a super noncommissioned officer in the form of my senior enlisted soldier, First Sergeant Paul Horn, to guide my development as a leader.

The Army decided that I was ready for graduate school and they were willing to pay the bills. My assignments officer told me that I had a choice of going to fully funded graduate school (all expenses paid by the Army and a paycheck on top of that) in Florida or going to a field assignment at Fort Hood, Texas. I opted for the graduate school. I assumed the options were designed as an idiot test: 18 months in a civilian graduate school or an assignment that would mean being in the field in Texas for the majority of a three-year assignment.

The Army sent me to the Florida Institute of Technology in Melbourne to study logistics management. This was probably the biggest turning point in my professional development. The time in Florida spurred my interest in studying this profession, not just in the classroom but also on my own time to become a better logistician. It was during the first year in Florida that I discovered something so amazing that I had to call my dad to tell him about it. What I discovered was if you go to class, read the assignments, and do additional reading on the topics, the classes actually make sense and I could actually tell what reference the instructor was using for the classes. If I had only discovered that during my first time in college I would probably have made it to medical school or at least earned a worthwhile degree.

I decided to use the discipline that I had learned in powerlifting to excel in graduate school. As a powerlifter I was successful enough to exceed the world record in the squat with a lift of 840 pounds at a body weight of 196 pounds and won national and international championships. This discipline taught me to apply myself to the classroom with the same enthusiasm and dedication. The result was admission to the Business Honor Fraternity at the Florida Institute of Technology. Not bad for a student that had less than a 3.0 average as an undergraduate.

Upon graduation, I immediately got started on the completion of a second master's degree on my time to complement the first degree. Upon completion of the second master's (MS, Systems Management), I enrolled in the U.S. Air Force Command and Staff College Correspondence Program to broaden my military education.

The next phase in my professional development was attendance at the U.S. Army's Command and General Staff College at Fort Leavenworth, Kansas. This was followed by an assignment to Germany and the chance to apply my logistics and leadership education and experience to being the second in command of the Army's only forward-deployed Logistics Management Center. While in Germany I continued my personal professional development by enrolling in and completing the U.S. Army War College Defense Strategy Course and enrolling in the U.S. Air Force Air War College. It was during this period that I first started setting aside at least one hour every morning for professional development reading. This practice has continued for the past 11 years.

The next step in my development came in the form of the opportunity to activate a brand new distribution management battalion at the Army's National Training Center at Fort Irwin, California. During this assignment, the Army started a new supply chain reengineering program. Luckily for me, one of the places that the Army wanted to test its new program was the National Training Center. This program was a Six Sigma-like approach to streamlining the Army's outdated processes. The opportunity to get in on the ground floor at the National Training Center led to the opportunity to lead this program after completion of my command.

As the program manager for the Army's reengineering program, I was given the chance to train with and under some of the nation's leading supply chain practitioners and academicians. My boss in this project made sure that I was afforded every possible opportunity to learn how commercial industry did its supply chain business so we could apply the same principles to the Army's supply chains. The efforts of this team were so successful that the techniques were adopted by the other branches of the service and were recognized by the vice president of the United States and the National Partnership for Reinventing Government for their efforts in significantly reducing the Army's customer order processing times. Chapter 7 goes into more detail on this program. While serving as the program manager, I started my in-depth personal professional development in supply chain operations. My initial goal was to learn the civilian language of supply chains to prepare for a new career outside the Army. During this assignment I discovered the Warehousing Education and Research Council (WERC) and APICS. My involvement with APICS at the time was limited due to the lack of offerings by the local chapter, but my involvement with WERC went a little deeper and I found myself in several volunteer positions. The key to volunteering in a professional organization is that it is a win–win situation. By volunteering you get the opportunities to learn more and serve the organization at the same time.

The program manager assignment led to attendance at the Army's Advanced Operational Art Studies Fellowship. This fellowship is a two-year program that one attends instead of going to the Army War College at Carlisle Barracks, Pennsylvania. This program afforded me the opportunity to conduct research into Six Sigma, just-in-time logistics, and reverse logistics while preparing for another master's degree in operational planning. It was during this period that I finally felt comfortable enough with my understanding of supply chains to start giving presentations at professional conferences and seminars. It was also during this time that I started working on my APICS certification, which I finished in 2003.

The sum total of my formal education and professional development and my own personal professional development resulted in my being selected to command the National Training Center's Theater Support Command and my assignment as the director of the Distribution Management Center for Operation Iraqi Freedom.

Professional Development Guidance

The bottom line to your personal professional development is that every corporation (the Army is no exception) will provide certain formal educational opportunities to keep you in the game. But it is every individual's responsibility to establish a personal professional development and education program if he or she wants to be more than just an average employee.

Read everything you can get your hands on about your profession. If you are in the supply chain leadership field, read leadership books, read supply chain books, and read the professional publications that cover supply chain topics. Take correspondence courses, attend online "Webinars," attend professional development conferences, and get involved in a professional organization. The key to success in any field is to gather the knowledge to enable you to get ahead. The choice is yours: stay in the middle of the pack or take it upon yourself to get ahead by gaining as much professional knowledge as you can. Contact leaders in supply chain leadership and ask them questions; find a mentor among the leaders.

There is a link among training, education, and your process or product quality. The test of the quality of your training and education programs will be the reaction of your customers. If you are training on customer relations, will the customer notice the difference in the attitudes of your personnel? If you are training on warehouse and distribution processes, will the customer notice the decreased wait times? What are the customer's perceptions of the outcome of your training programs and professional development programs? The quality of your training and professional development programs influences the company's reputation, operations efficiency, organizational effectiveness, and customer support.

On-the-job training is probably the most common form of training in industry. Just what is on-the-job training? It is a form of training where a formalized training plan is not necessary but the employee learns the job without any classroom instruction. Just because a formal training plan is not required and there is no classroom instruction associated with on-the-job training that does not mean it is not effective. On-the-job training is usually effective because it is entirely hands-on.

The Army employs a large amount of on-the-job training for its soldiers. However, this on-the-job training is usually structured to augment formalized training. The Army's school program has lost numerous hours of formalized, hands-on training for several reasons. The first is the move to keep the number of days in school to a set limit (remember, a soldier in school is not available to his or her unit for deployments or contingency operations) to get the soldiers to the field Army sooner. The second detractor from formalized training is the large number of mandated courses for trainees such as "Consideration of Others," and courses on equal opportunity and cultural awareness. These courses are designed to produce a better-quality workforce and they are indeed serving their purpose in that respect. However, these "detractors" reduce the time available to hone other professional skills. This puts the onus on the gaining units to provide skills training and certification on the job. The downside of on-the-job training is that it takes away from the productivity of the gaining unit because of the need to assign a trainer for every trainee to certify that the trainee is indeed mastering the skills.

How often do you depend on on-the-job training? Some companies adopt the attitude that on-the-job training in lieu of formalized training sends a message of "commitment by the company not to spend money on education." How many programs in education have been cut because they were perceived by managers as benefits for the employees and not viewed as requirements for job accomplishment?

Some companies augment initial formal training with additional formal training. Does your company have an equivalent of the Motorola University or Toyota University? Motorola University has a course catalogue just like any other university. Every employee has the opportunity to attend classes on one of the two company campuses if his or her job requires that particular skill or course information. The university is also used to improve or refresh skills for employees that may have been out of a particular field for a while.

How do you identify employees' requirements for additional or refresher training? In way too many companies, and again the Army is no exception to this, the employees that get to go to skill-improving schools or training are those employees that you can do without for the time of the training period. Are you making this mistake in your organization? What is the impact on the morale and motivation of the employees who deserve or really need the training? One of the trends that the Army discovered was that soldiers and civilian employees who went to formal training programs were promoted faster than the soldiers and civilian employees who did not. The impact on morale when the deserving individuals saw, in some cases, duds get promoted ahead of them because of education and training was telling.

Here is an example from the National Training Center of sending a person to formal training because he or she was "expendable" to the operation. We sent a senior civilian to a six-month professional development course in Virginia to get rid of the employee for a while. Did this employee really deserve to go to the school? Not at all, but because he or she was entrenched in the job and could not be fired and would not perform to the level that he or she should, the easy way out was to allow this employee to attend the course. In this case, it was a good decision to send this employee off for six months because we were able to see what an impact on morale he or she was having on the entire operation. However, in most cases what happens is that the unqualified or "expendable" employee gets the training at the expense of the workers that really could benefit the organization but are too valuable to allow to leave for any period of time.

Let's look at the concept that good people make bad decisions because they do not know better. How do we get employees to "know better"? It has to be through training. The Army has the National Training Center at Fort Irwin, California, the Joint Readiness Training Center at Fort Polk, Louisiana, and the Combat Maneuver Training Center in Hohenfels, Germany. The purpose of these training centers is to allow leaders to go through realistic, experiential learning exercises. Remember the words of Christopher Robin from the book *Winnie the Pooh on Management*, "Good judgment comes from experience, and experience comes from bad judgment." In order to gain the experience necessary to make good decisions, we have to put our employees through tough, realistic, and experiential learning exercises. At the Army's training centers, the concept is to allow leaders to learn from realistic combatlike situations to hone their leadership skills for the time when they may be needed in real combat. Likewise, we owe it to our employees and especially our leaders to allow them to undergo similar training to prepare them to make good decisions when they face difficult situations.

In the chapter on leadership (Chapter 6), we look at some of the ten imperatives for supply chain success as presented by Dr. John Langley to the Distribution Business Management Conference. One of the ten imperatives discussed by Dr. Langley was knowledge of the supply chain and the capacity to learn. This leads us to a discussion of lifelong learning. The Army is grappling with this concept. How do you stimulate this desire in employees? Can it be forced on them? How do you get employees to want to learn on their own? Part of this is through a corporate culture. The concept of corporate culture is discussed in detail in the next chapter.

The U.S. Army is transforming its leader development programs based on identified shortfalls and the need to provide better-trained leaders based on the changing world environment. Here is how the Army is transforming leader development according to the Center for Army Leadership in a recent position paper.

- To remain relevant, the Army's leader development and education system must train, educate, and grow leaders that are the centerpiece of a campaign-quality Army with a Joint and expeditionary mindset.
- The Army trains for certainty and educates for uncertainty.
- We must develop in our future leaders the right mix of unit experience, training, and education to meet the current and future leadership requirements of the Army and Joint force.

Is this plan for transforming leader development any different from what you should be looking at in your company? Do your employees, managers, and leaders need to remain relevant and current in your operations and business practices? Absolutely! Is there uncertainty in today's supply chains? Of course there is. Uncertainty is what causes variability in operations and if uncertainty is not trained for in supply chain operations, employees will not know how to react when uncertainty occurs.

Did you have a backup plan for distribution of goods during the 2002 dockworkers strike? I did not and, as I said, the gift for my wife for our 20th wedding anniversary sat on a ship outside the port of Los Angeles for an extra four weeks. If you do not have a plan or training for uncertainty, I can assure you that the cost to your company will be much greater than my costs. All I had to do was hastily find another comparable gift in addition to the one on the ship.

Do your employees need training, education, and experience in dealing with supply chain partners, other firms, or customers? Again, the answer is absolutely. Therefore, your training plan should look very much like the U.S. Army's plan to transform leadership development programs. Here is the training challenge for the Army according to Chapter 1, *Field Manual 7-1, Battle Focused Training.*

THE TRAINING CHALLENGE

1-5. Since the end of the Cold War, the world has been in a state of significant transition marked by increased uncertainty and vulnerability. The strategic environment is much less stable than in the past, and threats to American interests are more diverse and less predictable. In this era of complex national security requirements, the Army must embrace a wider range of missions that present even greater training challenges. To "train the way we fight," commanders and leaders must conduct training in a way that ensures mission performance in the contemporary operating environment.

1-6. Training for warfighting readiness is the Army's number one priority in peace and war. Army leaders at all levels are responsible for success on the battlefield. Training is a continuous, lifelong endeavor that produces competent, confident, disciplined, and adaptive soldiers and leaders with the warrior ethos in our Army.

1-7. Personnel turbulence, key-leader turnover, high operating tempo (OPTEMPO), and new equipment and systems fielding present a demanding set of training challenges. Resources for training are not unconstrained—they compete with other resource demands. Time is the inelastic resource.

The training challenge in supply chains is not much different. The supply chain industry has experienced periods of uncertainty, consolidations, expansions, mergers, and great changes over the past ten years. All of these create the need for increased training, refresher training, or simply requiring employees to learn different methods of supporting the customer. Many companies have experienced the need to "embrace a wider range of missions that present even greater training challenges" as more distribution centers are incorporating value-added services such as postponement operations. Every operation and every company has to deal with the inelastic resource of time.

Just as training for warfighting is the top priority for the Army, training for supporting the customer in the most effective manner should be the top priority of companies in the service industry and supply chains. Although the operations tempo may not be the same in the supply chain industry as it is in the Army, supply chains have to be ready to support the customer 24/7. And there are some companies in this industry that face astronomical personnel turbulence rates. There is a distribution center in West Memphis, Arkansas, that experiences over 50 percent personnel turnover monthly. Does this create a training challenge? So, how do we meet these challenges?

Based on the Army's plan, here are some important points to remember.

1. Professional development is accomplished in three domains: operational, institutional, and self-development

U.S. Army Field Manual 7-1 defines these three domains as follows.

THE OPERATIONAL ARMY

1-25. Training in the operational Army includes home station training, combat training center (CTC) rotations, joint training exercises, and operational deployments in support of national objectives. Each of these training activities and operations provides opportunities for experiential learning. They enable participants to conduct assessments, and to plan, resource, conduct, and evaluate training for soldiers, leaders, and units. Training in the operational Army is a team effort.

THE INSTITUTIONAL ARMY

1-30. The institutional Army focuses on educating and training soldiers, leaders, and the civilian work force on the key knowledge, skills, and attributes required to operate in any environment. Institutional training and education enhances military knowledge, individual potential, initiative, and competence in warfighting skills. It infuses an ethos of service to the nation and the Army, and provides the educational, intellectual, and experiential foundation for success on the battlefield. The institutional Army has many contributing components that affect the Army's training infrastructure.

INDIVIDUAL SELF-DEVELOPMENT

1-35. Individual self-development, both structured and informal, focuses on taking those actions necessary to reduce or eliminate the gap between operational and institutional experiences. Individual self-development is continuous. It should be emphasized in both institutional and operational assignments. Commanders and leaders provide feedback to enable subordinates to identify their own strengths and weaknesses and to determine the reasons for them. Together the senior and subordinate prioritize the subordinate's self-development goals and determine courses of action to improve performance.

1-36. Institutional and operational training and assignments and leader development programs alone cannot provide the insight, intuition, imagination, and judgment needed in combat. The gravity of the military profession requires comprehensive self-study and training. Individual self-development affects soldiers, civilian work force members, leaders, and supervisors of all grades, regardless of unit assignment, type of organization, current duty position, or location. The need for individual self-development requires commanders and leaders in the operational and institutional Armies, at all levels, to create an environment that encourages subordinates to establish personal and professional development goals. Successful self-development requires a team effort.

Operational training in supply chain organizations is that training which every employee goes through before starting the job. This may be any combination of classes including Warehousing 101, OSHA-mandated forklift training and certification, machine operator training, or driver's training. Operational training is that training mandated by corporate headquarters, the federal government, or OSHA regulations.

Institutional training is formalized training provided to employees to assist in their career progression and advancement. Institutional training in the Army takes the form of basic and advanced noncommissioned officers' courses, intermediate-level education for midgrade officers, and the War College for senior officers. Motorola University, Toyota University, and Disney University are examples of commercial operational and institutional training programs. They provide initial entry training for employees as well as career progression training and education. Figure 5.1 shows the Army's institutional courses for professional development.

Self-development training takes many forms. There is an operational and institutional responsibility for self-development. Some forms of this may come if an employee is changing jobs. In the Army if a soldier changes career fields, he or she must return to the formal institutions to undergo new skills training. The important part of this segment of the training trilogy is what an individual employee does to advance his or her skills or appeal. Earlier in the chapter we looked at some of the steps I took on my own time to improve my skills and knowledge.

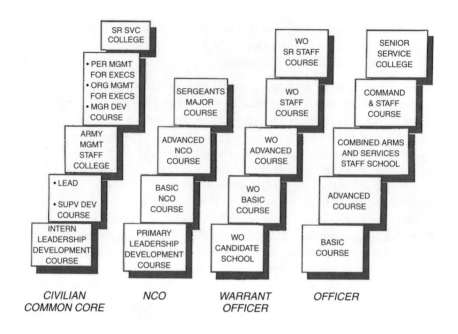

Figure 5.1 Professional development courses.

Employees and employers often overlook individual self-development. The opportunities for personal self-development are limitless with the advent of online courses and training programs. The Warehousing Education and Research Council, APICS, and the Council of Supply Chain Management Professionals (formerly known as the Council of Logistics Management) offer seminars and training courses for employees at all levels in a company. In addition, APICS offers courses and seminars leading to their Certified in Production and Inventory Management and Certified in Resource Management credentials. The simplest form of self-development training is reading books on your particular specialty.

2. Leaders and managers are involved in unit, individual, and collective training; training assessments; and feedback to employees

One of the primary responsibilities of leaders and managers is counseling employees on professional development needs.

In the U.S. Army professional development counseling is mandatory for all junior officers and civilian employees. There is a formal counseling checklist that must be completed, discussed with the officer or civilian employee, and attached to his or her performance appraisal worksheet. Everyone in the rating scheme reviews the worksheet and the counseling checklist. If properly done, this is not just a pencil drill at performance appraisal time. The checklist should serve as the guide for the annual training program for the employee. Figures 5.2 and 5.3 are examples of these counseling checklists. How do you formally counsel and develop your young employees, managers, and leaders? Do you only do performance and developmental counseling at evaluation time? All too often, this is the case in many companies. Worse still is a total lack of counseling, except when something goes wrong.

The Army developed these counseling forms and standards to augment the counseling that takes place in conjunction with the annual performance appraisal. The key to success with the use of these forms is an agreed-upon development plan between the supervisor and the employee. Without a mutually agreed-upon plan, there is no value in completing the forms. If your company has a professional development form or if you adopt one similar to the ones above, make sure you and your employees agree on the development plan and assess the progress throughout the year and not just at the performance-appraisal time.

Here is what the Army's *Field Manual* says about self-development training. The value of the training plan, like the civilian employee development plan, comes from identifying areas of need and then developing a mutually agreed-upon plan. By getting the employee to agree to the plan, you get employee ownership of the plan. With the ownership comes a commitment to making the plan work.

1-38. Self-development starts with an assessment of individual strengths, weaknesses, potential, and developmental needs. Commanders and leaders provide feedback that enables subordinates to determine the reasons for their strengths and weaknesses. Together, they prioritize self-development near-term and long-term goals and determine courses of action to improve performance. Self-development is—

■ A planned process involving the leader and the subordinate being developed. It enhances previously acquired skills, knowledge, behaviors, and experience; contributes to personal development; and highlights the potential for progressively more complex and higher-level assignments. Self-development focuses on maximizing individual strengths, minimizing weaknesses, and achieving individual personal and professional development goals.

JUNIOR OFFICER DEVELOPMENTAL SUPPORT FORM

For use of this Form, see AR 623-105; the proponent agency is ODCSPER

NAME OF RATED OFFICER (Last, First, MI)	SSN	GRADE	ORGANIZATION

PART I - INSTRUCTIONS. Use of this form is mandatory for Lieutenants and WO1s; optional for all other ranks.

Initial face-to-face (Part II and III)

- Discuss duty description/major performance objectives from DA Form 67-9-1.
- Discuss Army leader values, attributes and skills as related to future duty performance and professional development (Part II: Leader Character)
- Complete Developmental Action Plan (Part III)- Record at least one developmental task for each leadership action that targets major performance objectives listed on DA Form 67-9-1.
- Upon completion of the initial face-to-face counseling, date and initial Part IV (verification). Obtain senior rater's initials. Rated officer and rater retain file copy for use during later follow-up counselings.

Quarterly Follow-up Counselings (Part V- Reverse)

- Discuss major performance objectives and progress made. Adjust as needed.
- Discuss progress made on developmental tasks; update/modify tasks as needed to continue developmental process.
- Rater summarize key points in appropriate block of Part V.
- Rater and rated officer initial, date, and keep a file copy for use during later counselings.

NOTE: Reference for Army Leadership Doctrine is FM 22-100.

PART II CHARACTER. Disposition of the leader; combination of values, attributes, and skills affecting leader actions. (See FM 22-100)

ARMY VALUES

1. HONOR: Adherence to the Army's publicly declared code of values	5. RESPECT: Promotes dignity, consideration, fairness, & EO
2. INTEGRITY: Possesses high personal moral standards; honest in word and deed	6. SELFLESS-SERVICE: Places Army priorities before self
3. COURAGE: Manifests physical and moral bravery	7. DUTY: Fulfills professional, legal, and moral obligations
4. LOYALTY: Bears true faith and allegiance to the U.S. Constitution, the Army, the unit, and the soldier	

ATTRIBUTES Fundamental qualities and characteristics	MENTAL Possesses desire, will, initiative, and discipline	PHYSICAL Maintains appropriate level of physical fitness and military bearing	EMOTIONAL Displays self-control; calm under pressure
SKILLS (Competence) Skill development is part of self-development; prerequisite to action	CONCEPTUAL Demonstrates sound judgment, critical / creative thinking, moral reasoning	INTERPERSONAL Shows skill with people: coaching, teaching, counseling, motivating and empowering	TECHNICAL Possesses the necessary expertise to accomplish all tasks and functions
	TACTICAL Demonstrates proficiency in required professional knowledge, judgment, and warfighting		

PART III - DEVELOPMENTAL ACTION PLAN. Development tasks that target major performance objectives on the DA Form 67-9-1. (See FM 22-100)

INFLUENCING: Communicating, Decision Making, Motivating

COMMUNICATING. Articulates written and oral ideas/concepts clearly and concisely. Message received equals message sent. Displays effective listening skills.

DECISION MAKING. Reaches sound, logical decisions based on analysis/synthesis of information, and uses sound judgment to allocate resources and select appropriate course(s) of action.

MOTIVATING. Inspires, motivates, and guides others towards mission accomplishment. Sets the example by being in excellent physical / mental condition and consistently displaying proper military bearing.

OPERATING: Planning, Executing, Assessing

PLANNING. Uses critical and creative thinking to develop executable plans that are suitable, acceptable, and feasible.

EXECUTING. Shows tactical and technical proficiency; meets mission standards; takes care of people/resources. Maximizes the use of available systems and technology. Performs well under physical and mental stress.

DA FORM 67-9-1a, OCT 97

USAPA V1.00

Figure 5.2a Junior Officer Development Counseling Form.

ASSESSING. Uses after-action and evaluation tools to facilitate consistent improvement.

IMPROVING: Developing, Building, Learning

DEVELOPING. Teaches, trains, coaches and counsels subordinates increasing their knowledge, skills and confidence.

BUILDING. Develops effective, disciplined, cohesive, team built on bonds of mutual trust, respect, and confidence. Fosters ethical climate.

LEARNING. Actively seeks self-improvement (individual study, professional reading, etc.), and fosters a learning environment in the unit (IPRs, AARs, NCOPD, etc.)

PART IV - VERIFICATION: Rater initials _____ Rated officer initials _____ Date _____ Senior rater initials _____

PART V - DEVELOPMENTAL ASSESSMENT RECORD. Summary of key points made during follow-up counselings. Highlight progress and strengths observed as well as developmental needs across values, attributes, skills and actions.

1st Assessment — Key Points

Rated officer initials _____ Rater initials _____ Date _____

2nd Assessment — Key Points

Rated officer initials _____ Rater initials _____ Date _____

3rd Assessment — Key Points

Rated officer initials _____ Rater initials _____ Date _____

DA FORM 67-9-1a, OCT 97 (Reverse) USAPA V1.00

Figure 5.2b   Junior Officer Development Counseling Form.

BASE SYSTEM CIVILIAN PERFORMANCE COUNSELING CHECKLIST/RECORD
For use of this form, see AR 690-400; the proponent agency is ASA(M&RA)

RATEE	RATER
ORGANIZATION/INSTALLATION	INTERMEDIATE RATER *(Optional)*
PAY PLAN, SERIES/GRADE	RATING PERIOD	SENIOR RATER

PURPOSE. The primary purpose of counseling is to define organizational mission and values, discuss individual job expectations and performance, reinforce good performance/work related behavior, correct problem performance/work related behavior, and enhance the Ratee's ability to set and reach career goals. The best counseling is forward looking, concentrating on the future and what needs to be done better. Counseling should be timely. Counseling only at the end of the rating is too late since misunderstandings that impact performance and work related behavior cannot be resolved in time for improvement before the next annual rating.

RULES FOR COUNSELING.

1. Face-to-face counseling is mandatory for all civilians in the Base System.

2. Use this form along with a working copy of the Evaluation Form *(DA Form 7223)* and the Ratee's position description for conducting performance counseling and recording counseling content/dates.

3. Conduct initial counseling within at least the first 30 days of each rating period and again at the midpoint of the rating period.

AFTER COUNSELING

1. Summarize key points of the counseling on the back of this form and initial in the block provided. You may attach additional pages.

2. Give the Ratee the form to review/initial.

3. If the Ratee gave written input, attach it.

4. Forward the checklist through the rating chain to the Senior Rater *(if used)* who should review and, when satisfied that requirements are in line with mission needs, initial and date the checklist and return it to you.

5. Give the Ratee a copy and keep the original to use for the next counseling session.

CHECKLIST - LATER COUNSELING SESSION*(S)*

PREPARATION

1. Schedule the counseling session with the Ratee. Tell him/her to come prepared to discuss accomplishments and review requirements and effectiveness of any completed training.

2. Review notes from the last session.

3. Consider whether priorities or expectations have changed.

4. For each Value/Responsibility, answer these questions: What has the Ratee done? What was done well? Why? What could have been done better? Why?

5. Make notes to help focus when counseling.

CHECKLIST - COUNSELING AT THE BEGINNING OF THE RATING PERIOD

PREPARATION

1. Schedule the counseling session and notify the Ratee; suggest the Ratee write down or be ready to discuss ideas about expectations and requirements.

2. Get a copy of the Ratee's position description, rating chain, the counseling checklist, and a blank evaluation form.

3. Think how each Value and each Responsibility in Part V of the evaluation form applies.

4. Decide what you consider necessary for success in each Value/Responsibility. Be specific.

5. Make notes to help you with counseling.

COUNSELING

1. Explain the rating chain and the roles of each rater.

2. Discuss the position description. If the Ratee has worked in the job before, ask if he/she believes the description is accurate.

3. Discuss items that require top priority effort *(areas of special emphasis)*-realizing this may change later.

4. Discuss each Value/Responsibility in Part V of the evaluation form. Ask the Ratee for ideas about what Values mean and how he/she might perform assigned duties.

5. Review the Ratee's written input if he/she provides it.

6. Discuss what tasks and level of performance you expect for Success.

7. If you and the Ratee have different views, discuss them until you both are clear on requirements. Even if the Ratee disagrees, he/she must understand what you expect.

8. Using the DA-established performance standards and the tasks to be accomplished give examples of Excellence to give the Ratee specifics to aim for.

9. Ask the Ratee about career goals and training needs.

COUNSELING

1. Discuss job requirements and areas of special emphasis and priorities that have changed or that are new. Ask the Ratee if he/she is having problems and needs your help.

2. If the Ratee gives written input, review it.

3. Tell how the Ratee is doing. Talk specific examples of observed actions/results. Discuss differences in your views. Offer assistance if needed. The goal is to help the Ratee succeed.

4. Give examples of Excellence that occurred or could have occurred.

5. At least during the midpoint counseling session, discuss the Ratee's career goals, the effectiveness of training, and the Ratee's potential to perform higher level or different tasks.

AFTER COUNSELING

1. Follow the same procedures for documenting, initialing, and dating as you did for the initial session.

2. At the end of the rating period, use the checklist to prepare the Ratee's evaluation. Then attach the Counseling Checklist/Record to the performance evaluation for use by the rating chain. After the Senior Rater signs the performance evaluation, he/she returns it to the Rater to discuss with the Ratee, if a senior rater is used. After the Ratee signs, the Rater submits the evaluation with the checklist to the servicing personnel office for filing.

DA FORM 7223-1, AUG 1998   PREVIOUS EDITION IS OBSOLETE.   USAPA V1.00

Figure 5.3a Army Civilian Employee Counseling Form.

DA RESPONSIBILITIES AND PERFORMANCE STANDARDS

To derive Responsibilities ratings, think about the tasks that were performed under each Responsibility and apply the following performance standards which are written at the Success (Meets) level; e.g., the Ratee usually:

TECHNICAL COMPETENCE. Has knowledge, skills and abilities to do the work. Produces expected quality and volume. Meets deadlines. Works with right amount of supervision. Gets desired results.

ADAPTABILITY/INITIATIVE. Can work under pressure or during changing conditions. Is willing to try new ways. Suggests better ways to do business. Seeks/accepts developmental opportunities.

WORKING RELATIONSHIPS/COMMUNICATIONS. As a team member, works well with group and helps others get the job done. Expresses ideas clearly. Follows instructions or asks for clarification. Shows respect and is courteous. Shows concern for customer.

RESPONSIBILITY/DEPENDABILITY. Accepts responsibility for own actions. Keeps work area in order and equipment maintained. Uses supplies, equipment and time as intended. Complies with DA emphasis programs, e.g., Total Army Quality (TAQ), safety/security, internal control, inventory management, quality assurance, EEO/AA. Schedules nonemergency leave in advance to avoid adverse impact to work unit effectiveness.

FOR POSITIONS WITH SUPERVISORY DUTIES:

SUPERVISION/LEADERSHIP. Sets and communicates unit goals that reflect organizational goals. Implements/complies with appropriate DA emphasis programs. Sets standard/leads by example. Takes timely/appropriate personnel actions. Recruits/retains quality force. Motivates, challenges and develops subordinates, through counseling on expectations, performance, and career goals; evaluates timely. Resolves conflict and maintains order.

EQUAL EMPLOYMENT OPPORTUNITY/AFFIRMATIVE ACTION (EEO/AA). Applies EEO principles to all aspects of personnel management (e.g., hiring, training, work assignments/schedules, discipline, counseling and awards). As appropriate, takes immediate corrective action if sexual harassment or other discriminatory/unfair treatment is observed, reported or suspected. Provides leadership and emphasis to the execution of the Affirmative Employment Plan. Participates in EEO/AA activities and encourages subordinates to do so.

COUNSELING RECORD/INDIVIDUAL PERFORMANCE STANDARDS

DATE OF COUNSELING	RATEE/RATER/ INT. RATER/ SENIOR RATER INITIALS	KEY POINTS MADE
INITIAL		
LATER (Optional)		
MIDPOINT		
LATER (Optional)		

REVERSE, DA FORM 7223-1, AUG 1998 — USAPA V1.00

Figure 5.3b Army Civilian Employee Counseling Form.

■ Initially very structured and generally narrow in focus. The focus broadens, as individuals understand their strengths and weaknesses, determine their individual needs, and become more experienced. Each soldier's knowledge and perspective increases with experience, institutional training, and operational assignments, and is accelerated and broadened by specific, goal-oriented self-development actions.

3. Standards-based training and professional development programs are necessary to ensure that the proper skills are instilled through the training

Without standards for the training, there is no standardization or discipline. Here is the Army's definition and doctrine on performance-based training.

Performance-Oriented

1. *Performance-oriented training is hands-on and conducts the task under the conditions and to the standard specified.* Soldiers and leaders must be proficient in the basic skills required to perform their wartime missions under battlefield conditions. Units become proficient in the performance of critical tasks and missions by repeatedly practicing the tasks and missions to standard. Soldiers learn best through repetition, using a hands-on approach.

2. *Soldiers train better, faster, and to a higher degree of proficiency when they know the task, condition, and standard.* Likewise, training is more effective when it is performance-oriented and standards-based. *Enforcing standards allows leaders to identify and correct training deficiencies,* resulting in a more accurate assessment of combat capabilities.

3. *The complexity of the conditions is increased as soldier performance levels increase, while the standard remains constant.* Soldiers and leaders must execute the planned training, evaluate performance, and retrain until the Army standard is achieved under the most realistic conditions possible. They must evaluate and reinforce individual skills at each opportunity.

4. *The same standard must be enforced whether performed individually or as part of a larger operation.*

The italicized areas are the points that are important in developing your training programs. The training has to be hands-on, there has to be one standard, and the standard must be enforced across the board. Your employees will get more out of the professional development training if you standardize these three areas in your company.

According to the Warehousing Education and Research Council,

> Providing effective, results-oriented training to your warehouse and distribution center associates can pay off in increased productivity, higher morale, and lower turnover of staff. But it won't happen by itself. Training warehouse and DC associates has many components. A good training program addresses topics such as safety, warehouse functions, quality, systems, equipment, interpersonal relations, and government require-ments. . . . To implement an effective training program for warehouse associates, you need to have a full understanding of training needs across the facility or facilities.[3]

According to research conducted by the Warehousing Education and Research Council, Victoria's Secret's management explains to trainees the reason for each training session. In the Army, we set forth the purpose and the desired outcome for each training session. This process in the Army is known as providing the task, conditions, and standards. The task is the training subject for the session. The conditions are the conditions under which the training takes place. The standards set the bar for the training evaluation and what the trainees will learn during the session.

4. Build on experiences to enable lifelong learning

Lifelong learning is important not only to your employees' professional development but to the company's long-term goals as well. Coach John Wooden and President Calvin Coolidge are both credited with saying, "It is what you learn after you know it all that is important." At some point in everyone's career, they get to the point where they think they know it all about the job. This is where coaching, teaching, and mentoring will come in handy to spur the desire for further professional development.

5. Self-development and feedback are essential parts of lifelong learning

If the employee does not receive feedback or recognition for self-devel-opment activities and programs, he or she will stop doing them.

6. There are some other opportunities to professionally develop your employees that will help them hone their people skills

This comes from performing volunteer work in the community. Volunteer work provides goodwill for your company and allows your employees to hone their skills by helping others.

The Army sets aside a block of time every week for Sergeants' Time Training. Sergeants' Time Training is standards-based, performance-oriented, battle-focused training. Commanders emphasize individual soldier training in support of collective Mission Essential Task List[4] training by allocating dedicated training time for noncommissioned officers using Sergeants' Time Training. This training recognizes the first-line supervisor's primary role in conducting individual, crew, and small-team training. How much time do you set aside weekly for training? The Harley-Davidson plant in Kansas City has a program where the employees can request training on a particular topic. Although soldiers do not normally request the training topics for Sergeants' Time Training, the Harley-Davidson concept is similar in nature to the spirit of Sergeants' Time Training.

The Army has a Department of the Army pamphlet that deals with career progression and what schools and training a soldier needs for advancement. Do you have something similar? The Army's pamphlet gives timelines when a soldier should be promoted to the next rank, what key jobs the soldier should have during certain blocks of time, and what schools the soldier needs during certain phases of his or her career. In addition to career progression planning, the Army has a book known as the *Soldiers' Common Skills Manual*. This manual lists in detail all the common skills that every soldier must know to be successful on the battlefield. The training for the year for almost every unit in the Army is centered on these common tasks for individual training.

Training can cure most performance problems with employees. When you have a new employee or a problem employee, do you take the time to train him or her or do you find it easier to do the tasks yourself? As a company commander, I was finally given a company clerk to prepare all of the correspondence for my 550-soldier company. The newly assigned clerk was recently reclassified from another military occupational specialty. This meant that he had to learn the job of a company clerk while doing the job. Anyone who has ever seen an episode of *M*A*S*H* knows how much trouble Radar had trying to teach CPL Klinger to be the new clerk. This is exactly the situation that First Sergeant Horn, Sergeant First Class Brogsdale, and I faced when we got our new clerk. For the first several weeks we all found it easier to do our own typing rather than try to let the new clerk butcher the paper and redo it several times. Then it dawned on all of us that we were doing a great disservice to the clerk by not taking the time to teach him what he needed to know and let him make mistakes while learning so he would know what right really looked like. It was a frustrating month or two but in the long run the soldier, the company, and the Army were much better off because we decided to do the right thing and train him rather than take the easy way out and do it ourselves.

Training should use the crawl–walk–run approach. According to *Field Manual 7-1,*

> This allows and promotes an objective, standards-based approach to training. Training starts at the basic level. Crawl events are relatively simple to conduct and require minimum support from the unit. After the crawl stage, training becomes incrementally more difficult as the training progresses through the walk stage, requiring more resources from the unit and home station, and increasing the level of realism. At the run stage, the level of difficulty for the training event intensifies. Run stage training requires optimum resources and ideally approaches the level of realism expected in combat. Progression from the walk to the run stage for a particular task may occur during a 1-day training exercise or may require a succession of training periods.[5]

Summary and Conclusions

If you do what you've always done, you'll get what you've always got.

Darrell Waltrip[6]
Winner of 87 Winston Cup Races

Every year baseball players go to spring training in Florida or Arizona to get ready for the upcoming baseball season. During spring training, these professional ball players work on the basics such as base running, bunting, and hitting. Professional football players do the same thing every summer. They report to preseason camps and work on blocking and tackling. How often do you get back to the basics of your organization to get the most out of yourself and your employees? All too often we get caught up in the day-to-day pace and some of the basics are forgotten or in some cases with new employees, are never learned.

Studies show that employees work for the following reasons: work challenge, responsibility level, growth opportunity, and base pay, in this order. Are you developing, challenging, and retaining your people? Or are you simply trying to retain them by pay alone? If you want to keep quality employees, you have to give them the opportunity to grow and accept greater responsibility by providing them opportunities to professionally develop and acquire new and greater skill sets.

Dr. W. Edwards Deming set forth 14 points for the transformation of management.[7] Point 6 is, "Institute training on the job." Point 13 states, "Institute a vigorous program of education and self-improvement." That is the purpose of this chapter: to guide you in establishing training on the job and a vigorous program for self-improvement for all of your employees. Never let the schedule of operations prevent you from sending the right people to training. It is an investment in your employees and the future of your company.

When you are developing your training plans do not forget to plan the training for your successor. But be careful in training your replacement. All too often the training of the replacement yields the potential to teach the wrong things. This leads to a whole generation of employees that do not know what right looks like and presents the potential for a perpetually bad system. Train your replacement, make sure someone is ready to take your place in case something happens, but make sure you are training him or her in the right ways.

Whose job is it to make you the best you can be? The old Army slogan was "Be All That You Can Be!" Who is responsible for getting you there? I once heard a soldier say, "If this is all I can be, I am disappointed in my life!" Yes, you will have teachers, coaches, and mentors along the way, but the person that has to be responsible for helping you "Be All That You Can Be" is the person looking back at you in the mirror. People can only hold you back from reaching your potential if you let them. Or as Eleanor Roosevelt once said, "No one can make you feel inferior without your permission." No one can hold you back from becoming the best you can be without your permission. Do not grant that to anyone. The flip side is, whose job is it to assist your employees in becoming all that they can be? It is your job as a leader or a manager to help your employees reach their potential.

Unfortunately, it may take more than training to fix bad leadership. In an earlier example on changing for the sake of change, we discussed a leader who went out of his way to change everything that his predecessor did—right, wrong, or indifferent—just to make his mark on the unit. It took his replacement almost a year to get the morale back in the unit. It took just as long to get people in the unit to the point where they were comfortable enough to think for themselves and express opinions without fear of retribution. The bad news that most people did not see about this situation was that every one of the 30 lieutenants who were assigned to the unit during the reign of the bad leadership did not stay in the Army past their initial commitments. This style of leadership disillusioned the lieutenants. Because they only had that one point of reference with which to form an opinion of the Army, they all decided to seek other careers. In the next chapter, we look at leadership and how to use leadership to guide your organization to new levels of excellence.

Training and Professional Development Rules

1. Leaders and managers are responsible for the professional development training of their subordinates.
2. First-line supervisors train individuals and teams.
3. Train teams as a unit.
4. Train for operational efficiency. Training has to be performance oriented in order to provide effective feedback to participants.
5. Train to a set standard, not to time. If you have an hour to train but the standard is met in 30 minutes, then start training on a new subject. However, if you only have an hour to train and the subject requires more than an hour, find more time for training. Do not shorten the training to meet the abbreviated time schedule.
6. Take time to train employees on preventative maintenance of equipment.
7. Maintain individual and team proficiency. Use refresher training to keep employees current and ensure that they are not cutting corners because of a lack of training.
8. The future managers and leaders you train are your legacy and the future of the company. Take great care in ensuring the future of the company is sound. Do not adopt an attitude of "I am retiring soon, so that is someone else's problem." Do not allow the attitude of "I know you are leaving soon, so that is not your problem." If the future of your company is not sound, neither is your retirement check.

Questions for Thought and Discussion

1. When The Limited implemented a new Warehousing Management System, they provided 12 hours of training for employees. When the Army implemented the Standard Army Retail Supply System, they had 40 hours of training for all operators before implementing the system. For those units that had a long lag between the initial

training and the actual fielding date, there was a series of follow-up training sessions. These sessions lasted two to five days depending on the length of the time lag. The purpose of the follow-up training was to ensure that the operators of the system were comfortable with the hardware and software. How much time do you allocate to training for a new system?

2. Training and retention: is there a link? What are the costs of a quality training program and what are the cost savings? What is the cost of not conducting training? Is training a draw on the bottom line or an investment in the future of your company?

3. Participating in the activities of professional associations/seminars on your own, is there a benefit to you to doing professional development on your own time even if the company does not pick up the tab?

4. What are some areas that you need to focus on in your organization?

Book List for Chapter Five

1. Aguayo, Rafael, *Dr. Deming—The American Who Taught the Japanese About Quality*, Simon & Schuster, New York, 1990.
2. *Field Manual 7-1, Battle Focused Training*, Department of the Army, Washington, DC, September 2003.
3. Waltrip, Darrell, with Jade Gurss, *DW—A Lifetime of Going Around in Circles*, Putnam, New York, 2004.
4. *WERCwatch*, Warehousing Education and Research Council, Winter 2004. The Warehousing Education and Research Council puts out a monthly newsletter, *WERCsheet*, and a quarterly *WERCwatch*. Each of these publications contains valuable information on warehousing and distribution training topics.

Notes

1. From the back cover of the Council of Logistics Management Booklet, *Careers in Logistics*.
2. Interview published in the April edition of *DC Velocity Magazine*.
3. WERCwatch, Warehousing Education and Research Council, Winter 2004, p.1.
4. A Mission Essential Task List is a listing of all missions that a unit should be able to successfully accomplish based on their equipment and personnel.
5. *Field Manual 7-1, Battle Focused Training*, Department of the Army, Washington, DC, September 2003, p. 5-4.
6. Waltrip, Darrell, with Jade Gurss, *DW—A Lifetime of Going Around in Circles*, Putnam, New York, 2004.

7. For more on Dr. Deming's 14 points for transforming management, see *Dr. Deming—The American Who Taught the Japanese About Quality*, by Rafael Aguayo, Simon & Schuster, New York, 1990. In addition to being an excellent primer on Dr. Deming's work, the foreword is by Dr. Deming.

Chapter 6

Leadership and Lessons for Leading 21st-Century Supply Chains to the Next Level of Excellence

Leadership is "the accomplishment of a goal through the director of human assistants."

W.C.H. Prentice[1]

When you are dealing with people, you go much farther if you don't go so much by the book, but by the heart.

"Barney Fife"[2]

You can achieve supply chain excellence through the effective use of leadership. In this chapter, we look at the values of leaders and how those values contribute to the success of a company or organization. We contrast leadership and management and look at why they are different and why you need to have both in your organization.

Leadership remains a lot like love for several reasons, primarily because, just like love, everyone knows what leadership is and can recognize it when they see it but has great trouble defining what it is.

The other similarity between leadership and love is that both require a great deal of passion. Leaders have to be passionate about their jobs, their missions, and most important, about their employees. Leadership is about the people and getting them to achieve their best in any situation.

Much has been written about the different management styles. Let's take a quick look at these styles as an introduction to management. This will establish a management baseline that we can use to compare and contrast leadership and management.

Many managers still subscribe to the Machiavellian theory of management. Just what is the Machiavellian theory of management? Management by fear and retribution. A Machiavellian manager thinks nothing of denigrating an employee in front of everyone and certainly never thinks twice about firing an employee before investigating a situation.

Here is an example of a Machiavellian manager. During a recent meeting of a large professional organization, the president of the organization addressed the assembled crowd of volunteer leaders. In his presentation, the president stated, "Can you fire volunteers? I have no problem firing a volunteer if they are not putting in enough time." This presentation immediately followed a presentation on how to stop the decline in membership of the organization. With managers such as this placed in leadership positions, is there any question why this organization is faltering while similar organizations are continuing to prosper and attract new members?

Douglas McGregor postulated the concepts of Theory X and Theory Y management styles in 1960 in his book, *The Human Side of Enterprise*. These theories are still in use today. Theory X postulates that the average person possesses an inherent dislike for work and will do everything possible to avoid it. We have all had this type of employee work for us. Usually they possess the attitude of, "You want me to do some work for that paycheck?" McGregor felt that the average worker wants to be directed. The assumption of Theory X management is that people must be controlled because of their dislike for work and efforts to avoid working. I once had a young officer working for me who was perhaps the most brilliant person I have ever had work for me. However, he was a classic example of McGregor's Theory X. This particular officer would spend more time trying to find ways out of work than he would actually spend working. He would, in fact, spend exorbitant amounts of time trying to find a way out of a simple five-minute task. We revisit this officer when we get to the discussion on leadership.

The basic assumption of Theory Y is that working is a natural condition for employees. This theory assumes that workers enjoy working and therefore do not need the controls postulated by Theory X. Managing and leading this type of employee is much easier than a Theory X-type employee. Some academicians will tell you that neither of these theories is realistic. As we discuss leadership we look at the impacts and realities of these categories of employees.

William Ouchi developed the third major management theory, Theory Z. Theory Z is a byproduct of the swell in admiration for the Japanese management styles in the 1970s. Theory Z is more of a participative management style and assumes that a strong sense of commitment to be part of something worthwhile is the primary motivator. This is somewhat analogous to Maslow's hierarchy of needs, with self-actualization at the top of the pyramid.

Now that we have looked at the major management styles and theories, what is management and how does it differ from leadership? Also, do you need management and leadership to be successful and can you be both manager and leader at the same time?

> *No man is a leader until his appointment is ratified in the minds and hearts of his men.*

> **Anonymous, *The Infantry Journal*, 1948**

The U.S. Army *Field Manual 3-0, Operations,* states,

> The role of the leader and leadership is central to all Army operations. Leadership is influencing people—by providing purpose, direction, and motivation—while operating to accomplish the mission and improving the organization. Purpose gives soldiers a reason to do tasks. Direction communicates the way to accomplish the mission. Motivation gives soldiers the will to accomplish the mission. Leadership and the warrior ethos sustain soldiers during the brutal realities of combat and help them cope with the ambiguities of complex military operations.[3]

This *Field Manual* is the cornerstone of all Army operations. In the very next paragraph it says,

> Leaders create conditions for success. Organizing, equipping, training, and leading soldiers to accomplish operational missions are the goals of leaders. Will and determination mold soldiers into effective organizations. Full spectrum operations demand Army leaders who are masters of both the art and the science of military operations, and have the training and temperament to adapt to any situation. Success comes from imaginative, flexible, and daring soldiers and leaders.[4]

Leadership

What is leadership? The Army defines it as, "Leadership is influencing people—by providing purpose, direction, and motivation—while operating to accomplish the mission and improving the organization."[5] In an article in the *Harvard Business Review*, Abraham Zaleznik states, "Leadership inevitably requires using power to influence the thoughts and actions of other people."[6] Zaleznik's definition is very close to the Army's definition of leadership.

Is there a difference then between leadership and management? Which one do you need? In order to answer this question, we need to look at the definition of a manager. According to *Webster's Third International Dictionary*, a manager is "a person that conducts, directs, or supervises something as a person whose work or profession is the management of a specified thing (as a business, an institution, or a particular phase or activity within a business or institution)."[7] Although we have already looked at a couple of definitions of leadership, to provide a balance, we use *Webster's* again to define a leader: "a person who by force of example, talents, or qualities of leadership plays a directing role, wields commanding influence, or has a following in any sphere of activity or thought."[8] The keys to defining the difference between a manager and a leader from these definitions is the "force of example, talents, or qualities of leadership" that a leader uses in directing and influencing whereas a manager usually manages specified things.

Management is a subject and discipline that can be taught in a classroom without any hands-on experience. This is evident in the number of schools that teach management courses. Leadership is a skill set that requires experiential learning. A leader needs a mentor and coach and an atmosphere that allows the leader to make decisions in a nonthreatening environment to gain experience and confidence.

How does this translate to commercial supply chains? Every link in the supply chain requires a manager for the specific functions of that link in the chain. The supply chain manager focuses on the operations and managing the resources. The supply chain leader focuses on inspiring, influencing, and guiding the people who work in the supply chain. The key is that you lead people and you manage things.

> The attribute—the gifts and skills—that allow a person to lead are timeless and indifferent to whether the individual is Casper Milquetoast or a braggart. And just as personal style doesn't determine the ability to lead, that ability is no guarantee of virtue. The ultimate test of leadership is having willing and inspired followers.
>
> **Warren Bennis**[9]

This quote from Warren Bennis about the attributes of leaders makes a good lead-in to a discussion of the attributes of world-class leaders. In a previous work, I listed the attributes of quality leaders as an acronym that spelled LEADERSHIP.[10] Further research into the habits and attributes of great leaders in history has prompted an update of the list. The new list of qualities and attributes looks similar to the original LEADERSHIP acronym but there are more attributes. After looking at the attributes in the LEADERSHIP format, we reorder them based on the priority of the attributes. The new list looks like this.

Loyalty/Respect

A true leader has to be loyal not only to those above him or her, but equally as important, to those that work for him or her. General Patton once said, "I prefer a loyal staff officer to a brilliant one." Employees know when the leadership is loyal to them and concerned about their welfare and professional growth. Loyalty from your employees is something that you must earn; you cannot buy loyalty. During the days of Sun Tzu (500 BC) and during the days of the Napoleonic Wars, loyalty could be bought and sold. The problem with purchased loyalty is that someone else can purchase the loyalty just as easily. The free-agent "wars" after the end of each professional sport season are a good example of purchasing loyalty, or better yet, an example of loyalty only to the dollar. You cannot force loyalty on an individual, nor can you buy it as you could during the Napoleonic days. The quick collapse of the Hussein regime in Iraq is an example of the fickleness of "forced" loyalty. As soon as the forcing force is out of power, the "forced" loyalty will quickly evaporate or switch to another leader.

Here is a good example of loyalty from World War II. Anyone who has seen the movie *Patton* is familiar with the "slapping incident." During the campaign on Sicily, General Patton visited a field hospital where he came across a soldier suffering from battle fatigue. General Patton regularly visited to check on the soldiers that served under him. In this particular incident, General Patton slapped the soldiers who suffered from the then-unknown ailment, battle fatigue. Rather than letting the press have a field day, General Eisenhower tried to keep a lid on the story. General Eisenhower knew that General Patton had the ability to get the most out of his soldiers and realized that the story had the possibility of ending the career of his long-time friend. General Eisenhower knew that he would need such an exceptional officer and leader for exploiting the Normandy Invasion.

Respect

Respect for employees and co-workers is necessary for a productive work environment. Although a leader must earn respect, the respect for subordinates must be constantly present. In his book, *Ground Rules for Winners,* Joe Torre writes, "To get respect, you have to give respect."[11] There is a difference between the respect for a position and the respect for the person in that position. You have to strive to earn the personal respect afforded your job or position. It is more important to the success of your supply chain to earn respect from your subordinates for your abilities to produce results and take care of them than just to be respected for your position.

One area of respect for others that many leaders violate is the respect for the employees' time. President Eisenhower did not like making people wait for him to show up; consequently he showed up ten minutes early for every appointment. Coach Vince Lombardi operated on a very similar concept that he called Lombardi Time: always arrive ten minutes early for every meeting. Coach Lombardi's concept was if you showed up five minutes early, you were actually five minutes late.

How many times have you had to wait for the boss to show up for a meeting? I have seen "leaders" who intentionally made people wait for them to show up for a meeting, "Because I am the boss." Your employees may not make the same amount of money that you do, but their time is just as valuable to them as yours is to you.

Ethics/Integrity/Honesty/Courage

> *A leader has no asset more valuable and no tool more effective than the truth.[12]*

These qualities are very closely related. The original list of world-class leadership attributes listed these related attributes separately. Compromising any of these qualities will affect your ability to lead.

There is no "right way" to do something that is wrong. Pete Rose, when asked why he continued to bet on baseball when he knew it was wrong, stated, "I did not think I would get caught." Does that make it right? No! When the former president was asked why he had had an affair with an intern he answered, "Because I could." No matter how hard you try to justify it, if it is wrong, it is wrong, and not being caught does not make it right. Another baseball player of note, John "Buck" O'Neil,[13] makes this point very clear when he says, "Always tell the truth, and if that is not possible, tell the truth anyway."

Today's headlines are full of examples of unethical behavior by leaders of major corporations. As with integrity, once you have compromised your ethics, it is hard for employees to follow you. If something does not feel right, it probably is not right. Most world-class leaders have an ethical compass inside them. However, every so often, that compass goes out of whack and greed takes over. The Enron debacle is a good example of this. Insider trading is another good example of this type of behavior.

"When making a decision, ethical leaders should ask themselves whether they would like to see the action they are contemplating on tomorrow morning's front page."[14] In an article in the *California Management Review*, Trevino, Hartman, and Brown explain this as the *New York Times* test. Other tests that I have found of great value are, "How would I explain this to my children?" and, "What would I tell my parents if I did this knowing that it was wrong?" But probably the greatest test of all is in the poem by Dale Winbrow, "The Man in the Glass." Can you look yourself in the eye in the mirror when you are shaving or putting on your makeup? If you cannot look yourself in the eye after committing an act because you know it was not ethical, then why do it?

The best way to squash rumors in your organization is to tell the truth. Unlike good wine, bad news does not get better with age and as we have all seen even in the highest levels of government, leaks will occur. When leaks occur, the employees start talking and spreading their version of the truth. Get the truth out to the employees and let them know what is going on. In today's electronic age, an unconfirmed rumor can be around the world in less than a few minutes and could potentially cause extreme problems on Wall Street.

Honesty is important for your employees but it is also important in how you treat applicants for jobs in your company. If the applicant is not qualified for the job or was not the most qualified for the job, be honest and at the same time tell the person what he or she can do to be better prepared. It may be as simple as taking additional courses or being better organized at the interview. Do not tell the applicant or candidate after a series of interviews that you picked a more experienced person if the real reason was a forced hire of an internal applicant or because the candidate's salary requirements were outside what you could afford. This happened to me during my job search. After already telling a company that their offer was only about one-half of what I was looking for and politely telling them that I was not interested in the position for that amount, I received a call from the company officer with whom I had previously spoken. I was told, "We found someone with more experience for the job." Being the inquisitive person that I am, I asked how they found someone with more than 26 years of experience who was willing to work for so small a salary. After reviewing my qualifications and reminding the interviewer of our previous conversation, she admitted that they could not afford my salary requirements. I politely thanked her for calling me back but could not help thinking that she would have preserved her integrity and trust by being honest at the beginning. Unfortunately, trust that is lost is hard to regain. Be honest with your employees and prospective employees; you never know when you may need their skill sets in the future.

Honest and open communications are necessary to establish and maintain your credibility. In 1993, the *Stars and Stripes* newspaper in Germany ran an article that the Army was going to deactivate the 11th Armored Cavalry Regiment, stationed at Fulda. The 11th Armored Cavalry Regiment had served as the guard for the Fulda Gap, the supposed path that the Soviet Union would use to invade West Germany from East Germany. With the fall of the Berlin Wall and the reunification of Germany, this was no longer a viable threat to the security of Germany and Europe. The Army vehemently denied this "rumor" and insisted that the 11th Armored Cavalry Regiment would not be deactivated. Less than three weeks later the newest list of units to deactivate or return to the United States as part of the "drawdown" of U.S. forces in Germany was released. The 11th Armored Cavalry Regiment was indeed on the list. This caused a loss of confidence on the part of many soldiers that the Army would continue to be straightforward and honest about the future of the force and the units in Germany.

Courage

Closely related to the other three attributes in this section is the attribute of courage. In this attribute, we are not talking about the courage exhibited by Audie Murphy or numerous other soldiers in the heat of combat. That kind of courage is an attribute of leadership but not one that all leaders will need to possess in their careers. In this case, courage is the courage to do what is right. Let's look at an example of courage and doing what is right with a problem employee. When you have a problem employee, do you prefer to talk to everyone about that person's behavior except for the person that has the behavior problem? You have to have the courage to face your employees and discuss their strengths as well as their weaknesses. When you make a mistake, do you have the courage to admit it, apologize, and move on?

One of the Mary Kay Cosmetics rules for leaders is, "Always do what is right, honorable, and ethical." Not a bad rule. This should be the rule for every leader in every organization.

Attitude

The great motivational speaker Zig Zigler tells audiences, "Your attitude and not your aptitude will determine your altitude." Your attitude gives you the power to add or detract from the happiness of everyone you meet. As a leader, your attitude permeates throughout your organization, no matter how large or small. Sam Walton, the founder of Wal-Mart, was convinced that the attitude you show your employees will be reflected within two weeks in the attitude that your employees show your customers. What attitude do you want your customers to see? I keep a note on my desk at home with a quote from Kansas City Chiefs Head Coach, Dick Vermeil. Coach Vermeil tells his players, "There's only one thing more infectious than a good attitude. And that is a bad attitude."

What about negative thinking? As a competitive powerlifter for over 20 years and a coach for several more years after that, I tried to focus on positive thoughts, especially on the day of a big competition. What do you think would happen if while standing under 800 pounds I started thinking, "This is heavy, it may crush me"? In business, there is little difference; you have to focus on positive thoughts and keep your employees doing the same thing. Negative thinking will give you exactly what it promises: that would be nothing, almost like a self-fulfilling prophesy. Positive thinking will produce something. Something is definitely better than the nothing you get from negative thinking. Negative thinking usually comes from a fear or false expectation of reality or a lack of confidence. If you expect the worst, you will not be disappointed. If you expect to fail, you probably will. You need to have a plan in the event the worst-case scenario does happen, but do not sit around thinking negative thoughts.

Here is an example of the power of negative thinking. The famous magician Harry Houdini provides this example for us. Houdini was proud of the fact that he could escape from any jail cell. One time he was locked in a prison with no clothes and told that he could not get out of his cell. After the cell door was closed, Houdini produced a wire from his mouth and started working on the door. After more than an hour of trying unsuccessfully and sweating profusely, he finally leaned on the door and it opened. You see, the door was never locked, except in Houdini's mind. The moral of this little vignette is: are you working against a locked door or a locked mind? Do not let negative thoughts limit your potential or the potential of your employees.

D4: Devotion/Dedication/Determination/Discipline

These are the four corners of motivational success! These four attributes of world-class leadership are closely linked to attitude. How often have you heard, "I've been there, done that, and it did not work"? Is that indicative of a lack of determination and dedication? With the right devotion to getting the mission accomplished coupled with a devotion to taking care of your people, there is no limit to what your organization can accomplish. There is no sign that says, "STOP—You have reached the limits of your potential!"

Dedication and determination are necessary for seeing a project to completion. How often in history has a person stopped just short of a goal and missed something great? Legend has it that Alexander Graham Bell took that extra step after one inventor stopped literally one screw turn short of inventing the telephone. In Calico, California, one of the country's richest silver strikes took place. Desert lore has it that the original miners stopped only a few feet short of the silver strike because of frustration and a lack of dedication. The next set of miners to try the same stake and the same hole hit the strike. How often have you stopped a few feet short of a record strike? Worse, how many times have your employees stopped "just a few feet short" of a record strike?

I recently heard Dr. Robert Schuller say, "I would rather attempt to do something great and fail, than to attempt to do nothing at all." This is a good example of devotion, dedication, and determination. Wayne Gretsky, the great hockey player, put it a little differently than Dr. Schuller. Gretsky's slant on determination is, "You miss 100% of the shots you never take." The fourth square of D4 is discipline: discipline in your professional life, discipline in your personal life (this includes your diet and exercise), discipline in your personal professional development, and discipline with your operations and personnel. Habits lead to standards, standards lead to discipline, and in any endeavor, with discipline all things are possible.

Here is an example from my life. How do you go from being a 98-pound wrestler as a sophomore in high school to being an international powerlifting champion and bodybuilding champion at 198 pounds over a ten-year period of time? Only by applying dedication and discipline to a grueling workout regimen and listening to my coaches and teachers. By applying dedication and discipline to my workouts, I was able in 1984 to win the Hawaii International Powerlifting Championships, two European Armed Forces Championships in 1993 and 1994, and in 1987 I was fortunate to exceed the existing world record in the squat by 14 pounds with a lift of 840 pounds.

The same application of discipline to your personal life and to your professional life will enable you to reach any goal to which you set your mind. Your limits to your career and accomplishments are within you.

In business, as in combat operations, without leadership and discipline, bad things happen. This generation saw that at the Abu Ghraib prison. But we also saw what happens without leadership and discipline at

WorldCom, Enron, and Global Crossing. Discipline is necessary in all aspects of business, just as it is in all aspects of military operations. Good order and discipline help in motivating your employees, just as bad order and discipline can do the opposite.

Here is an example of discipline that negatively motivates employees. Let's look at the motivational techniques of Shaka Zulu. "Every day, Shaka's men would be put through their paces, marching forty or fifty miles at a time, practicing army maneuvers and, although Shaka looked after his men well, if anyone fell out of rank during these marches they were ruthlessly executed on the spot by a rearguard hand-picked by Shaka for this very purpose."[15] Is that the kind of motivation you need to reach your goals? Most definitely not; the motivation you need comes from within by applying D4.

It is up to you to use D4 to motivate your employees. Look at the words of General Patton: "It is up to the manager to motivate his people, and the most important ingredient in motivation is knowledge of goals, objective, purpose. . . . Communicate. Don't just give pep talks. Communicate facts."[16]

Equality/Example

Equality is an interesting topic. The fact that inequality exists at all is unfortunate but it is a reality. The U.S. Army and the other armed services are probably the best examples of equal treatment for everyone regardless of sex or ethnic background. But even that does not always work the way it is supposed to. In Kuwait, I had an African-American lieutenant reporting to me at the Theater Distribution Center. This lieutenant came to me one day and said he refused to work with the Bangladeshi forklift drivers and stated that he wanted them gone and would replace them with soldiers. I asked why and the reply was, "I don't like them and they don't speak English." His reasoning caught me off guard. I asked if he had ever experienced discrimination. I knew this was a stupid question but I was trying to make a point. He answered yes with a very puzzled look on his face. I then asked, "How did you like it?" (I know, another stupid question, but the question did make the point.) After a long talk about the quality of work that these forklift drivers were doing for me despite not speaking the language and a longer talk about how to treat people, the lieutenant made the decision to work with the forklift drivers. I mention this story because no matter how hard you try and how far we progress as a country, prejudice still exists.

America's history with racial inequality is evident in the displays at the Civil Rights Museum in Memphis, Tennessee, and at the Negro Leagues Baseball Museum in Kansas City, Missouri. For way too many years, people assumed that "separate but equal" was okay; even though it was separate it was far from equal. Thankfully, we have moved past this as a nation. Unfortunately, we have not moved past it completely everywhere.

But there are other forms of equality or lack thereof that also have an impact on your supply chain operations. Do you have a favorite department that you show the boss every time he or she comes by? Do you have a favorite division, section, or office staff? Does it appear that you do? At the National Training Center, the commanding general rarely came by the shops or warehouses of the Theater Support Command. The commander was always at the offices of the Operations Group and the 11th Armored Cavalry Regiment or out in the field with these units. After being approached by a large number of soldiers wanting to know why the general never visited them, I approached him about it. I told him that my soldiers felt like they were not important because he did not visit them. What I found out was, "Be glad I do not have time to come down there. I only have time to be where there are problems. Since you do not have any, I have to focus my attention elsewhere." When I passed this on to the soldiers, they were happy and proud that they were doing so well that the general did not have to visit them. Nevertheless, the perception before the explanation was that the other units were receiving preferential treatment. Do you have a perception problem like that?

Here is an example from the sports world of how to handle equality and favoritism. In his book, *Coach Wooden One-on-One,* Coach John Wooden says,

> Each year before our first practice I would tell my players something like this: 'I will love you all the same, but I won't like you all the same. You won't like each other all the same; you won't like me all the same. I understand that.
>
> You may feel, at times, that I have double standards, as I certainly will not treat you all the same. I think treating everyone the same shows partiality. However, I will attempt to give each player the treatment that he earns and deserves according to my judgment and in keeping with what I consider the best interest of the team.[17]

The key for a successful leader is the ability to treat every employee as an individual. Treating employees all the same can create some morale problems. If you are going to treat employees differently based on their needs and abilities, make sure, like Coach Wooden, you tell them up front.

Example is the second attribute of world-class leadership that starts with "E." All leaders must lead by example. The Army has a philosophy, although not subscribed to by everyone today, that you should never ask your soldiers to do something that you are not willing to do yourself. Obviously, there are some tasks that everyone would prefer not to do. Setting up and taking down tents is an example of this. My philosophy is if you sleep in the tent, you should help set it up and take it down when the time comes

Driving the forklift at the open-air Theater Distribution Center in Kuwait is an example of leading by example. When the soldiers were tired but there were still supplies to move, I thought nothing of getting on the forklift and doing some of the work. One officer who would rather complain than work made the comment to a group of people in an e-mail that "seeing the colonel on the forklift is an example of everything that is wrong with logistics in this operation." I guess everyone is entitled to his or her opinion. I can assure you his supplies would have made it to his soldiers faster if he had been willing to get on a forklift and help load his trucks. A person's rank or title does not preclude him or her from doing a little work if it will inspire the workers to work harder at taking care of the customer.

Responsibility

Not only do you have to take responsibility for your actions, you must also take responsibility for the actions of your organization. You may not need to subscribe to the military theory that the commander is responsible for all of the actions of his or her command. However, you still need to accept the responsibility for what your section or division does.

You cannot delegate your responsibility. You must take an active interest in your daily operations to ensure the right things are happening and are happening when they should be. Not knowing or "not being in the loop" are not valid excuses; you are still responsible for your actions.

You have a responsibility to take care of your employees. They need to know that you are providing top cover for them so they feel comfortable in taking calculated risks because they know that you will back them up. You have a responsibility to your employees to make sure they are professionally developed and prepared for any contingency that may affect their performance and that of their section.

Self-Development

This topic received full coverage in Chapter 5, however, always remember: it is your career and no one has a greater stake in your success than you do. Take the necessary steps to remain current in your profession. Do this even if it means you have to do it on your own time and maybe with your own dime. This is a small investment in your future. In addition, make sure your employees get the opportunity to develop themselves as well. Give them the opportunities and encourage them to take advantage of the opportunities available.

Humor

Harvey MacKay, the author of such classics as *Swim with the Sharks, Shark Proof,* and *Dig Your Well before You Are Thirsty,* tells readers and audiences, "Take your job seriously, but do not take yourself so seriously that you cannot laugh at yourself." Do not take yourself so seriously that you cannot laugh at yourself when you do something stupid or something that is funny. I often ask audiences, "How many of you, by show of hands, have never done anything stupid at work?" Amazingly, no one has ever raised his or her hand. If you do something stupid, be able to laugh at yourself. I assure you everyone else will be laughing. It is better to laugh with them rather than have them laugh at you.

Reader's Digest started a column over 40 years ago called "Laughter, the Best Medicine." This was a true statement then and it still is. Take time to laugh! As a Hawaiian friend told me once, "It won't make your face break to laugh or smile."

As a leader or manager, the attribute of humor should not be misconstrued as a license to tell offensive or foul jokes. Moreover, you need to set the example for your employees in this area. However, humor as an attribute of leadership does mean that you can laugh at things that are funny. As a leader, you must set the example and create a climate in your organization where people can have fun, laugh, yet still get the job done.

Interest in Employees

The opening quote for this chapter from the *Andy Griffith Show*'s "Barney Fife" is an example of taking interest in your employees. Sometimes you really do have to deal with employees from the heart. Dealing with employees from the heart rather than the rulebook does not mean break the rules but always remember to take care of your employees. Get to know your employees and what their interests are. General Patton told his staff over 60 years ago to take a genuine interest in the things that were of interest to the soldiers. What is going on with your employees? What are their hobbies? How many children do they have? If a good worker suddenly starts having problems, find out why. If you have to write down items of interest about a worker on an index card, do it. Then refer to the card before you know you will see that employee. Salespeople do this all the time with clients. Do you think a salesperson knows everything about a client? More than likely, he or she has a memory good enough to write down items of interest after a sales call and a good enough memory to read the card before the next sales call.

You will be amazed at how surprised some of your employees will be when you ask about their spouse or children by name, or ask about a hobby. Watch their eyes light up when they realize that you "remembered" that small piece of information. Taking an interest in your employees is a very inexpensive way to build morale and motivate your workers. Workers would much rather work for someone who cares about them and takes an interest in them and their families. On a visit to an old unit that was experiencing leadership problems, I asked one of the soldiers about his hobby of racing cars. Not only did he want to bring me up to date on what he was doing but the initial response was, "Sir, you remembered!"

Credibility is important to success as a leader, but so is compassion and taking an interest in your employees. Your employees will not care how much you know until they know how much you care.

Take the time to take an interest in your employees and then watch the morale start improving at a rapid rate. Remember, this attribute of leadership is very inexpensive yet will pay you and your company huge dividends. Help your employees achieve what is important to them. The great negotiator Ron Shapiro told an audience at the Logistics and Supply Chain Forum, "To get what you want, help others get what they want." You can do this by taking an interest in what interests them.

One of the best ways to find out what is important to your employees is through the use of sensing sessions. The Army conducts regular sensing sessions with the commander, command sergeant major, and a randomly selected group of soldiers to get a feel for what soldiers are thinking. If the leader is out of the office on a regular basis, there should be no surprises. How do you get your employees to open up and be candid about problems, perceived problems, or potential problems? You have to build trust.

This comes from knowing the soldiers and solving the problems that they bring up. The word will spread like wildfire if you solve their problems and the next group will be eager to open up and tell you what is bothering them. As the Commander of the National Training Center's Theater Support Command, I held monthly and quarterly sessions with my soldiers. The sessions were initially set up to discuss any particular equal opportunity problems, but I found them to be an opportunity to speak to smaller groups of soldiers about what we were doing to improve their quality of life and work conditions. I made it very clear that I was taking notes but unless it was a personal problem that only affected one particular soldier, I was not taking names. I showed the notes to all of the attendees to reinforce the notion that I was not taking names, only issues. I then had one of my noncommissioned officers get the e-mail addresses of the attendees and I had that NCO e-mail each of the attendees the results of the problem-solving processes. The word spread quickly: if you wanted a problem solved, bring it up at the sensing session, but make sure you had your facts straight before bringing the issue to the commander.

One of the benefits of spending time observing operations and talking to the soldiers in the motorpools, warehouses, and other work areas was that most of the issues were not surprises and in most cases a solution was being worked on. The other benefit was that without asking, I could usually identify the unit that a soldier was in just from the morale, attitude, and answers to questions that I posed to him or her at the sessions.

Here is an example of problems that could be identified from holding regular sensing sessions. This example is from a memo written by an employee of a major logistics software provider.

> 1. No one respects our Director, her decisions or motives. 2. We are treated like children. 3. We consistently get the message that we aren't trusted. My question is this: why hire us if you do not trust us?
>
> Reporting is ridiculous. We spend an inordinate amount of time making tic marks, discussing reporting, reporting . . . just so our Director can disappear and promote herself wherever possible. If something goes wrong, we are the first to receive the wrath (filtered thru her poor managers) but if something goes right, she's first in line for credit. There is an "oppressive" feeling among management . . . seems to be quite a bit of pressure to make a certain appearance at all times and to always say the right things. It appears that managers often are forced to carry out or voice decisions they don't necessarily stand behind, having been coerced (or dictated to) in order to further a personal agenda.
>
> Communication from the top is laughable. The director is never here and does not make herself available. A big deal is made of her "open door" policy but nothing could be farther from the truth. It only takes once to learn that it won't pay to go to her for help on a problem. Problems aren't allowed. Only positives.

Taking an interest in your employees also means taking an interest in why subordinate supervisors want to fire an employee. The book, *Life's Little Instruction Book,* provides us with some very good insights on life and leadership. Rule number 43 states, "Never give up on anybody.

Miracles happen every day." Let me tell you a story that emphasizes that. As a brigade commander at the Army's National Training Center, I had legal jurisdiction over my brigade's soldiers, as well as the soldiers of the garrison command (all of the soldiers involved in the day-to-day running of the installation), the hospital, and the dental clinic. One of my duties in this capacity was to review every action that would result in putting a soldier out of the Army. The Army can put a soldier out of the Army for a variety of reasons including being overweight, failure to pass a physical fitness test, drug and alcohol abuse, repeated acts of indiscipline, or because of not conforming to the Army's standards or lifestyle. Soldiers with drug problems leave very little latitude for the chain of command because we cannot afford to have soldiers with this type of problem handling weapons or working on equipment or injured soldiers. Soldiers with repeated problems or those who "do not conform" usually are a different matter. Some of the soldiers that were referred to me for determination of whether to keep in the Army or discharge were obviously a problem to the unit and needed to leave the Army.

I personally reviewed every case that came to my office, much to the chagrin of the other commanders. I later found out that my predecessor had simply signed the necessary paperwork without ever talking to the soldier. I made it a policy to see the entire packet and talk to the soldier. I did this for two reasons. The first was that I wanted to hear the soldier's side of the story and wanted to ask questions about the incidents that led up to his or her coming to my office. The second reason was to talk to the soldiers who were going to be released from the Army to (1) make sure they understood the consequences of being released from the Army and (2) to see what their plans were for their future and give them some advice about how to turn their lives around and become productive.

Some cases were cut and dried, like the soldier who was assigned to a local recruiting office after completion of basic training and her advanced individual training courses. The Army does this on a routine basis. The premise is that the "local" soldier will have more credibility in selling the Army than the recruiter. In this particular case, the soldier decided she did not like the recruiter and went Absent WithOut Leave (AWOL). She was apprehended because she used the recruiter as a reference when she applied for a job at the local Wal-Mart. Some cases were a little more complicated.

Two particular cases drive home the point that you need to know all of the information before firing a person from the job. In the first case we will call the soldier Specialist Smith. Specialist Smith was being put out of the Army because his first-line supervisor had convinced the chain of command that he was incompetent and a risk to soldier safety as a medical specialist. When I reviewed the packet on the soldier I discovered that he had been recommended for promotion only a few months earlier and sent to the Army's Primary Leadership Development Course at Fort Lewis. He had been removed from that course because he failed his map reading course (there is a big difference between the terrain at Fort Irwin, California, in the middle of the Mojave Desert and the terrain at Fort Lewis, Washington). I found out that no one from the chain of command had taken the time to ensure that Specialist Smith knew how to read a map and compass in mountainous terrain. Failure to pass the course is cause for removal from the promotion list and requires the soldier to go before a promotion board again. I also discovered that Specialist Smith had recently reenlisted in the Army to stay at Fort Irwin. Further questioning revealed that after coming back from Fort Lewis, he was reassigned to a different section with a new supervisor (new as a supervisor and new to the section also).

All of the problems with Specialist Smith came after his transfer to the new section and after his removal from the promotion list. The "leaders" of the unit told me that they did not have time to train this soldier for the new job, and that he should already know it, and that they were not willing to put him in another position because they were too busy to train him there also. Interestingly enough, the unit did not know that the soldier's wife had severe medical problems and could not drive, which required him to take her to the clinic for treatments, nor did they know that the soldier had two daughters who would have been forced to leave school with only about eight weeks left in the school year if the soldier were put out of the Army. The final decision was to move the soldier to another unit on Fort Irwin that had a need for that specialty. The result was that the soldier stayed in the Army and at last report was doing very well in the new unit.

The second case involved the same unit. This soldier — we will call him Private Jones — was erroneously promoted while temporarily away from the job in support of another ongoing operation. The easy fix would have been to reverse the promotion and promote the soldier two months later as originally scheduled. What actually happened was that the soldier was somehow blamed for the erroneous promotion and his supervisor took it out on him by constantly telling him that he was not performing at the appropriate level. The policy of this particular unit was that three counseling statements would result in what the Army calls an Article 15 (based on the article of the Uniform Code of Military Justice) and a reduction in rank. Over a three-month period, this young soldier went from a Specialist to a Private First Class to a Private. Again, I called the soldier and his supervisors in to discuss the situation. Everything continued to point back to the erroneous promotion. The final reduction in rank came because of three counseling statements that all stemmed from the same incident. The soldier was caught speeding. During the routine check after pulling the soldier over, it was discovered that he had an expired driver's license (some states allow soldiers to carry an expired license until they return to their home state for renewal), and it was noted by the military policeman that the soldier was wearing an earring (this is against Army regulations for male soldiers). These three incidents were each treated as separate and Private Jones was again reduced in rank. When I spoke with the chain of command, they all said that he was a good soldier going through a bad time. Because Private Jones wanted to stay in the Army, because the proverbial straw that broke the camel's back really did not merit the punishment imposed, and because the supervisors said he was a good soldier, we kept him in the Army.

The lesson here for leaders is to know your employees and make sure you are asking the tough questions if the personnel action you are approving will have an impact on the lives of your employees. Who are your Specialist Smith or Private Jones whom you have passed on to someone else or let go because you did not ask the right questions or did not get involved in the process?

By all means, if you have to fire an employee, do not be like the Kansas City Chiefs a few years ago and allow the person being fired to find out on the Internet before you make the announcement. This ties leadership to security. If you want something to be held close to the vest, then keep it to yourself and you will not have a leak.

P2. Professional Pride and Passion

Figure 6.1 shows an example of professional pride found in a garment pocket. This shows that Inspector 29 is proud enough of the job that he or she did in inspecting the garment, as well as the job the other workers did in making the garment, that he or she is willing to put this notice in the garment. Every Mercedes-Benz has a little sticker in the window signed by Mr. Daimler as a sign of quality. Are your workers willing to put their names on their work? After all, they do whether they want to or not.

If you asked them to put their names on their work, would they view it as a way of finding out who was not producing quality work? Many companies have employees who feel this way. It is a great leadership challenge to instill enough professional pride that employees want their names on the product.

Taking an interest in your employees helps you to take care of them. Treat each employee as an individual. Take care of your people. General Patton referred to his soldiers as four-star soldiers and as such he felt that they deserved the best. He constantly reminded his commanders that an Army is only as good as its soldiers. This lesson is applicable today. A company is only as good as its employees. What have you done today to raise the morale of your employees?

"I have personally examined every
detail of this garment to make
sure it meets our high quality standards.
Thank you for buying our product.
Inspector: 29"

Figure 6.1   Professional pride found in a garment pocket.

Passion

Not only do you need to have passion for your work, you must instill this passion in your employees. What do I mean by passion? What we are talking about here is a passion for the business; the supply chain business is such an exciting profession that having a passion for this business is not difficult. But can you get your employees to share that passion? Of course you can. This ties back to leading by example. We are talking about a passion for excellence, a passion for quality, a passion for taking care of customers, and a passion for inspiring employees to achieve at new levels of excellence. This is a passion for seeing your employees get recognized for performance, even if it is a simple pat on the back and telling them, "Great job. I am proud of you." Every employee yearns to hear those words. To emphasize this, think back and remember how good you felt when your mom or dad told you they were proud of you. Your employees will feel the same thing when you tell them that. As exciting as this business is, how can you not have a passion for it? Like a winning attitude, passion is contagious. Sometimes you may even catch the passion from one of your employees that inspires you to greater levels of achievement and personal excellence.

Meaning of Attributes

Does this listing of the attributes by order of importance to your success as a leader (see Figure 6.2) mean that some of the attributes are of lesser

Attributes of World-Class Leadership

LEADERSHIP	Order of Importance
• Loyalty/Respect	• Ethics/Integrity/Honesty
• Ethics/Integrity/Honesty	• Loyalty/Respect
• Attitude	• D4 – Devotion/Dedication/Determination/ Discipline
• D4 – Devotion/Dedication/Determination/ Discipline	• Equality and Example
• Equality and Example	• Attitude
• Responsibility	• Responsibility
• Self-Development	• Interest in employees
• Humor	• Humor
• Interest	• P2. Professional Pride and Passion
• P2. Professional Pride and Passion	• Self-Development

Figure 6.2   The attributes of leadership in the LEADERSHIP format in order of importance.

importance than the others? Absolutely not. What it does convey is that if you compromise your integrity, I don't care how well you score in the other attributes, you will not be successful as a leader. Do you have to have all of the attributes to be a world-class leader? No, history is full of "leaders" who did not meet the definitions of the attributes. However, if you want to be truly successful, although you may be stronger in some of the attributes than in others, you should score well in each of the attributes.

Here are some examples of successful leaders who violated some of the most important attributes of leadership. General Omar Bradley, known as the soldier's soldier, was a very successful World War II general and later served as the chief of staff of the U.S. Army. General Bradley retired as a five-star general. Yet look at his lack of loyalty toward his superiors and lack of respect for a superior and subordinate. General Bradley criticized General Eisenhower for being too weak to stand up to the British. This would have been acceptable if he had had the personal courage to say this to General Eisenhower's face when it could have influenced decision making during World War II. However, he was not strong enough to say it while Eisenhower was still alive. He waited until after Eisenhower's death to make his statements.

General Bradley also despised the command style of General Patton who served as General Bradley's superior early in World War II and later as one of Bradley's subordinate commanders.[18] The movie *Patton* depicted some of General Bradley's attitude toward General Patton.

Another example of General Bradley's violation of the attributes of leadership is seen in his response to the slow pace of the battles after the D-Day invasion. Rather than trying to find out why the pace slowed,

General Bradley's response was to fire subordinate commanders without trying to find out what was causing the slowdowns.[19]

Examples of Good and Bad Leadership

We first look at some examples of bad leadership styles. The first example comes from Operation Iraqi Freedom. Before the start of Operation Iraqi Freedom, one senior logistics general told his staff, "We will take a picture every morning; that way we will know who died the previous day because they will not be in the picture." These words were spoken to a staff with no battle experience who were already worn out from the excitement and nervousness of facing uncertainty in combat. Do you think this speech produced positive motivation for the staff?

Now compare the leadership of this modern-day general to the leadership words of General Eisenhower just prior to D-Day on June 4, 1944. General Eisenhower told the Expeditionary Force, "Your task will not be an easy one. Your enemy is well trained, well equipped, and battle-hardened. He will fight savagely. . . . I have full confidence in your courage, devotion to duty, and skill in battle. We will accept nothing less than full victory. Good luck! And let us all beseech the blessing of Almighty God upon this great and noble undertaking."[20] Which of these two leaders would you rather follow?

Here is an example of good leadership from Operation Iraqi Freedom. During Operation Iraqi Freedom, all of the drinking water was provided in the form of bottled water. For some reason the shrinkwrap around the pallets of water bottles was not sufficiently thick to prevent some of the bottles (okay, a lot of the bottles) from falling off or shifting while in transit. On one occasion as the truck was preparing to depart the Theater Distribution Center, a whole pallet of bottles shifted as the truck turned and the entire pallet of one-liter bottles fell off the truck. Lieutenant Colonel Wayne Tisdale was on the site as the Deputy Director of the Distribution Center. Instead of getting upset because this created a delay or yell at the soldier because he had made a quick turn, Wayne quickly realized that the soldier felt bad enough and made a game out of picking up the bottles. The soldiers all pitched in, in record time had the bottles back in a box for shipment downrange, and actually seemed sorry to see the last bottle picked up. Wayne made it fun for the soldiers to do a job that otherwise would have seemed boring. That is the mark of true leadership: getting workers to do something mundane and enjoy doing it. This is the challenge of many of today's warehouse supervisors: there is perhaps no job in the supply chain that is more boring than driving a forklift and packing orders all day. However, a good leader can make it fun for the workers and motivate them to do it with a winning attitude.

Leadership Styles

Leadership styles vary along a spectrum between autocratic and hands-on. The autocratic leader gives direction and orders and then has his or her subordinates enforce the orders. The hands-on leader gets out of the office, is not afraid to get dirty hands, and knows what is going on in the organization from first-hand knowledge of the operations. How does your leadership style affect your employees? Are you hands-on, compassionate, and concerned about your employees? If so, you will probably notice that you have employees who are hands-on, compassionate, and concerned about their employees and fellow workers. Do you shoot the messenger and throw violent tantrums? How do you think this affects your employees?

Look at Machiavelli; his influence came from Cesare Borgia, the duke of Romagna. Borgia was despised, cruel, and cunning. From Borgia, Machiavelli came to feel that "anyone compelled to choose will find greater security in being feared, than loved." Machiavelli developed his leadership style of punishing subordinates by watching Borgia. Even though Machiavelli in his book, *The Prince*, advocated the need to break promises to protect the state, he did acknowledge that a prince who keeps his word earns respect and praise.

Leadership in Action

You have to get out of the office to really know what is going on. Figure 6.3 is an example of making the wrong assumptions from behind a computer screen. During OIF, I frequently drove a forklift, a habit that earned me the nickname "The Enlisted Colonel" from some of my soldiers because it was apparent that I was not afraid of working. I did this for a couple of reasons. The primary reason was to experience what my soldiers were experiencing, thereby giving me an insight into what was needed to improve the flow of supplies. The other reason was to show some of the younger soldiers that the mission could be accomplished with the equipment available. I tried to drive the forklifts with enthusiasm to show that this was not a bad job and to emphasize the importance of the mission. Try to imagine a colonel on a forklift laughing, smiling, and appearing to be having fun doing what is considered a dull job. This is what my soldiers and Bangladeshi workers saw: a simple plan to show the importance of the mission and make the soldiers feel good about what they were doing. During the Korean War, "The Chinese commander in Korea, General Peng The-huai, was famous for himself taking up a porter's 'chogie stick' or 'A-frame' and trotting off a mile or so to encourage the other bearers."[21] Driving a forklift, moving supplies, and loading trucks in Kuwait had the same effect on the soldiers.

Figure 6.3 From a briefing by the Deputy Undersecretary of Defense, Logistics, to the military's Council of Logistics directors.

The goal of the Deputy Undersecretary of Defense, Logistics, by showing this picture was to illustrate the disarray in the Theater Distribution Center in mid-April 2003. The reason for showing this picture here is to illustrate the method used to identify pallets and boxes for movement by the Bangladeshi forklift drivers. Because of the communication barriers between the American soldiers and the forklift drivers, a simple system was devised to identify the customers' shipments using the three letters from the unit's routing identifier code (see the pallet just right of center in the lower half of the picture with RWM). The routing identifier code is the three-letter code for the parent support center. In some cases, it was easier to simply use the unit's identification as shown by the big 3ID marked on the shipment on the left. The use of these codes allowed the forklift drivers to match the three letters with the 4' × 8' signs at the end of each customer lane and the same-size signs posted by each truck being loaded for delivery. This simple system, in spite of all the technology available, also allowed us to quickly check the customer staging lanes for shipments in the wrong lane before they were loaded on the wrong truck. Sometimes, it's the simplest ideas that are the best.

One of the responsibilities of leaders is to develop subordinates. Your legacy to your organization will be the people you develop and this legacy will last long after you are gone from the organization. It is your choice whether this legacy is one of quality developed personnel or substandard undeveloped personnel. The key to developing subordinates is to do so through mentoring and the use of carefully planned development counseling. This is best accomplished through the use of developmental counseling. The Army has established tactics, techniques, and procedures for counseling subordinates. The following is an adaptation of those procedures.

The Army breaks down the counseling tactics, techniques, and procedures into four major areas. These areas are visualize, describe, direct, and assess. The use of this program will produce better employees, better leaders, and will prevent the surprises at evaluation time. This is not a once-a-year program. To be successful, counseling and mentoring have to be an ongoing program.

- Visualize
  - Developing subordinates to promote the organization's end state.
  - Complementing performance counseling and mentoring.
- Describe
  - Perpetuating counseling at every echelon.
  - Collaborating to identify competencies, skills, and behaviors for improvement.
- Direct
  - Coaching the employee in developing a performance and development plan.
  - Linking counseling to the development plan.
- Assess
  - Exploiting opportunities for counseling. Formal versus informal. Location of each.
  - Defining measures of success: feedback and assessment plan. Keep an open mind during the feedback portion of this plan. If you ask for input from the subordinate, listen to what he or she has to say and do not get defensive if the opinion or view of a situation differs from yours.
  - Develop a developmental counseling form.
  - Schedule time for feedback and use the feedback to revise the leader's plan, if necessary.

The Role of Leadership and Customer Service

As a leader you have to set a work climate where the employees can make customer-focused decisions without having to wait for management approval or wade through a sea of red tape. This is especially true for repeat customers. The Hilton Hawaiian Village is a good example of this. They have their customer database that tells them when a repeat customer is arriving. Before arrival, the guest receives a letter from the manager thanking them for choosing the Hilton Hawaiian Village Resort again and telling the guest about upcoming activities and programs for the family. Upon arrival, the repeat customer is called by name, welcomed back to the resort, and given a special phone extension to call and request any assistance necessary to make the visit to the resort a pleasant stay. The Ritz-Carlton chain is another good example of taking care of the customer without having to go to a manager. Every employee is authorized to spend up to $1500 to accommodate a customer to make his or her stay more productive and pleasant. At one stay at the Ritz-Carlton in Pasadena, California, I returned to my room to find the battery to the electronic key reader dead. I called the front office and the night manager came to the room with the maintenance man to fix the door. The time to fix the door took longer than they expected, so I was treated to an open bar and complimentary meals for the remainder of my stay.

Compare lack of customer service at Northwest Airlines to the customer service of The Hilton Hawaiian Village and Ritz-Carlton, above. Northwest has become famous for their lack of customer service, even to their frequent flyers. The June 2004 edition of Northwest Airlines' *World Traveler* magazine had an article by Richard Anderson, CEO of Northwest Airlines, that stated, "At Northwest we are committed to using technology to provide you with choice, convenience and—above all—the best customer service available." But if there is a problem, they simply throw customer service out the window.

On a recent trip to Hawaii, the group in front of me in line had been traveling together for over three weeks and had purchased their tickets six months earlier. For some reason, Northwest was not able to put this group of seven on the same return flight from Hawaii because the plane was overbooked. When it was my turn, I found out that my family did not have seats at all, even though we had purchased our tickets several months in advance. The agents at the gate and the manager for the terminal were not only unhelpful but rude and discourteous to all the passengers who were in the same situation. Calls to Northwest's elite Silver World Perks line resulted in my being hung up on twice. I tried to explain that I was traveling with my children. I was pointedly told, "I don't care about your children." Obviously, for Northwest Airlines, the best customer service available is not the best customer service for the customer. This is perhaps a goal of the management that does not reach down to the workers. When we finally got seats on a flight out of Hawaii (there are worse places to be delayed) I told one of the Northwest flight attendants that for some reason they have some of the best and friendliest flight attendants and some of the rudest gate agents. His response to me was,

"Everyone is cutting back and feeling pressure." Not exactly what I expected to hear and definitely not an excuse for rudeness. True leadership is needed to set the standard for customer service and attitude toward customers.

Leadership and Vision

One of the roles of leadership is to provide a vision and the goals for the organization. Here are some examples of visions and goals in corporate America. Wal-Mart set a goal a little over six years ago to become the nation's largest grocery retailer within five years. A large number of their competition laughed at that goal. However, the vision was transferred to the employees of Wal-Mart and today they are indeed the largest grocery retailer in America.

Cabela's is another leader in their field. Cabela's has a stated vision of being "Dedicated to connecting customers to products through excellence in service." This commitment is demonstrated in the knowledge and enthusiasm of their telephone center personnel. As a result of the operator knowledge of the product, Cabela's experiences a returns rate of less than 10 percent in catalogue sales compared to the 30-plus percent average for catalogue sales.

What is important to remember about a vision? A vision must be clearly stated, clearly articulated, and most important, clearly understood. Just as we did with LEADERSHIP®, let's take a look at VISION®.

- ■ Vital to the organization
- ■ Integrated throughout the organization
- ■ Sustainable and achievable
- ■ Important from the viewpoint of the employees
- ■ Organizational goals
- ■ Not necessarily a one-size-fits-all vision

Vital to the Organization

The vision for a company has to be vital to the mission and core competencies of the company. The vision is the company's statement of where they want to be in the future and drives the operational strategy of the company in achieving this vision.

Integrated Throughout the Organization

This is where it is important for the vision to be clearly articulated and clearly understood. For every employee to share a vision, they have to understand it and buy into it. Understanding a vision includes understanding, "What's in it for me?"

Sustainable and Achievable

Like goals, the vision for the organization must be an achievable vision. A railroad certainly would not have a vision to be a world-class airline. At the same time that it is achievable, it must be a vision that the employees and the company can sustain. Look at the Cabela's vision again: "Dedicated to connecting customers to products through excellence in service." To sustain that vision, the employees have to understand it and buy into the vision for the company. So far, Cabela's has sustained this vision.

Important from the Viewpoint of the Employees

If the employees do not see the importance of the vision from their "foxhole," they will not buy into the vision and the vision will not be sustainable and achievable. Employees must see the vision as important to their careers and need to know that the vision for the company allows them the opportunity to display initiative and innovation in achieving the vision.

Organizational Goals

The vision provides the company with a set of goals for reaching the destination set forth in the vision. It is important to point out that in some cases the overall vision may create a situation that promotes activities at lower levels in the organization which may prove to be suboptimal to the overall vision of the company. If the goal is to save money, what saves money in one department may very well raise operational costs in another department. This is why the process maps developed as a result of the methods discussed in Chapter 4 are important in developing a vision for the company.

Not Necessarily a One-Size-Fits-All Vision and Goals

Sometimes the goals at the corporate level need to address specific areas of the company. What may indeed be perceived as achievable by one part of the company may not be perceived that way by another division. If the workers do not perceive the goals to be achievable, they will not work hard to achieve them.

Conclusions and Summary

Lead as you would want to be led. By yourself, you cannot be a George Patton, a Dwight Eisenhower, a John F. Kennedy, or a Martin Luther King. If you are acting, your people will know it. Be sincere; be genuine; be compassionate. Remember, your employees will not care how much you know until they know how much you care. Never argue for personal gain: "If we do this I will get promoted." Or worse, and this is an actual quote from a senior Army commander, "I don't care how you do it as long as it makes me look good." Remember, you are in the people business.

General Patton once said, "Supply and administrative units and installations are frequently neglected by combat commanders. It is very necessary to their morale and efficiency that each one be inspected by the senior general of the unit with which it is operating." The same is still true today, and not just in the military. How many supply chain operations receive the personal attention of the CEO? Would the morale of your employees improve if they did visit? At the National Training Center at Fort Irwin, California, this is very evident. The commanding general is very involved in the day-to-day operations of the training units and the units stationed at Fort Irwin to facilitate that training. However, most commanders shy away from the logistics units because it is not a glamorous activity. One such commander had to have his aide call ahead to get directions to one maintenance facility after being on the installation for over three years. As a leader, you have to get out and see all of your operations. There are still leaders who shy away from their logistics activities unless there is a problem. The workers want to see the boss at times other than problem times. One prominent logistics executive once said, "Logistics done well is all but invisible." Sometimes it is still nice to see the boss and for the boss to see the workers who are "invisible."

Sun Tzu spoke of leadership habits and examples over 2500 years ago. Albert Schweitzer spoke of the power of example from leaders when he said, "Example is not the main thing in influencing others, it is the only thing." What Dr. Schweitzer is telling us is what we all learned from our parents as children, "Your own behavior speaks louder than your words."

Dr. John Langley, director of the Supply Chain Executive Forum for Georgia Tech, during a presentation to the Distribution Business Management Conference in Las Vegas in June 2003, listed ten imperatives for success in a supply chain. Two of these imperatives are directly related to leadership. These two imperatives are the need for enlightened leadership, which ties to the need for training and professional development, and the belief that people are the most important assets in the supply chain. I tell senior leaders learning to be commanders in the Army that the only reason we exist as leaders is to take care of our people.

A third of these imperatives presented by Dr. Langley is the ability and willingness to change. As a leader, you have to lead the change. Peter Drucker tells us, "If people are committed to maintaining yesterday, they are not available for tomorrow." Leaders have to lead and champion the change process. There is a need for senior leadership commitment to the change and not just support for the management of the change. To stop people from being committed to maintaining yesterday, you have to get them to understand clearly, "What's in it for me?"

Always remember that you are leading people and not the organization or section or division. Never lose sight of the people aspect of your job. And when one of your people makes a mistake, do not give up on him or her. Remember the words of Jimmy Valvano, the great coach of North Carolina State University in the 1980s. When Coach Valvano was dying of cancer, he called all of his friends, former players, and family together and told them, "Don't give up. Don't ever give up." Coach Valvano was not specifically talking about employees here but it is just as applicable. Quality leadership and genuine concern for the employee as a person will usually provide the motivation necessary to get even a bad employee on the right track. Never lose sight of the mission but always keep an eye on taking care of the employee.

President Franklin Roosevelt had a famous quote on hope and not giving up. His quote is similar in spirit to the words of Coach Valvano. President Roosevelt put it this way: "When you get to the end of your rope, tie a knot and hang on." In other words, if you think you are at the very end, be glad you still have some rope left. Do not give up hope. The same is true for your employees. If they are at the end of their rope, help them tie a knot in it by giving them the training and encouragement necessary to start climbing the rope again.

Regardless of what business you may think you are in, supply chain, distribution, warehousing, maintenance, or fleet management, you really are in the people business. Every business is really a people business. Alan Axelrod in his book on President Roosevelt, *Nothing to Fear,* states this concept very clearly:

> Leaders must never make the mistake of believing that they lead a company, a department, or a unit. What they lead are the individuals who make up the enterprise. It is all too easy to think of an organization as a monolith, a single, solid thing that can be pointed unerringly in a particular direction. In fact such a group is a collection of people, each of whom is subject to distraction and each of whom may, for a variety of reasons, begin to follow a separate agenda.[22]

As Roosevelt tried to keep the coalition together during World War II, "He faced a problem many leaders of major projects face: maintaining momentum toward the final goal."[23] All too often, teams miss the final goal and become fixed on the intermediate goals. For the Allies in World War II, these intermediate objectives such as individual battles or individual theaters of operations clouded the vision of the leaders and created a situation where the senior leaders had to constantly refocus the lower-level leadership on the final goal of defeating the Axis powers.

A good leader does not need to push his or her employees along, nor does he or she need to pull them toward the mission accomplishment. The good leader will serve as a coach, mentor, teacher, and guide.

What is success as a leader? For me it is watching the people who worked for me get promoted and selected for command positions. For you it is watching your employees develop and progress and become leaders in the company. Leadership is motivating the people to execute the plan as if it were their idea. Leadership is validated when times are tough. It is not about being the Boss!

W. Edwards Deming tells us that the aim of leadership should be to help people and machines and gadgets to do a better job. Leadership of management is in need of overhaul as well as leadership of production workers. In his twelfth point on quality, Dr. Deming reminds us to remove barriers that rob people of their right to pride of workmanship. In other words, you should develop a sense of professional pride in your employees.

Ego was not discussed in this chapter. The reason for this is that there is no place in leadership for ego. Being a leader is not about your career and promoting yourself. It is about your employees and promoting them. If doing this helps your career, that is a corollary benefit, but it should not be your driving motivation.

One final thought on leadership: watch your language. The rule number 110 from the *Little Instruction Book* is, "Never use profanity." You never know who is watching you and whom you will influence. Look at the words of General U.S. Grant, "I never learned to swear as a child and when I got older, I saw the folly of it."

If you offer quality, world-class leadership you may not be the most popular leader, but your employees will know what right looks like. As long as you are able to accomplish the mission, meet the goals, and inspire the employees to achieve what they would otherwise not achieve while thinking it is their idea, you will be a successful leader.

Discussion Questions and Topics for Thought

1. How do you set your goals?
2. What is your company vision? Can you sum it up on a 3×5 card? Do your employees know what it is? Your suppliers? What about your customers?

3. Setting the corporate culture. How do you treat your employees in the first 72 hours? How do you treat them in the last 72 hours? The first 72 hours set the stage for the time they are with your company and the last 72 hours will tell the employee what you really felt and how the employee will represent the company when he or she leaves. The Army established the Army Career and Alumni Program to assist soldiers and their families in transitioning from the Army to a civilian career and to ensure that former soldiers are the best spokespersons for the organization.

4. How much training do you do annually? How is it done? Do your employees simply read and sign? Do they attend classes? Do they get hands-on training?

5. Are you doing business the same way you did last year? Are you doing business as usual? Do you do routine things routinely?

6. Have you become efficient at being inefficient?

7. Are you doing things wrong for so long that wrong looks right?

8. How important is the training of your first-line supervisors? This is the first leader in the chain and can easily affect how employees "see" the company.

9. Sensing sessions. Do you do sensing sessions? Are they beneficial? Why or why not?

Book List for Chapter Six

1. *Field Manual 3-0, Operations*, U.S. Army, Fort Leavenworth, KS, 2001.
2. *Field Manual 22-100, Leadership*, U.S. Army, Washington, DC, 1997.
3. Walden, Joseph L., *The Forklifts Have Nothing to Do!* Lessons in Supply Chain Leadership, iUniverse, Campbell, CA, 2003.
4. Torre, Joe, *Ground Rules for Winners*, Hyperion, New York, 1999.
5. Axelrod, Alan, *Nothing to Fear—Lessons in Leadership from FDR*, Penguin, New York, 2003.
6. Klein, Shelley, *The Most Evil Dictators in History*, Michael O'Mara, Great Britain, 2004.
7. Wooden, John and Carty, Jay, *Coach Wooden One-on-One*, Regal, Ventura, CA, 2003.
8. D'Este, Carlo, *Eisenhower: A Soldier's Life*, Henry Holt, New York, 2002.
9. Pogue, Forrest C., *The Supreme Command*, Office of the Chief of Military History, Washington, DC, 1954.
10. Shrader, Charles, *Communist Logistics in the Korean War*, Greenwood Press, Westport, CT, 1995.
11. Brown, H. Jackson, Jr., *The Complete Life's Little Instruction Book*, Rutledge Hill, Nashville, TN, 1997.

Notes

1. Prentice, W.C.H., "Understanding Leadership," *Harvard Business Review*, January 2004, p. 102. This article first appeared in the *Harvard Business Review* in 1961. It was reprinted in the January 2004 edition as part of the "Best of HBR" series.
2. A character on *The Andy Griffith Show* speaking about what he learned from the main character, "Andy Taylor."
3. *Field Manual 3-0, Operations*, U.S. Army, Fort Leavenworth, KS, 2001, paragraph 1-56.
4. Ibid., paragraph 1-57.
5. *Field Manual 22-100, Leadership*, U.S. Army, Washington, DC, 1997.
6. Zaleznik, Abraham, Managers and leaders—Are they different?, *Harvard Business Review*, January 2004.
7. *Webster's Third International Dictionary*, Encyclopedia Britannica, Inc., 1981, p. 1372.
8. Ibid., p. 1283.
9. Bennis, Warren, Substance over style, *CIO Insights*, February 13, 2003.
10. Walden, Joseph L., *The Forklifts Have Nothing to Do! Lessons in Supply Chain Leadership*, iUniverse, Campbell, CA, 2003.
11. Torre, Joe, *Ground Rules for Winners*, Hyperion, New York, 1999, p. 42.
12. Axelrod, Alan, *Nothing to Fear—Lessons in Leadership from FDR*, Penguin, New York, 2003, p. 50.
13. Buck O'Neil was a star in the Negro Leagues as a player as well as famed as the manager of the Kansas City Monarchs. Mr. O'Neil was the first African-American coach in the major leagues. In addition, Mr. O'Neil serves as the honorary chairman of the Negro Leagues Baseball Museum.
14. Trevino, Linda, Hartman, Laura, and Brown, Michael, Moral person and moral manager: How executives develop a reputation for ethical leadership, *California Management Review*, 42: 4 (Summer) 2000.
15. Klein, Shelley, *The Most Evil Dictators in History*, Michael O'Mara, London, U.K., 2004, p. 38.
16. Axelrod, Alan, *Patton on Leadership*, Prentice Hall, Paramus, NJ, 1999, p. 92.
17. Wooden, John, and Carty, Jay, *Coach Wooden One-on-One*, Regal, Ventura, CA, 2003, p. 82.
18. D'Este, Carlo, Eisenhower: A Soldier's Life, Henry Holt, New York, 2002, pp. 441, 548, 561.
19. Ibid., p. 548.
20. Pogue, Forrest C., *The Supreme Command*, Office of the Chief of Military History, Washington, DC, 1954, p. 545.
21. *Communist Logistics in the Korean War*, p. 136.
22. Axelrod, *Nothing to Fear,* p. 29.
23. Ibid., p. 39.

Chapter 7

Speed and Velocity: How to Achieve Them

Speed is rapidity of action. Like concentration, speed applies to both time and space. And, like concentration, it is relative speed that matters. . . . Speed over distance, or space, is velocity—the ability to move fast. . . . Speed is a weapon. . . . Speed provides security.[1]

Started in 1995, The Army's Velocity Management initiative sought to improve the responsiveness, reliability, and efficiency of the Army's then outdated logistics system. Through the implementation of a simple yet powerful process improvement methodology, the Army has dramatically streamlined its supply process, cutting order and ship times for repair parts by nearly two-thirds nationwide and by over 75 percent at several major installations.[2]

Speed is the essence of warfare.

Sun Tzu

Just as "speed is the essence of warfare," speed is the essence of successful businesses and supply chains. Speed is important in getting items through the supply chain from your suppliers' suppliers to your customers' customers. It is also important to have speed in the reverse supply chain in order to get serviceable items (unused returns or items with no defects or mechanical faults noted) back on the shelf as soon as possible, to get unserviceable items (defective or damaged) into a repair system quickly, or dispose of items that cannot be resold or auctioned off. This chapter addresses speed and velocity in both the forward and reverse supply chains and provides methods to assist you in achieving world-class speed in both directions.

An APICS-sponsored presentation and courseware developed by Bill Walker, CFPIM, CIRM, discusses the five defining principles of supply chain management. The first principle is to "maximize velocity through the supply chain network" with a focus on both the forward and reverse supply chains.

Similarly, in a presentation to the Warehouse of the Future Conference (now known as the Distribution Business Management Conference) attendees, Dr. Jim Tompkins discussed what he saw as the six levels of Supply Chain Excellence.[3]

1. Business as usual (After September 11, 2001, there is no more business as usual. And, if you are still doing business the same way you were on September 10, 2001, you need to take a close look at where you are going.)
2. Link exchange
3. Visibility—both up and down the supply chain
4. Collaboration
5. Synthesis
6. Velocity

From a customer's perspective you can never have enough speed in your system. Success from the customers' point of view is to have the desired item at the very instant that they decide they want it. This is what customers want from the supply chain. The speed of your supply chain in meeting the customers' needs affects the reputation of your company and is dependent on the efficiency and effectiveness of your supply chain. The key to speed, efficiency, and effectiveness is that they must be consistent. You cannot have a speedy, efficient supply chain today and not tomorrow if you want to keep your customers. Even the military has found this out. The philosophy used to be, "Our customers have no choice but to come to us for their supplies." In some cases such as parts for the M1A1 Abrams main battle tank this is still true, but parts for trucks, trailers, and Humvees are available through other sources of supply. This reality forced the U.S. Army and other Department of Defense activities to adopt a new mindset of "faster, better, cheaper." After years of supply chain inefficiencies, it took several years to regain the confidence of our customers. You do not have that luxury.

Rick Blasgen, the vice president of distribution and supply chains for ConAgra foods, is emphatic that the key to success in supply chain operations is to increase the velocity of information and goods passing through the supply chain. Doing this will compress your supply chain response time, assist in providing more accurate invoices, and will assist in getting your supply chain integrated end to end. The Department of Defense has long worked under a system of silos for its logistics functions. As a result of the cooperation during Operation Iraqi Freedom, the Department of Defense is moving to an integrated, end-to-end supply chain, as opposed to unintegrated logistics operations.

Is speed important to your company? One would expect everybody to answer emphatically yes. However, this was overheard at the APICS 2003 International Conference and Exposition in Las Vegas, NV. A vendor (who will remain nameless to protect the guilty) was talking rather loudly on a cell phone and was heard to say, "If we don't get the parts there when they want them, we are screwed up. I am tired of customers that have that attitude." If you cannot deliver when the customer wants it, someone else will.

Some companies forget that the reason that we are here is the customer. We could use the *Green Eggs and Ham* approach. We could create our demand and finally convince the customer that what we have is really good and that is what he or she wants. This is the approach that Sam-I-am took in *Green Eggs and Ham*, the popular children's book by Dr. Seuss. Such an approach is sometimes used by software and enterprise resource planning program vendors. But in reality, we have to provide what the customer wants, when they want it, in the quantity and packaging that they want, and at a competitive price. FedEx has proven that you can charge more for expedited services. And, in fact, FedEx has built an entire industry around expedited services.

Dell has learned that lesson and, in fact, according to a Dell supply chain evangelist, they make more money from the charges for expedited services than they do from the computer itself. If you decide you need a new computer in less than the normal seven-day timeframe that Dell promises, you can pay a hefty fee to expedite your order. Dell simply moves your order to the top of the list and you pay for a production schedule change. In addition, you pay for the expedited shipment. Like FedEx, Dell found a need and created a system to fill it. And this need is built around our desire to have what we want right now.

Velocity and visibility are your links to satisfied customers and supply chain security. FedEx and UPS not only provide customers with expedited service, they also provide visibility throughout the distribution channel. This visibility helps improve customer confidence in the system. Another benefit for FedEx is that they realized an 80-percent reduction in tracking costs by allowing visibility online for every package versus having to operate an 800 number and call center for tracking.

Before we look at the Army's approach to velocity management and supply chain process improvements, let's take a look at the supply chain times for some commercial firms. The "world's foremost outfitter," Cabela's, has a lead time of one day from their distribution centers to their stores, and, if the item is a direct vendor delivery to the store, the lead time increases to three days. To facilitate postponement and accommodate regional sales or in-store specials at Cabela's retail store, an item is not priced until it is picked. When the item is picked, a price label is printed with the pick ticket and applied to the item before it is packed for shipment. This reduces cycle times for processing the products at the stores.

This is a great contrast to Walt Disney World. The distribution center at Walt Disney World may price the same item numerous times depending on the season and the sales volume for an item. If there is a price change on an item or if the item is being placed on sale, the items are returned to the central distribution center and retagged and then returned to the stores for sale. Not only does this increase the workload for the distribution center personnel, the additional handling times mean that the items are not available for sale.

Alternatively, contrast Cabela's efforts to reduce processing times with the practices of Grainger's distribution centers. Grainger works on a 4×10 (four 10-hour days) schedule with outbound shipments processed on the day shift and inbound shipments processed on the night shift. The items at Grainger that are to be shipped on Monday are picked and packed on Thursday night. This shipment then sits over the weekend before actually being pulled on Monday. This adds three days to the customer wait time as the items sit waiting to move. Conversely, the items that arrive on Friday morning are not processed into the distribution center until Sunday's night shift comes to work. Another three days of cycle time are wasted and all of these items are not available for sale. Because these items are not processed into the system, there is the opportunity cost of ordering additional items to fill customer orders. The combination of these two practices could very well add up to an additional six days to the customer wait time cycle. In addition, these practices add to the necessary safety stock inventory to support the artificially long wait times and artificially self-induced stockouts.

The successful business strategy has to be customer-centric with fast cycles of innovation and doing better what the customer wants. It requires responsiveness to the customer expectations. The speed of business depends on creating relationships around the customers and the suppliers while creating new partners in the supply chain, creating new value, preparing for growth, and creating first and then innovating and improving.

You cannot afford to continue to do the same old thing in a new way. This is a new ball game. Business is now a 24×7×365 operation: this drives the need for reliability and performance. This also drives smaller batches and smaller orders, but more frequently. There are more item picks than case and pallet picks. This is the downside of velocity. You have to pick more orders but the good news is that they are usually smaller. A Web site can make the promises and bring the customers in, but someone still has to deliver the goods.

Just-in-time and quick response/enhanced customer response drive more small shipments and in some cases have quadrupled the workload in the warehouses. This produces a situation where service failure equals out of stock and out of stock often enough (one time too many, which may only be once in today's economy) equals lost customers. Can you afford to add six days to your customers' wait times?

The Army started its velocity management program in 1995 as a way of improving customer order cycle times for repair parts. The results for the Army from using some of the techniques discussed in this book were a decrease of customer wait times of over 70 percent, a real dollar savings of over $300 million over a two-year period from an investment of less than $3 million, and a corresponding reduction in maintenance repair cycle times of over 50 percent.

What are some ways to add velocity to your supply chain? Here are a few that will supercharge your supply chain.

Cross-Docking to Improve Velocity

What is cross-docking and what does it have to do with velocity? The *APICS Dictionary* defines cross-docking as "The concept of packaging products on the incoming shipments so they can be easily sorted at intermediate warehouses or for outgoing shipments based on final destinations. These items are carried from the incoming vehicle docking point to the outgoing vehicle docking point without being stored in inventory at the warehouse."[4]

In 2000, The Warehousing Education and Research Council published a handbook on cross-docking, *Making the Move to Cross-Docking*. This handbook states,

> Some define it as the movement of full pallets from inbound trucks directly to outbound trucks with the load never touching the warehouse floor. . . . Cross-docking is defined as a process where product is received in a facility, occasionally married with other products going to the same destination, then shipped

at the earliest opportunity, without going into long term storage. It requires advance knowledge of inbound product, its destination, and a system for routing the product to the proper outbound vehicle.[5]

The earliest cross-dockers in America were the riders of the Pony Express. In fact, these pioneers epitomized cross-docking. Look at their operation. One rider simply cross-docked his express package to another shipper, and so on down the line until it reached the ultimate customer.

What are the benefits of cross-docking? The greatest benefit of cross-docking in improving the velocity of your supply chain is that there are fewer touches of the merchandise as it moves through the supply chain; velocity is added. Information is the key to making this happen. The closer to real-time information, the more successful the move to cross-docking will be. This need for real-time or near real-time information ties cross-docking to the impacts of security on supply chains.

The other benefits of cross-docking include the following.

1. Labor savings. The labor savings come from not having to put the inbound material into storage and later retrieve it for issue to customers. The labor savings are a direct result of the reduced number of touches.
2. A reduction in inventory coupled with a requirement for less storage space, the need for less inventory investment, and a potential reduction in the damage to supplies on the shelf, not to mention a reduction in obsolete and pilfered supplies.
3. A faster flow through the distribution center because the material is not going into storage and is moved directly to the outbound shipping dock or at a minimum to a temporary consolidation point. This is the goal of velocity management: to get the items through the center and to the customer faster.
4. Just-in-time logistics supports the move to cross-docking. The advantage of the smaller shipments associated with just-in-time and the information requirements to make just-in-time work contribute to the success of cross-docking.

What are the types of cross-docking? There are three formal forms of cross-docking and one informal but widely used method for cross-docking.

1. Pre-allocated and supplier consolidated. In this case, the suppliers prepackage and preload shipments to arrive at the distribution center or warehouse for cross-docking to outbound transportation to the ultimate customer or to another distribution center. W.W.

Grainger uses this form of cross-docking when moving supplies from one regional distribution center to another.

2. Pre-allocated and operator consolidated. In pre-allocated and operator-consolidated cross-docking, the distribution center personnel consolidate the outbound shipments at the dock without moving the items to the storage locations. In some major distribution centers, there is a formal cross-dock area between the receiving dock and the shipping dock. The key to this form of cross-docking is advanced shipping notification from the suppliers or shippers to the distribution center. Information is key in all forms of cross-docking, however, in this form of cross-docking it is imperative to know what is coming in and what is going out to ensure that the cross-docking effort is successful.

3. Post-allocated. Post-allocated cross-docking, like pre-allocated cross-docking, requires advance shipping notification from suppliers or shippers. This form of cross-docking is usually a procedure reserved for shipments to fill past-due orders or back orders. Rather than preplanned cross-docking, this form of cross-docking is a method to expedite shipments to catch up based on back orders.

4. The most common form of cross-docking and the one the U.S. Army subscribes to the most is what I refer to as a miracle or coincidental cross-docking. Miracle cross-docking occurs when the items for a customer just happen to arrive about the same time that an outbound shipment is being prepared for that customer.

During Operation Iraqi Freedom, we established the Theater Distribution Center to be a cross-dock facility. For the first two weeks of operations, the only real cross-docking we did was to employ the miracle form of cross-docking. As the noncommissioned officers and officers working the Theater Distribution Center got the operation working, it became more of a planned cross-dock operation, but it never reached the point of a total cross-dock facility. The packaging of the supplies coming into the theater prevented pre-planned cross-docking. To be a true cross-docking facility required the defense depots to package the supplies into pure pallets or pallets for one consignee.

To implement cross-docking, you have to have a detailed plan. Although this is not rocket science, it is a drastic change from business as usual. Do not try to change your operation from a traditional distribution center to a cross-dock facility in the midst of your busiest time of the year. In other words, if your busiest time of the year is in preparation for the Christmas season, you probably need to start the move to cross-docking immediately after the Christmas season and the Christmas returns season. To make the move a success, you need to make sure you have a cross-docking area and the information technology is in place, and then phase in the move over a couple of months rather than making a drastic move overnight.

Warehouse/Distribution Center Layout and Velocity

Can the layout of your distribution center affect velocity in your supply chain? Absolutely! Numerous time–motion studies in warehouses and distribution centers reveal that the majority (in some cases as much as 55 percent) of a warehouse worker's time is spent in movement in the warehouse.[6] A good distribution center/warehouse layout can significantly reduce this movement in search of a location or between locations during the pick process. One of the definitive guides to warehouse layout and design is the Navy's publication, *Navy Supply Publication 529*.[7] Pages from this publication are included in the appendices as examples of warehouse/distribution center layout and design.

Is there a difference between the layout and design of a small warehouse and a large distribution center? My experience runs the gamut from my first warehouse in Hawaii that was about 10,000 square feet to the 4.2 million square-foot Theater Distribution Center in Kuwait in support of Operation Iraqi Freedom. The principles for the layout and design are almost the same. The only real difference between a small warehouse and a large distribution center is the allocation of space for cross-docking. In the smaller warehouses that I have worked in or worked with in redesigning the layout, the need for cross-docking was as important as the need in larger distribution centers, but there was no real space to set aside specifically for cross-docking. In the smaller warehouses the customer staging areas served as cross-docking and consolidation points.

APICS stresses an application of A-B-C storage[8] to determine which are the fast-moving items. These items should be located close to the outbound doors to reduce travel time for the warehouse workers. One prominent automobile parts distribution center in Virginia failed to adopt this concept and during a visit to the distribution center, workers were observed walking past very slow-moving parts to get to the fast-moving parts. The distribution center manager kept complaining about a shortage of workers to meet the demands, but was not willing to reorganize the distribution center to put the slow-moving parts at the back of the aisles and the fast-moving parts close to the shipping dock.

Slotting methodologies also contribute to warehouse velocity. Dr. Ed Frazelle refers to a slotting technique called "golden zones." In addition to the APICS A-B-C inventory management concept, a golden zone methodology puts the fast-moving items in locations that do not cause the workers to bend or reach to pick the items. This not only improves velocity but it also reduces worker injuries.

Another methodology that increases velocity in the warehouse or distribution center is the concept of profiling. L.L. Bean uses a profiling technique that puts items that are habitually ordered together in locations close together to reduce travel time. This is somewhat similar to the "warehouse in a warehouse concept." Home Depot and Lowe's both do this with tools. Not only does this put all of the tools together in close proximity locations, but it also improves control of the tools and prevents theft. At the National Training Center, the Army's contractor-operated warehouse uses this concept. All of the items that are habitually used for servicing a vehicle are stored together and then kited together when ordered to speed the picking process.

Another use for profiling is to ensure that items are properly slotted. Has demand for the item increased the necessary stockage levels? Does this require a larger slot in the warehouse versus slotting in multiple slots? Multiple locations not only have the ability to decrease velocity in the warehouse, but they can also create inventory accuracy problems or warehouse denials of an item. In other words, your system says that you have stock in a location, but when the worker gets there, the location is empty. Has the item become a slow mover and does it need to be moved to a less velocity-oriented location?

So, why have a warehouse at all? Wouldn't omitting the warehouse improve velocity? Here is why warehouses will never go away.

1. *Having a warehouse close to the customer assists in improving customer service.* Toyota and Dell have mastered the concept of having items stored close to the point of use to improve supply chain velocity. The Army uses a concept called Prescribed Load Lists and Authorized Stockage Lists to allocate fast-moving items close to the users. The Army uses the Prescribed Load Lists and Authorized Stockage List to put repair parts closer to the units to improve readiness. In commercial operations, readiness equates to having it when the customer wants it in the quantity the customer wants, and when does the customer want it? Try yesterday.

2. *Value-added service.* More and more warehouses provide value-added services for customers. These services range from special packing to adding pricing labels to the merchandise before shipping it to the retailer. Another term for some of the value-added services at the warehouse is postponement. This concept allows for such services as custom labels or final assembly of products to take place at the warehouse prior to shipment to the customer.

3. *Transportation consolidation.* One of the major values of warehouses is to serve as a consolidation point for shipments to customers. Consolidating shipments, either via cross-docking or

convenience of pack, is a way to speed up shipments and save shipping costs.

4. *Reverse consolidation.* Just as warehouses serve as a consolidation point for items going forward in the supply chain, they also serve as a location for consolidating items in the reverse supply chain. These items are either serviceable and being returned for resale or repacking prior to resale or may be heading to a repair facility or disposal.

5. *Procurement efficiencies.* Using a warehouse for temporary storage allows a company to take advantage of volume discounts on items that they know they will use in a relatively short period of time. As long as the cost of storage does not exceed the value of the volume discount, this is a good reason to keep a warehouse.

Inventory Turns and Velocity

How often have you complained to your boss that you need more distribution space? I heard that complaint at a major distribution center (greater than one million square feet under roof) recently. When I asked further questions about the needs, what I found out was that in some cases there was over a one-year's supply of items on hand and in another case over six months of supply on hand. In fact, the average turns for this center were about two turns per year. More questions about some of the "stuff" on the shelves revealed that a marketing error resulted in over $700,000 worth of stuff[9] coming in with no demand. A reverse auction sold this "stuff" for $100,000 and then this distribution center (that "needed" more space) volunteered to store the "stuff" for free until the new customer could arrange shipment.

Another prominent automobile manufacturer's distribution center manager expressed a need for more space. Again, questions were asked and the processes observed. There was a large amount of obsolete, slow-moving, and nonmoving supplies at the front of the center and the "popular" or fast-moving items were at the back of the center. As much as many folks hate to hear the word "rewarehousing," sometimes it is a necessary evil. Rewarehousing sometimes is necessary to get the flow of the distribution center right and get the obsolete, or as one major distribution center manager called it, "dormant stocks," out of the distribution center and put the fast-movers closer to the pickers and the shippers.

One of the Department of Defense distribution centers discovered it was easier to move to a new facility for its active stocks and leave the "dormant stocks" behind to be disposed of or reduced in quantity. At one point in time in the late 1990s, this particular distribution center had over 60 percent of its stocks that met the center's dormant criteria. And, like the automobile distribution center above, they had dormant stocks up front and fast-moving stocks in the remote locations in the center. The amount of dormant stocks, besides detracting from the efficiency and velocity of the center, significantly affected this distribution center's inventory turns calculations.

What is the impact of inventory turns on your operation? Everyone seems to be concerned with the number of turns for inventory in a distribution center or warehouse. Does a high number of turns mean that you have achieved high velocity for your activity or supply chain? Not necessarily, because turns are a measure of the average inventory turns for your activity. Some very fast-moving items can skew your data. Do not confuse data with information and remember that you do not want to manage to averages. Here are some of the aspects of inventory turns and velocity.

- *Accuracy and speed.* The accuracy of your inventory information is important to the measure of turns. Having high velocity turns and poor inventory management is not a good thing. In fact, depending on what method you use to calculate your turns, the poor inventory management may be the reason for the high number of turns. Lost or stolen merchandise is not a good measure of turns.
- *On-time delivery.* This is a good measure of your inventory turns. On-time delivery in the quantity requested means that you have a good inventory management system. However, on-time delivery in the right quantity needs to be balanced against the number of turns that you have. You may find that the reason for your consistent on-time delivery is not that you have good velocity in your supply chain, but it is more a result of having way too much stuff on the shelf.
- *Forecast and collaboration.* Good forecasting coupled with strong, honest collaboration with your supply chain partners will not only reduce your on-hand inventory, but will also increase your turns and your supply chain velocity.
- *Housekeeping.* There is nothing worse than thinking you have a stockout and failing to meet customer demand because the items are in the wrong location. This will not only slow the velocity of your supply chain, but will also have an impact on customer confidence and may result in lost orders. With fewer orders you may improve your velocity but this is not a desirable way to do so.
- *Point-of-use storage.* Storing items for manufacture close to the point of use will definitely improve your velocity. In addition, this methodology will reduce the need to stock the items in the warehouse except for safety stock.

- *Order-processing time.* Obviously, longer order-processing time produces the need for larger piles of supplies. Whenever you increase the piles of supplies, you are risking a slowdown in the velocity of your supply chain.

Vendor-Managed Inventory and Velocity

What is the advantage to vendor-managed inventory from the velocity viewpoint? To answer that question we need to start with a standard definition of Vendor-Managed Inventory (VMI). In simple terms, VMI may be company-owned merchandise or parts, but managed by the supplier. Or VMI may be owned by the supplier and managed by the supplier and becomes the property of the company when the item is used or purchased by a customer. The Opel plant outside Wiesbaden, Germany, has employed VMI for its assembly line for over a decade. There is a line on the floor of the assembly plant. When the part crosses that line it is purchased by the Opel plant for use. Until the part crosses the line on the floor, the part still belongs to the supplier. Dell uses the same concept with a warehouse directly behind its assembly plant in Texas. The master of VMI is Wal-Mart. Wal-Mart and Proctor & Gamble epitomize the efficiency and collaboration of VMI.

In VMI the role of the supplier includes the following.

- *Capture data.* This requires close collaboration between the supplier and the using company and usually involves sharing close-hold type information. This aspect of VMI requires a great deal of trust and cooperation between the firms.
- *Guide decisions on products.* Based on the supplier data and expertise, the supplier provides assistance in making stockage decisions.
- *Replenish as needed.* This is the critical part of VMI and will make or break the collaboration. No one is going to allow a company to serve as a VMI partner if it does not replenish the items prior to a stockout.
- *Eliminate obsolescence.* Obviously, if the items are not stocked at the retail location or assembly line, the items will have a much lower chance of becoming obsolete. If the supplier owns the parts or merchandise until it is sold, as in the Opel example above, the supplier will ensure that items do not become old or obsolete on the shelves.

What is important in choosing a partner for VMI? Does that have an impact on velocity? Choosing the wrong VMI partners could very well have a negative impact on your supply chain velocity and the image of your company.

- *Experience.* What is the experience of your partner in supporting VMI and a just-in-time-like resupply system? What is their past performance for those companies that they have supported with VMI efforts?
- *Workforce.* Does the prospective partner have the workforce to properly support this effort? If not, are they willing to increase their workforce to make the VMI partnership successful?
- *Automation.* What is their automation capability? A full-scale VMI initiative is no place for manual techniques. Experience in supporting VMI may help in providing a sense of judgment on what needs to be on the shelves, but automation is required to process the shared sales data.
- *Financial stability.* What is the financial stability of the potential partner? How many times have you seen a company contract out a function only to find out that the contractor was not stable enough to provide the product, resulting in a loss of business for the partner?
- *Expansion capability.* Does the potential VMI partner have the capability to expand their operations in order to expand the VMI partnership as the partnership matures?
- *Backup plan.* What is the backup plan for the VMI supplier in the event of a supply chain disruption or interruption?
- *Ability to capture data.* Do they have the ability to capture the necessary data in order to provide the level of support that you desire and the level of support necessary to keep your customers satisfied?

There are some other advantages of VMI in addition to adding velocity to your supply chain. These corollary benefits are as follows.

- *Reduction in orders generated.* The time and money spent in traditional replenishment systems is saved because of the reduction or even elimination of the ordering process under VMI.
- *Reduction in receipts processing.* Just as with the ordering process, with VMI there is a significant reduction in the amount of receipts processing and stocking of the shelves. Under VMI programs such as the Wal-Mart and Proctor & Gamble model, the vendor stocks the shelves, eliminating the need for a stock clerk and receiving clerk to receive the shipments, open the boxes, and replenish the shelves. The Home Depot has a number of vendors that do the

same thing for their stores. One of the benefits to the vendor is usually a better location on the shelves and access to sales data.

■ *Reduction in inventory counts and personnel.* Because the vendor is responsible for stocking the shelves and ensuring that the items are always on hand in preset quantities, there is a reduction in the need for inventory personnel. There is also an increase in the inventory accuracy for the items delivered and managed by the vendor. Why? Because the vendor does not want to take the chance of having an empty shelf; plus, the vendor usually has access to sales data, and is better able to forecast how much needs to be on the shelves on what days to meet customer demands.

Visibility and Velocity

Visibility provides timely information and assists in meeting the supply chain need for security. Visibility relies on and provides the timely transmission of data required to accurately plan distribution operations. This ties visibility to the importance of securing the information pipelines and communication networks and nodes. What happens to visibility when you have a node failure? Here is an example of node failure: the Command and General Staff College network was infected in February 2004. The e-mail system was infected with the "Beagle" virus. The virus infection shut down the e-mail servers for the college. This resulted in the use of faxes and phones for routine staffing. This was only a minor inconvenience but the node failure prevented access to information stored in the e-mail files. The same thing can happen to your system and the loss of visibility will have a negative impact on your supply chain's velocity.

In a presentation to a conference sponsored by the U.S. Army War College and the University of Pittsburgh, James Rosenau from George Washington University said, "I believe that the information revolution, by providing technologies that have continued to greatly accelerate the collapse of time and space, has added substantially to the complexities that mark our time."[10] But at the same time that they have added to the complexities, the information systems provide visibility that increases not only the velocity of your supply chain, but also the customer confidence in the system. This confidence provided by visibility will reduce the number of redundant orders and requests for information and order status. The ability to provide visibility access to the customer, such as what UPS, FedEx, and the United States Postal Service now provide, also saves the companies money in call center staffing.

Visibility is based on a continuum of logistic data from origin into and through the processes of the distribution system. Visibility comes in a variety of means, including the following.

- *In-process visibility.* This form of visibility allows manufacturers to see the status of the product throughout the manufacturing process. It also allows customers to see the progress through the system.
- *Supply visibility.* The U.S. Army, like many major corporations, has visibility of where every item in the Army's supply system is stored. With over 440 local storage sites scattered around the world, this allows the Army to know where critical items are and provides the ability to direct the release of a part from a storage facility closer to the customer whenever possible. The prevailing logic is that if an item is in Hanau, Germany, why ship one to Wiesbaden, Germany, from the Pennsylvania depot? Cummins Diesel provides the same supply visibility to its customers and dealers. NAPA auto parts provides a very similar capability to customers and dealers in order to shorten the order delivery cycle and improve supply chain visibility.
- *In-transit visibility.* This is the ability to track an item as it moves through the supply chain. The U.S. military has this capability. In-transit visibility provides a certain level of confidence for soldiers, sailors, airmen, and marines that the part really is coming. UPS and FedEx provide the same level of in-transit visibility for every package in their system. In-transit visibility enables the customer to know exactly where the package is and provides a good idea of when the item will be delivered based on the available data.

Information must be accurately captured and entered into the information networks. This is another tie to supply chain and information security: the accuracy of the data input into your system. Inaccurate visibility data is of no value to the customer. The more data that can be entered through automated means, the better the fidelity and security of the data. This was the impetus for the use of bar codes, radio frequency readers, portable data collection devices, radio frequency identification tags, the acceptance of global positioning satellite systems, and other automated tracking systems that provide not only visibility but also automated data capture.

Reverse Logistics/Reverse Supply Chains

What is the impact on the forward velocity of your supply chain from the reverse supply chain? In 1999, Drs. Rogers and Tibben-Lembke completed the first study of reverse logistics in the United States. The results of their study, sponsored by the Reverse Logistics Executive Council, the University of Nevada—Reno, and the Council of Logistics Management, was published as *Going Backwards.*[11] The opening of this book states, "Now, more than ever reverse logistics is seen as being important."[12] That was 1999. In 2003, a new company was formed to look at the "emerging" reverse logistics problem. Reverse Logistics Trends, Inc.,[13] was formed as a professional organization to address what is becoming a very visual part of the supply chain. As companies continue to squeeze efficiencies out of the forward supply chain, they are starting to realize that there is a lot of money tied up in products in the reverse supply chain that could immediately affect corporate profitability.

Here are some examples of reverse logistics problems in commercial industry.

- After the 2003 holiday season, Wal-Mart experienced over 2000 containers of returns at their returns distribution center. According to senior Wal-Mart personnel, these containers were "packed full" and could best be described as "a mess." Inside these containers that represented about four days of supply for Wal-Mart were serviceable and unserviceable items that had to be sorted and either resold, repaired for discounted sales, or disposed of.
- Palm One experiences approximately a 25 percent return rate on its Personal Digital Assistants (PDAs). This produces a warehouse of items marked "broken," whether or not the items are actually broken. These items have to be sorted and tested. Based on the test results, the returned PDAs are repackaged for resale, repaired for discounted resale, or disposed of. To help reduce the warehouse contents, Palm One now has a program in place to track the call center personnel and can identify those personnel who account for higher-than-average returns.
- Hoover, the vacuum cleaner manufacturer, experiences approximately $40 million in returns each year and to date, simply crushes and destroys the returns rather than refurbishing and selling through reverse auctions or liquidators such as E-bay.
- Before getting into a reverse logistics program, Estée Lauder dumped approximately $60 million in returned cosmetics into landfills.
- Kmart, the year before filing for bankruptcy protection, took in over $800 million in returns. It is really hard to turn a profit when you have that much stuff coming back into the store.

In the early 1970s, the country music group the Statler Brothers had a hit song titled, "Do You Remember These?" See if you remember some of these about reverse logistics.

- Do you remember when reverse logistics was considered the seedy side of your business and no one wanted to touch returns? This is only recently turning the corner as companies realize that there is money in reverse logistics. Previously, a return meant a bad product and no one wanted to admit to a bad product. Now, companies are starting to realize that there are lessons to be learned from the reverse logistics system such as, what is wrong with the product or why did the customer not like it?
- Do you remember when reverse logistics was the last thing anyone in your company wanted to focus on or even think about? There are still companies that refuse to think about reverse logistics. This has spawned a whole industry for third-party providers that manage the reverse process for the companies.
- Do you remember when anything that was returned that was "broken" or defective was simply thrown into a landfill? Look at the figures above for Estée Lauder. Could you afford to throw that much stuff away?

It is hoped that no one falls into these categories or can remember these as recent occurrences in their company. However, if the interest displayed at the shows of Reverse Logistics Trends, Inc., is an indication, there are still a large number of companies that fall into these categories, but have realized that they need to do something quickly to remain profitable and competitive.

Reverse logistics as a "green" initiative has its roots in Germany. In 1991, the newly reunified Germany passed an ordinance that really put some teeth into the reverse logistics business. This ordinance, among other things, put the onus on the producer to take responsibility for the disposal of an item after the consumer was through with it. In addition, it makes the producer responsible for the disposal or recycling of the packaging materials. This ordinance also put legal teeth into the handling of hazardous materials. As the chief of the Supply Management Division for the Army's Third Corps Support Command,[14] I was responsible for the distribution of all supplies throughout Europe for Army forces. This included, among other items, the distribution of batteries for trucks, tanks, and Humvees. These batteries contain acid. The provisions of the law stipulated that I was responsible for the shipment, therefore any acid spilled or not properly disposed of was my responsibility and the failure to properly ship these items would lead to my responsibility to pay the fine in German marks. In addition, the transportation of engines for rebuilding or repair had to be drained of all fluids, steam cleaned, and placed in a sealed container to prevent spilling of fluids on the roads—another fine.

Many companies are finding it profitable to use returnable totes and containers. The use of returnable/reusable containers traces its roots to Marks and Spencer in Great Britain as early as 1970. The use of reusable containers is starting to catch on in the United States with such firms as Food Lion, Target, Books-a-Million, and Wal-Mart shipping from distribution centers in reusable totes and containers.

The European Union set a goal of 50 to 65 percent of all shipping containers and packaging waste to be recovered, recycled, or reused by 2001. The impact for the rest of the world is that to do business with the EU will require adopting their standards for reducing repackaging waste. This affects the reverse supply chain and has an impact on the velocity of the forward supply chain as the reusable, recycled, or recovered items consume space in the finite supply chain.

Is reverse logistics something unique to commercial industry? Do the Army and the Department of Defense have problems with reverse logistics? If so, what can we learn from them? Reverse logistics is not unique to the Department of Defense. According to an article in *Inbound Logistics* in January 2004, "Reverse logistics is the backward flow of what we all wish would be a forward-only process. If you expect zero product returns in your supply chain, you are living in a dreamland."[15]

In preparation for the actions of Operation Iraqi Freedom, the United States Army moved the equivalent of approximately 150 Wal-Mart Super Centers into Kuwait in a matter of only a few months. A few months later, *Jane's Defence Weekly* reported that there is a 40-hectare area in Kuwait adjacent to the Theater Distribution Center stocked with items waiting to be retrograded to the United States. A report by the Government Accounting Office in December 2003 provided Congress with pictures of the "excess" items awaiting the return to the United States to be placed back in the supply system for future use, or worse, awaiting disposal as a result of exposure to climatic elements.

The buildup of excess is not something unique to Operation Iraqi Freedom. During the United Nations missions to Somalia, Croatia, and Bosnia, excess items started coming back to the Theater Distribution Center in Kaiserslautern, Germany, within days of soldiers arriving in these countries. Chapter 9 looks at the lessons from these operations and other military operations in greater detail.

Part of this problem stems from the desires (not necessarily the needs) of soldiers in combat and the attitude of the supply personnel to meet their needs and then worry whether the item is really needed. It is awfully hard to sit in an office in the United States and tell a soldier being shot at that he or she does not really need an item. General George S. Patton was accurate when he said, "In battle, troops get temperamental and ask for things which they really do not need. However, where humanly possible, their requests, no matter how unreasonable, should be answered."

Is this attitude to give customers whatever they request a purely military problem? Not really. Companies all over the world have adopted the same attitude for their customers. Even though the item may not really be needed, it is not our place to tell the customer that he or she does not need it. As a result, items do indeed come back through the reverse supply chain. In a perfect world there would be no need for a reverse supply chain, but obviously, our supply chains do not have the luxury of operating in a perfect world.

The problem for velocity management is that items processed in reverse have an impact on the time, personnel, and resources necessary to process items through the forward supply chain. And if a supply chain is only as strong as its weakest link, this may be the weak link in the chain.

Do you know what is affecting your reverse supply chain? The following areas are necessary to know in order to get control of this valuable process and improve the velocity of your forward supply chain.

1. What is your rate of returns and what percent of your orders' dollar value is represented by the returns? In the Army, after spending several years to streamline the forward supply chain operations, we started looking at the volume of returns. Our hope was that by getting a grip on the reverse supply chain processes we could squeeze more efficiency from the forward supply chain. What the Army discovered was that the rate of returns was approximately 20 percent of all orders. Although this was not as bad as some commercial operations and although it was down from a high of almost 50 percent of orders from only a few years earlier, what we discovered was that the 20 percent returns represented almost 50 percent of the dollar value of all orders. If you assume that the Department of Defense has the same level of returns as the Army (a safe assumption for illustration purposes inasmuch as all of the Department of Defense uses the same catalogue data), this means that there could be as many as 11 million items in the reverse supply chain every year. How many companies actually have that many orders in the forward supply chain? This gives you an idea of the size of the problem at the Department of Defense level and why it is getting so much attention from the General Accounting Office and Congress. Imagine the velocity impact of 11 million items going backward in your supply chain in addition to the programmed return of repairable items such as engines, starters, and transmissions.

2. What does it cost to process your returns? Are you spending more money on the return processing of your items than the item is

actually worth? Although estimates are as high as $85 for the processing of a single return, the Army set the dollar figure at an arbitrary $50. Any item above $50 that is "excess"[16] to an organization is returned through the reverse supply chain. Items costing less than $50 are either disposed of through the Defense Reutilization and Marketing Office or are maintained on the shelf locally for future use. When this $50 criterion is extrapolated against the potential items for returns in the Department of Defense, the candidates for return drop to approximately 1,650,000 down from the original 11,000,000. This indicates that perhaps the Department of Defense prior to this decision was processing approximately 9,500,000 items at a cost greater than the value of the item. How many companies are doing the same thing in their reverse supply chains? In addition to spending money unnecessarily to process "worthless" returns, the items that are being processed are constipating the supply chain.

3. Therefore, the next question is, how long does it take to process a returned item through the supply chain? By using the techniques described in Chapter 4, "Knowing Yourself," the Army discovered that it took an average of eight and one-half days to process a serviceable return back into the system. This data is meaningless until it is compared to the average dock-to-stock time of just over one day for items in the forward supply chain. The critical information for the Army was not so much the seven-plus day difference between the processing times, but the times revealed to actually get the item from the customer back to the dock for processing. In some cases, this exceeded 100 days. To prevent a stockout from occurring, this means that the wholesale and retail systems have to carry additional stocks on the shelves to cover the unavailable stocks that are tied up in the reverse supply chain. The carrying of additional inventory in the distribution centers can affect velocity. If the right items are stocked closer to the customer, velocity is improved. However, if the reverse logistics problems mean stocking more of the same items in a fiscally or spatially constrained center, the impact is adverse on velocity, because this demands stocking fewer SKUs.

4. What are your costs, above the cost of the item, for processing returns? Here is what you are spending money on in the reverse supply chain.

   a. The processing of merchandise credits back to the customer. Even if this is an automated system, there is a cost of doing business to include the cost of the electronic transfers and the software to make these happen.

b. The transportation costs of moving the items from the customer to the dock for processing. This may be borne by the customer, but if so, may result in displeased customers and lost future business.

c. The cost to repackage serviceable/resaleable items for return to the shelf.

d. The cost of warehousing the items awaiting disposition. We previously discussed the distribution center that not only stored items for reverse auctions but also stored the auctioned items for the customer until they could accept delivery. One of the managers was proud of the fact that they had sold the $700,000 items in a reverse auction for $100,000. (Wow, only a $600,000 loss. Now that is something to be proud of. Not!) The interesting information was that they were now storing these items for free for the reverse auction customer. What do you think the customer will say when some of those items are missing because a distribution center worker picked from the wrong location?

e. And, of course, there is the cost of disposing of items that are either obsolete (a very common occurrence in the electronics business), unserviceable (broken but repairable), or damaged beyond repair and awaiting disposal. This takes on a whole new level of concern if your products contain precious metals that can be recovered, items with mandatory recycling (a very common situation in Europe), or hazardous materials.

5. What went wrong and why do we have returns? The final question is what can you learn from your returns to reduce the number of returns in the future? Returns have to be viewed as an indicator of a problem. Data that can be mined from returns includes the following.

a. Why was the item really returned? Defective, not needed, wrong size, only needed for a day, used and returned?

b. Is there an indication of a problem in the packaging material that allows damage in shipment?

c. Is there an indication of a problem in the production process that is allowing the production of defective items?

d. Do we have a faulty supplier?

e. Are we not meeting customer expectations with the item?

When we walked the process in the Army, we discovered a reverse process that looked like the diagram in Figure 7.1.

This processing can result in a continual do-loop if the items are repaired and are then discovered to be excess to the unit, or if the item is returned to the supply system and then needed again at a later date,

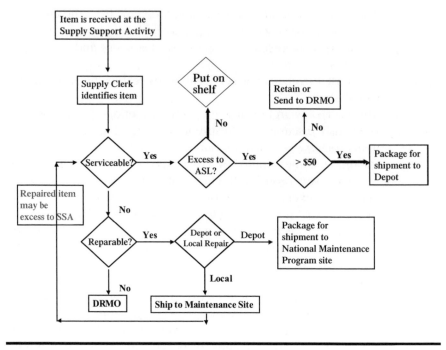

Figure 7.1   Processing returns in the Army.[24]

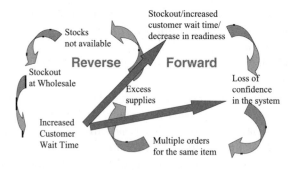

Figure 7.2   The return supply chain do-loop and impact on the forward supply chain.

or is needed immediately by another unit. This do-loop looks something like Figure 7.2.

In reverse logistics there is another impact on velocity. The multiple handling of returns is not uncommon. This multiple handling of returns, just like the multiple touches in a forward supply chain, is inefficient and affects velocity.

Another impact of returns that affects the bottom line, but not really the velocity of the supply chain, is worth mentioning. For items that are defective or otherwise not repairable or resaleable, the carrying costs for the items are 100 percent at disposal. This represents a large controllable opportunity cost that can affect profits, especially when you consider that almost half of what goes into landfills is logistics related: either packaging products or items damaged in shipment. In 2001, the amount of returns for commercial industry reportedly reached $60 billion, of which approximately $52 billion was excess to the supply system. Corporations spent almost $40 billion to process these items and usually were lucky to recover 7 percent of the costs. Do the quick math. First companies spent 66 percent of the value of the items to process them and then received 7 percent of the value in return. This is not a good return on investment.

What corporate America discovered was that in some cases the handling of the returns was as much as three times as costly as selling an item in the forward supply chain. And, research shows that as many as 80 percent of the returned items are not actually defective, a condition in the military known as "No Fault Noted." Kmart discovered this when lawnmowers started coming back in after the summer grass-cutting season, but were still under warranty and thus were taken back in the stores. What do you do with a used lawnmower that someone just used for free for three or four months?

Historically, most companies have ignored the reverse supply chain and have not measured the impact of the items going backward on the items going forward. One of the ways to get visibility in the forward and reverse supply chains is through the use of radio frequency identification tags.

Reverse logistics is not a new problem. During World War II, it surfaced as the war was winding down. In fact, by May 1946 there was a storage area of approximately 77,000,000 square feet in Europe that contained over $6.3 billion in stuff waiting for the reverse logistics process to return it to the United States, donate to war-torn countries, or dispose of it. As the U.S. Army is learning during Operation Iraqi Freedom, the use of radio frequency identification tags helps to reduce some of the reverse logistics backlogs and visibility problems.

RFID/AIT and Velocity

In 2003, Wal-Mart, followed by the Department of Defense, Target, and a few other major firms, announced programs that required their top suppliers to use Radio Frequency Identification (RFID) tags on pallets and cases by January 1, 2005. The rationale for the use of RFID is to improve velocity in the supply chain by increasing visibility of goods, materials, and merchandise moving through the system. The Department of Defense adopted the use of active RFID tags on pallets in 1995 in Europe and by 1998 for most shipments in the continental United States. The purpose of these active tags was to provide greater visibility and tracking of supplies in the supply chain.[17] The additional benefit to the visibility was a greater confidence by the users in the supply system to provide the items because the customer had visibility as well. Proctor & Gamble believes that the use of RFID will enable the company to cut its inventory in half. As we discussed earlier, smaller inventories usually contribute to the velocity of your supply chain. Another benefit of the RFID tags is the reduced time to process receipts and the reduced time necessary for inventories.

RFID and automated information technology data capture improve distribution-based logistics by automating information at the source for use throughout the supply chain, provide in-transit visibility, and provide the customers with increased confidence in the system, thereby reducing redundant orders and preventing potentially returned merchandise.

The use of RFID and AIT has raised security concerns. The possibility of intercepting RFID data is very remote. With the use of passive tags, the ability to intercept data is reduced even more because of the required close proximity of the reader to the tag (see Figure 7.3).

Figure 7.3 An RFID tag on an Air Force pallet.

One potential benefit for the use of RFID tags to add velocity to personal lives is in the sorting of baggage at airports. With the use of barcodes and RFID, airlines could perform a presort of baggage before loading the plane. While standing at the Kansas City Airport, I watched as the bags were unloaded from the small commuter plane and taken to the center of the terminal where they were unloaded and sorted for transfer or for delivery into the terminal for the passengers that were at the end of their journey. A presort could prevent having to handle all the bags multiple times and could reduce the passenger wait time for bags. Satisfied passengers would definitely be something new for most airlines.

Achieving Velocity in Your Supply Chain

The real competition is between supply chains.

Dr. Eli Goldratt

Now that we have looked at what velocity management is and how the reverse supply chain can affect the forward supply chain, it is time to take a look at how to achieve velocity in your supply chain. The end of the chapter contains a checklist for achieving velocity. Let's take a look at some of the best ways to achieve velocity in your supply chain.

The most effective way to supercharge the velocity of supplies moving through your supply chain is to use the techniques in Chapter 4 to map the process and identify the non-value-added activities in your processes. This will lead to increased responsiveness to the needs of the customer. Your responsiveness is the measure of the reaction time for the service provided. How fast can you respond to changes in customer orders? Having contingency plans on the shelf to respond to almost any demand from your customer is a method for reducing your reaction times.

Providing the customer with assurance of time-definite deliveries will enable the customer to be ready to receive the shipments from you. In the Army, we discovered that providing the customer with a small window of when a truck would show up at their dock enabled the warehouses to have a maximum amount of their workforce ready. This provided the customer with predictability and shortened the time that the truck spent at that warehouse before departing for the next one. The new hours-of-service rules almost dictate the same mentality in commercial operations. If customers have a high level of certainty regarding the quality of service provided, they can schedule their workload to adopt a pit crew mentality on unloading their merchandise or materials from the truck and reduce the time the truck is at their dock, thus reducing the unproductive time for the driver.

A recent FedEx commercial showed a customer in his bath towel calling to complain that his FedEx package arrived exactly when he had requested delivery. The gist of this commercial hints at the need for assurance and confidence by the customer. Apparently this customer, based on previous experiences, did not expect delivery at the promised time and was caught, literally, unprepared when the package arrived.

Empathy for the customer is important. This is the understanding of the customer's situation. By understanding the situation, you can tailor your support to your customer to meet his or her needs. A good example of this comes from Operation Iraqi Freedom. Some of the support personnel in Camp Arifjan, the logistics headquarters for the operation, were content to stay within the confines of Camp Arifjan well away from any action.[18] By staying away from the action, these managers could not fully understand the needs of the soldiers in combat or preparing for combat. Not understanding the needs and conditions of your customers does not allow you to adequately meet their needs.

During Operation Iraqi Freedom, this led to misplaced priorities. As the Third Infantry Division moved from their base camps in the Kuwaiti desert to their staging areas to prepare for crossing into Iraq, they discovered that no one had placed portable latrines in the staging areas. Although the distribution priorities for that particular day did not include moving portable latrines, a decision was made to divert supply trucks to moving portable latrines forward. The soldiers at Camp Doha, the headquarters for the Combined Land Component Command (all United States and British soldiers and marines), and at Camp Arifjan all had either portable latrines or actual indoor latrines and therefore did not grasp the need for the portable latrines in the very forward areas.

One of the requirements in today's environment to improve your velocity is to master the art of the smaller shipments. For years every distribution center focused on case lot picks and pallet load shipments. Today's customers are ordering in smaller quantities. Have you mastered the art of the smaller shipment? This is critical to improving your responsiveness and velocity. Maybe it is time to change the way your suppliers pack your items. If what the customer is ordering does not match your current unit of pack, change it to match what the customers are ordering and you for all practical purposes will be back to "case" picks.

Time is a competitive advantage and weapon in the competition between supply chains. Take the non-value-added processes out of your supply chain, adopt the techniques discussed in this chapter, and not only will you supercharge the velocity of your supply chain, but you will improve customer support and confidence in your ability to meet their needs, regardless of how ridiculous some of their demands may seem.

Velocity management for the Army is based on the concept of replacing mass with information. But, if the information that you collect is not accurate or if the information sits in someone's in-box, it is of no value. When the Army started the velocity management program and established the baseline measurements for the program, they discovered that it took as long to move information through the system as it did to physically move the supplies through the distribution system. In today's commerce, there is no excuse for information at rest.

Velocity over mass was the basis of the Army's success. Replacing the stockpiles of supplies with information systems and best business practices provided success for the Army. In addition, the adoption of speed and accuracy produces the ability to replace mass with velocity and improve the flow through the supply chain. The goal is to substitute velocity coupled with reduced cycle times for the historical mass or mountains of supplies, sometimes known in the Army as "iron mountains." These iron mountains gave the title to Gus Pagonis's book, *Moving Mountains.*

To achieve velocity you have to maximize throughput. Throughput is defined as prepacking merchandise or supplies to move through the distribution system by reducing the number of touches to as few times as possible. One of the ways to maximize throughput is by cross-docking when possible. Partners should pack for direct and time-definite delivery to minimize handling and reduce customer wait times. This is the culmination of effort of velocity over mass.

Maintain minimum essential stocks. Although this is a goal of just-in-time (JIT) and lean programs, it is not a new objective. Maintaining minimum essential stocks to improve the speed of the supplies moving through the supply chain was a goal during World War II. This does not mean zero inventory or a total reliance on JIT. Even with minimum essential inventories, you may need some just-in-case stocks. An example of this is the use of small, fast-moving supplies at lower levels. The Army does this with Prescribed Load Lists (usually about 100 fast-moving SKUs), Authorized Stockage Lists (several hundred fast-moving critical SKUs), and limited "Theater" stocks to reduce the long supply-chain reaction times from the continental United States to operations in foreign countries.

Confidence in the system eliminates the need for large stockpiles. Confidence in the system comes from velocity management techniques such as time-definite delivery, and perfect order fulfillment (delivering the right material at the right place and time and when the customer expects it or at least when we promised the customer it would be there) coupled with providing the customer with visibility of the system.

Measuring Velocity

What are the metrics of velocity? It involves a shift in how things are measured and what is measured. If your metric does not measure what is important to the customer, take a look at it. Are you measuring the same things as last year? In the same way?

- Throughput
- Number of touches: use the example of OIF. Take a look at the number of times an item could be touched before getting to the soldier who ordered the item.
  - Item is picked from the shelf at the national depot (for simplicity we assume the part needed was stocked in the Susquehanna Depot in Pennsylvania; if the item came from another source or storage location, the number of touches would increase).
  - The part goes through the sort process at the depot and comes out the chute at the packing station.
  - A clerk at the depot pulls the item out of the chute and places it in a large tri-wall multipack box. (Again, for this example we assume that all of the items in the multipack box are for the same customer unit. Otherwise the number of touches would again increase at the other end when these items are sorted into customer boxes or lanes.)
  - The multipack box is loaded onto an Air Force 463L pallet and loaded on a truck for the airport.
  - At the airport, the pallet is loaded onto a plane heading to Charleston Air Force Base. With any luck at this point the entire pallet is cross-docked at Charleston to an intercontinental airlift asset or a commercial airplane in support of the operations as part of the CRAF (Civilian Reserve Air Fleet) program.
  - When the plane arrives at the Kuwait City International Airport, the pallet is removed from the plane.
  - The pallet is then placed on the shuttle truck to move to Camp Wolf (less than one-half mile away).
  - The pallet is again downloaded and placed in the Wolf staging area.
  - When the transport trucks arrive for movement to the Theater Distribution Center, the pallet is loaded for the 30-minute ride to the Theater Distribution Center.
  - At the Theater Distribution Center, the pallet with the multipack box is again downloaded.
  - If the pallet is not a pure pallet (all for one consignee) the box is removed and placed in the customer location. If the box is for the General Support distribution center, it is placed in that shipping lane.
  - The box going to the General Support[19] DC is loaded on a truck and shipped to Camp Arifjan.

- At Camp Arifjan the box is unloaded, sorted, and put on the shelf (at least two touches).
- The part is pulled off the shelf to fill a request to replenish the Direct Support distribution center.
- The part is received at the Direct Support center.
- The part is placed on a shelf at the Direct Support center.
- A supported customer unit requests the part and it is picked and packed.
- The box with the part is put on a truck to go to the Theater Distribution Center to be consolidated with other shipments going to the customer in Iraq.
- The box is downloaded at the Theater Distribution Center and placed in the customer shipping bin (again, for this example we are not considering the chance for cross-docking).
- The box is loaded on the truck going forward to the ultimate customer's support unit.
- At the support unit the part is taken out of the box and given to the requesting soldier's unit.
- The unit gives the part to the customer repair parts supply clerk.
- The supply clerk gives the part to the mechanic and the part is placed on the vehicle that had the deficiency that caused the part to be ordered.

A total of 22 to 23 touches are possible in this scenario. Is there any wonder why the customer wait time for the soldiers of Operation Iraqi Freedom averaged 49 days? Any wonder why one captain said he did not get any repair parts until July? And this is the product of a system that only a few years earlier produced over 50 percent reductions in customer wait times and repair cycle times for equipment, and produced a real dollar savings of over $300 million in one year. This is an example of the tie between knowing yourself by walking the process and the velocity of your supply chain.

- Total hours, not days, to meet customer demands. It was not that long ago that the time buckets for measuring the supply chain were in days, but in today's supply chains, the measure of effectiveness is in hours to be competitive.
- Total customer wait time. How long does it take from the time your customer places an order until the item is in his or her hands? Do you know? You can bet your competition probably knows.
- What is the cost of quality? The cost of good quality for supply chains is much lower than the cost of poor quality. In addition to the cost of replacing a damaged item, the additional cost for supply

chains is that of the reverse supply chain and repairing or disposing of damaged products.

■ What is the handling cost per unit? Do you know how much it costs to handle items forward and reverse in your supply chain?

■ Dock-to-stock time. Remember the examples of Disney and Grainger. This is the measure of how fast your inbound items are available for sale to customers. The longer the dock-to-stock time, the slower your velocity, and the more inventory you have to carry.

■ Stock-to-shipping dock. Is this important? You bet it is. This is a matter of items in motion (not wasted motion), items at rest, and items that may very well get lost.

■ Dock-to-customer. Are you measuring the transportation leg of your supply chain or are you trusting your sources that all is well? At the National Training Center at Fort Irwin, California, when the logistics community started watching shipping times, they discovered that they were paying for premium service and were actually getting two-week service from northern California. The supplier's response was, "No one ever questioned it before so we did not think these shipments were important." I hope you do not have suppliers like that.

■ Customer promise fulfillment. This is critical. Are you meeting the promised delivery dates, with the promised quantity, and with the promised quality of product?

Examples of Improving Velocity

The same techniques discussed above and some of the techniques and methodologies used by the Army have proven to be successful for other organizations. Here are some examples of velocity management and improvement.

At the Food Lion distribution centers in North Carolina, the managers took a look at the handling of perishable foods. No one wants to buy perishable foods that are a day or two late getting to a store. The distribution center managers looked at how each product was handled and stored. Some of the ideas considered and adopted to increase the velocity of the perishable goods was to increase the number of receiving docks to facilitate faster receiving, use standardized pick patterns, and review the slot sizes. The teams looking at the distribution centers recommended improved center layouts and warehousing operations. The result of these actions was an increase in productivity at the distribution centers of between four and six percent.[20]

After the success of the Army's velocity management program, the Joint Chiefs of Staff for the Department of Defense established a similar program for the entire Department of Defense. In the *Joint Publication 4.0*, the new doctrine established the tenets of joint (all of the U.S. armed services) distribution. The tenets are as follows.

1. Visibility: "This is an essential component of distribution management. It can serve as a positive indicator that the distribution pipeline is responding to the needs of the customer." Just as discussed earlier, visibility is not only a tenet of distribution but also a method to improve the velocity in your supply chain. The use of technology to provide total asset and in-transit visibility contributes to velocity by reducing the number of redundant requisitions and improving velocity in your supply chain.
2. Capacity: "The capacity of the system is dictated by the constraints of the infrastructure." The capacity of the supply chain is a constraint on the velocity of your supply chain. The ability to anticipate bottlenecks (similar to the techniques described in the Theory of Constraints), disruptions (as discussed in Chapter 3 on security), and potential changes in the distribution plan (a requirement to maintain flexibility in the supply chain) allows managers to optimize the supply chain capacity. The greater your supply chain capacity, the greater the potential for high velocity in your supply chain.
3. Control: "centralized vs. decentralized." The Department of Defense rationale for this tenet is that centralized control reinforces the authority of the distribution manager. Where the control is in the supply chain depends on who is the focal point of your distribution operations. Centralized control reduces your supply chain flexibility. The reduced flexibility to respond to customer requirements may in fact reduce your velocity.

Velocity of the time-to-market for high-fashion designers is costly but not as costly as not having velocity in the system. According to the *Wall Street Journal*, the "knockoffs" or inexpensive copies of fashion garments habitually beat the big fashion houses to the stores with new fashions. "To eliminate this edge, the Italian fashion company, Ferragamo, has been investing heavily behind the scenes to speed up its production cycle. By improving information technology and streamlining its supply chain during the past year, Ferragamo has shaved about 20% off the time it takes a product to get from sketchpad to store, bringing it down to about ten weeks from three months. . . . The fast-fashion retailers are changing customers' expectations for speed and variety."[21] Ferragamo discovered what many of you in the supply chain industry have known for years: the faster you can get the product to the customer, the better your chances of being competitive and the better you will meet the customers' needs.

Figure 7.4 Pallets awaiting distribution.

Ferragamo is also discovering what many of you already have experienced: the faster you get merchandise to the customer, the faster they want it the next time (see Figure 7.4).

Conclusions and Summary

Ultimately, the transformation of Army logistics, much like commercial supply chains, must create a seamless system that extends from the factory to the foxhole. Beyond that, the system needs to extend to the cockpit, the bridge, and all other elements of a force that contain the other Department of Defense services and allied partners. The same is true in your industry; logistics cannot be treated as an afterthought. Properly organized, managed, and supported, a modern logistics system of the kind the U.S. Army is creating is a potent force multiplier. In commercial terms, a force multiplier is a supply chain that although smaller and more streamlined, gives you the capabilities of a much larger system.

Using an analogy between the Army's logistics system and football, when retired General Fred Franks, one of the principal commanders during Operation Desert Storm, talked to the senior logisticians in Kuwait prior to Operation Iraqi Freedom, he told them, "If you move the ball ninety yards but can't move it the final ten yards, you have failed to score." The ability to move supplies into Kuwait but not the "final ten yards" to the soldiers could be considered a failure in the eyes of the logistics community. Some company commanders reported not getting repair parts from the time they went into Iraq until July. This is a failure of the system and a situation that does not create the confidence necessary to have velocity in your supply chain. It is not the velocity in the individual links of the supply chain that the customer cares about. What your customers care about is how fast you can get the items they want to them, in the quantity and quality that they expect. For the Army the velocity to Kuwait was fantastic; it was the velocity from Kuwait to Iraq that was abysmal and created concern on the part of all involved.

If you can take an order; pick, pack, and ship the order; but not get the goods to the customer in the timeframe expected or when the item is really needed, you have failed to score.

Here are some examples of commercial failures in the supply chain. In August 2003, I ordered a Dell laptop computer online. The laptop did not arrive when promised because the Dell partner, United Parcel Service, "Did not know where the address was," and in fact, posted online status on their tracking site that the "Address was unknown and delivery was not possible." It took several calls to UPS to get them to understand that the address was new and that FedEx knew where it was because they had delivered a package that same week.

Another example, this time with the United States Postal Service, occurred in January 2004. As I attempted to deliver a compact disk to the *Supply and Demand Chain Executive* magazine offices, I was told that the location did not exist. Then I was told that the "Property manager did not know what suite to take the package to." Both times the Express Mail package was returned to Kansas to start over. However, there is a good news ending to this story. Finally, a very courteous employee in the Birmingham Express Mail office called and got a confirmation of the suite and the contact phone number and the package was delivered. The elapsed time was almost two weeks.

In the book, *Adapt or Die,* the authors state on the first page, "It's a simple fact: The rules of business have changed. In the New Economy, it's all about speed and service. With today's instantaneous availability of information, new cultural trends can take hold globally within weeks—and fade just as rapidly."[22]

The authors of *Adapt or Die* go on to say, "To play by the new rules of today's fast-moving economy, businesses need mechanisms to allow them to swiftly react and change direction—even when they cannot foresee what lies ahead."[23] This is the purpose of velocity management, to provide you with the tools to supercharge the velocity of your supply chain in order to compete successfully in the 21st century.

Just as the Army has discovered, there are great advantages to streamlining your supply chain and getting merchandise to the customer faster. The next section provides a list of questions and techniques for supercharging your velocity.

Velocity Improvement Techniques and Questions

1. *Use of automation.* Are you using automation to enhance the velocity of your supply chain or have you, like the Army in the 1990s, simply automated the old manual systems without eliminating non-value-adding procedures? Are you taking advantage of technology to improve the visibility of items as they pass through your supply chain?

2. *Case picks and loose picks.* Obviously, the more case picks you do, the greater the velocity in your distribution center. However, lean logistics and just-in-time concepts drive customers to more frequent orders of smaller quantities. Do you know the ratio in your distribution center between case picks and individual or loose picks?

3. *Slotting/Storage areas.* Most warehouse management systems incorporate an automatic slotting feature. Does this automatic slotting put your items where they can best affect your velocity?

4. *Golden zones.* The majority of the items picked are at an ergonomic level. The results of what you learned from the time mapping and process mapping discussed in Chapter 4 will assist in finding out what your workers are doing and what percentage of their time is productive.

5. *Postponement and the impact on velocity.* In most cases, postponement operations in your distribution will reduce the velocity in your center. But, if properly coordinated and controlled, will enhance the overall velocity in the supply chain.

6. *Batching orders together.* Do you pick the orders as they come in, or do you try to batch orders to level the workload? There are some distribution centers that "bank" orders from one day to the next to create a balanced workload for the distribution center workers. As nice as a balanced workload sounds, this technique adds time to your supply chain.

7. *Prioritize sequence of picks.* Do you pick orders for priority customers first? Do you pick for past-due orders first? How you prioritize the sequence of your picks can have an impact on your velocity.

8. *Popularity of product.* Do you conduct an A-B-C analysis of fast-movers and variation based on seasonality? This analysis has an impact on your slotting decisions and the layout of your warehouse or distribution center. It can have an impact on your velocity.

9. *Profile activity.* Do you have items that are ordered together on a regular basis? If so, do you slot these items together? Do you have a warehouse-in-a-warehouse concept to place these items in a central location?

10. *Throughput.* Throughput in your distribution center is increased through the use of cross-docking. The less handling in the center, the faster the velocity.

11. *Inventory at rest.* How much inventory do you have at rest or dormant in your facility? Are these resting or dormant stocks stored in locations that are more convenient to the workers than the fast movers?

12. *Service offerings.* This ties to the previous discussion on postponement. What additional services are you providing for your customers in your distribution center? The more services done in the warehouse, the slower the velocity coming through your operation.

13. *Accuracy.* What is your inventory accuracy and picking accuracy? The inventory accuracy has an impact on your ability to fill orders. Your picking accuracy affects the amount of additional picks and returns processing. These two activities can have a negative impact on your velocity.

14. *Inventory available.* Obviously, the more inventory you stock, the shorter the response time should be to the customer. However, you have to balance the cost of mountains of merchandise against the reduced times. In some cases, the increase in the amount of SKUs actually decreased velocity because of the increased storage and inventory problems and the additional travel times in the warehouses or distribution centers.

15. *Warehouse order cycle.* Do you know the total time it takes to get an order processed, picked, packed, and shipped out of your warehouse or distribution center?

16. *Value-added services.* If you take a narrow view from the viewpoint of the distribution center, additional value-added services might appear to slow the supply chain. However, when a global view is taken, the supply chain velocity should actually improve.

17. *Returns policy.* If you take back any item bought from your store regardless of the reasons, you may find yourself inundated with used and abused items that will clog your supply chain operations and reduce your velocity.

Book List for Chapter Seven

1. Heinrich, Claus and Betts, Bob, *Adapt or Die,* Wiley, Hoboken, NJ, 2003.
2. Pagonis, Gus, *Moving Mountains,* Harvard Business School Press, Boston, MA, 1992.
3. Rogers, Dale and Tibben-Lembke, Ronald, *Going Backwards,* University of Nevada, Reno, 1999.
4. *The Information Revolution and National Security,* ed. Thomas E. Copeland, Strategic Studies Institute, Carlisle Barracks, PA, 2000.
5. *Navy Supply Publication 529, Warehouse Modernization and Layout Planning Guide,* U.S. Navy Supply Systems Command, 1985.
6. Napolitano, Maida, *Making the Move to Crossdocking,* Warehousing Education and Research Council, Oak Brook, IL, 2000.
7. *APICS Dictionary,* Tenth Edition, APICS—The Educational Society for Resource Management, Alexandria, VA, 2002.
8. *Warfighting,* United States Marine Corps, 1989.
9. Dumond, John, Eden, Rick, and Folkeson, John R., *Velocity Management: An Approach for Improving the Responsiveness and Efficiency of Army Logistics Processes,* RAND, Santa Monica, CA, 1995.
10. Girardini, Kenneth, et al., *Establishing a Baseline and Reporting Performance for the Order and Ship Processes,* RAND, Santa Monica, CA, 1996.
11. Wang, Mark Y. D., *Accelerated Logistics,* RAND, Santa Monica, CA, 2000.

Notes

1. *Warfighting,* USMC, 1989, p. 40.
2. From the preface to Dr. Mark Y. D. Wang's book, *Accelerated Logistics,* RAND, Santa Monica, CA, 2000.
3. For more on the works of Dr. Jim Tompkins go to www.tompkinsinc.com.
4. *APICS Dictionary,* Tenth Edition, APICS—The Educational Society for Resource Management, Alexandria, VA, 2002, p. 25.
5. Napolitano, Maida, *Making the Move to Crossdocking,* Warehousing Education and Research Council, Oak Brook, IL, 2000, p. 6.
6. According to Dr. Ed Frazelle, director of the Logistics Institute at Georgia Tech, 55 percent of a warehouseperson's time is traveling to a location; 15 percent is spent searching for the item once he or she arrives at the location; 10 percent of the time is actually spent picking the items; and 20 percent of the time is spent on other functions and miscellaneous activities.
7. *Navy Supply Publication 529, Warehouse Modernization and Layout Planning Guide,* was published by the U.S. Navy Supply Systems Command in 1985. This publication is still the best book published on warehouse layout and design. Unfortunately, it is out of print.
8. A-B-C slotting is a method of analyzing your inventory and stratifying the inventory by the frequency of customer demands for the items. With this methodology you put your fast-moving items in a convenient pick location.

9. The difference between supplies and stuff is that stuff is not needed and should not be in your warehouse. Stuff has the tendency to accumulate in warehouses. One particular warehouse had lots of stuff outside in open storage. This stuff was obsolete, unnecessary, and in some cases unknown. Every couple of months the warehouse manager would move this stuff around to give the illusion that it was moving. The leader in charge of monitoring this third-party logistics provider caught on to the manager. It took this manager over six months of dedicated work to clear the stuff out of the yard. At least he quit complaining about a lack of storage space in his yard.

10. *The Information Revolution and National Security*, ed. Thomas E. Copeland, Strategic Studies Institute, Carlisle Barracks, PA, 2000, p. 9.

11. *Going Backwards* remains the standard on reverse logistics studies five years after its publication. This study provides great insights to the background of reverse logistics and how companies have overcome reverse logistics obstacles to improve their bottom lines.

12. Rogers, Dale and Tibben-Lembke, Ronald, *Going Backwards,* University of Nevada, Reno, 1997.

13. For more on Reverse Logistics Trends, Inc., and their sponsored trade shows go to http://www.rltshows.com.

14. The Corps Support Command is the organization responsible for supplying all of the tactical units in an Army corps. The Third Corps Support Command in Wiesbaden, Germany, supported the 65,000 soldiers of the United States Fifth Corps in Europe, and more recently in Iraq and Kuwait. This support was provided in the mid-1990s by 27 different distribution activities stationed throughout Germany and Italy.

15. Robert Malone, "Closing the Supply Chain Loop," *Inbound Logistics*, January 2004, p. 217.

16. The term excess is placed in quotation marks because in 2000, the Department of Defense received so much bad publicity from Congress for excess items that the use of "excess" became taboo and the new euphemistic term became "redistributable assets." Items that exceed your requirements are excess and excess by any other name is still excess and can have an adverse impact on the velocity of your supply chain.

17. An active RFID tag has an internal battery that allows it to continually send out a signal capable of being read or monitored at multiple points in the supply chain. Because of the internal battery, the range of the signal from the tag is significantly longer (depending on battery size) than the signal for a passive tag. A passive tag can only be read from short distances and is not always on. The passive tag has to be interrogated within a few feet of the reader to be effective. Because of the internal battery, the active tag is considerably larger than the small passive tag.

18. One higher-ranking officer told his family that there was nothing to worry about; the worst thing that could happen to him would be an infection from a paper cut because he was not planning on leaving the safe confines of Camp Arifjan.

19. A Direct Support unit is a logistics unit that provides support to individual companies and units. A General Support unit provides support to the Direct Support units. A General Support supply unit usually has greater storage and distribution capacity so it can support multiple Direct Support units. The relationship is similar to having a regional distribution center supporting a "warehouse" style retail center with the retailer providing direct support to the customers. A dedicated shipment is one that is all for one customer and does not need additional processing before cross-docking to the ultimate consignee.

20. "Food Lion Gets Ready to Roar," *Inbound Logistics*, January 2004, p. 134.

21. The *Wall Street Journal*, February 2004.

22. Heinrich, Claus and Betts, Bob, *Adapt or Die,* Wiley, Hoboken, NJ, 2003, p. 1.

23. Ibid., p. 4.

24. Every brigade-sized element (approximately 4000 soldiers) has a Supply Support activity or distribution center to support all supplies for the unit. The distribution activity stocks a certain number of lines of supply in what the Army calls the Authorized Stockage Lines (ASL). Items not retained on the ASL and less than $50 in value are sent to the Defense Reutilization and Marketing Office (DRMO).

MILITARY THEORY, PRACTICES, AND LESSONS LEARNED AS THEY APPLY TO 21ST-CENTURY SUPPLY CHAINS

III

Everybody likes to talk about and analyze strategy, for there is about it the attractive quality of intellectual contest. Logistics, on the other hand, is the more pedestrian application to war of the factors of time and space; it does not determine the course of action to be taken, it does set the stage for the action and its limits, and often will indicate a preferred course of action. War frequently is likened to a game of chess, but chess is not a strategic game, for there is no logistics.

James A. Huston, *Sinews of War*, p. 424

Section III looks at lessons from the U.S. Army and the Department of Defense that are applicable to today's supply chain operations.

Chapter 8 looks at the Army's After Action Review process and how to apply this process of seeing yourself to improving today's supply chains. This chapter builds on the "Seeing Yourself" discussion from Chapter 4.

Chapter 9 looks in great detail at military operations from Sun Tzu to Operation Iraqi Freedom. It analyzes the lessons learned in these operations or from the recorders of operations in history and how those lessons can be applied to 21st-century supply chains. There are a great number of observations about the importance of supply chains to the success of military operations. The key is to take these observations and apply them so that they become lessons learned and not mere observations. Just as the evolution of the modern battlefield has produced what is known as the nonlinear battlefield, today's technologies have produced a nonlinear supply chain that must be capable of operating in any environment and in any country in the world, 24 hours a day, seven days a week.

Chapter 8

The After Action Review

The After Action Review is a powerful tool that makes the U.S. Army unique with respect to all other armies. It provides the means to attain and sustain the Army's readiness and to ensure that the deficiencies in performance are corrected. Effective, mission-focused, standards-based feedback to unit leadership through the After Action Review process should parallel the performance-oriented counseling and mentoring process commanders owe their subordinates as a cornerstone of the Army's commitment to leader development.

All leaders have an obligation to teach subordinate leaders how to conduct an effective After Action Review and how to create an effective mentoring environment in their units.[1]

The National Law Enforcement Trainers Association online magazine in the January 2002 edition contained an article by Bryan D. Cox, the president of the association at the time. In his article Mr. Cox writes,

> The US Army has used the After Action Review process for several years to identify training strengths and areas for improvement. The After Action Review process has been so successful in the military that several multi-national companies have implemented the process throughout a variety of activities. The After Action Review also represents an extremely effective way for law enforcement to maximize the learning opportunities during our day to day job performance.[2]

Just as the U.S. Army and the law enforcement community have learned, the After Action Review is a valuable tool for identifying shortcomings and ways to prevent future occurrences of similar problems in your organization.

The preface to *Army Training Circular 25-20, The After Action Review,* states:

> Modern combat is complex and demanding. To fight and win, we must train our soldiers during peacetime to successfully execute their wartime missions. We must use every training opportunity to improve soldier, leader, and unit task performance. To improve their individual and collective-task performances to meet or exceed the Army standard, soldiers and leaders must know and understand what happened or did not happen during every training event.
>
> After-action reviews help provide soldiers and units feedback on mission and task performances in training and in combat. After-action reviews identify how to correct deficiencies, sustain strengths, and focus on performance of specific mission essential task list training objectives.
>
> Key is the spirit in which after-action reviews are given. The environment and climate surrounding an after-action review must be one in which the soldiers and leaders openly and honestly discuss what actually transpired in sufficient detail and clarity that not only will everyone understand what did and did not occur and why, but most importantly will have a strong desire to seek the opportunity to practice the task again.[3]

A recent search of the Internet revealed over 200 sites that reference After Action Reviews in the military and commercial sectors. The majority of these Web sites shows the pages from the Army's *Training Circular* and shows them as copyrighted to the authors of the Web page without any further explanation of the concepts and terms associated with an After Action Review. What is an After Action Review and how can you use it to improve your operations? This chapter answers these questions and provides some useful checklists for organizing your After Action Review and making sure that every participant gets the most out of the process.

The Army's lessons learned database contained the following guidance on After Action Reviews.

> After-action reviews were conducted throughout the Warfighting Exercise. Their purpose was not to criticize, but to guide the participants through a professional dialogue consisting of an

honest, candid self-examination of what occurred, why it occurred and how to improve. To reiterate, the after-action review was a professional deliberation, which required active participation; it was not a critique. After the exercise's conclusion, the unit received a Final Exercise Report, which included an executive summary, a Battlefield Operating System analysis, a graphics package, videotapes and written material from the exercise and the after-action reviews.[4]

Okay, so what does that have to do with your operations and how do you conduct an After Action Review? The answers to these questions form the purpose of this chapter.

Chapter 1 of *Training Circular 25-20* defines the After Action Review:

An after-action review is a professional discussion of an event, focused on performance standards, that enables soldiers to discover for themselves what happened, why it happened, and how to sustain strengths and improve on weaknesses. It is a tool leaders and units can use to get maximum benefit from every mission or task. It provides—

■ Candid insights into specific soldier, leader, and unit strengths and weaknesses from various perspectives.
■ Feedback and insight critical to battle-focused training.
■ Details often lacking in evaluation reports alone.[5]

Let's start with the benefit of an After Action Review to your operations using this definition from the Army's *Training Circular.* How many projects has your company started that were completed without any glitches or problems? How many times has a program not produced the results that you expected? How many times has a project produced better-than-expected results and your boss asked, "What did we do different that produced such phenomenal results?" If every project or program that you have been associated with experienced no problems and all of them achieved exactly the desired results, then you do not need to read this chapter. If you have experienced any of the other above situations, this chapter is for you.

The benefits of doing an After Action Review are that you can identify what went wrong with a process or project, what went as planned, ways to fix the problems, and ways to sustain the things that went right without placing blame for the situation. In addition, if the After Action Review is properly conducted, the key players will buy into the solutions and accept responsibility for ensuring the next mission or project is successful.

The U.S. Army's *Training Circular* goes on to say,

> Feedback compares the actual output of a process with the intended outcome. By focusing on the task's standards and by describing specific observations, leaders and soldiers identify strengths and weaknesses and together decide how to improve their performances. This shared learning improves task proficiency and promotes unit bonding and esprit. Squad and platoon leaders will use the information to develop input for unit-training plans. The After Action Review is a valid and valuable technique regardless of branch, echelon, or training task.
>
> Because soldiers and leaders participating in an After Action Review actively discover what happened and why, they learn and remember more than they would from a critique alone. A critique only gives one viewpoint and frequently provides little opportunity for discussion of events by participants. Soldier observations and comments may not be encouraged. The climate of the critique, focusing only on what is wrong, prevents candid discussion of training events and stifles learning and team building.[6]

Notice that the After Action Review is not a critique session or a performance appraisal; it is a discussion of the mission or project with input from all of the participants. During an After Action Review, all participants have the same level of say and can add comments without fear of retribution.

There are several types of After Action Reviews used by the Army to assess training events and operations.

> All After Action Reviews follow the same general format, involve the exchange of ideas and observations, and focus on improving training proficiency. How leaders conduct a particular After Action Review determines whether it is formal or informal. A formal After Action Review is resource-intensive and involves the planning, coordination, and preparation of supporting training aids, the After Action Review site, and support personnel. Informal After Action Reviews (usually for soldier, crew, squad, and platoon training) require less preparation and planning.[7]

The two forms of reviews include the following.

- *Formal Reviews.* These reviews have external observers. The external observers are fully trained in the mission and receive classes in the conduct of the After Action Review as well as a full set of classes on the standard operating procedures of the unit that they are observing. This is done to ensure that the observers know what the unit or section is supposed to do and what their standard operating procedures say about how they should accomplish the mission. A formal review usually takes more time than informal reviews. For the Army, a formal review usually uses complex training aids. At the Army's National Training Center a formal review will use computer-generated graphics of the training exercise and show the commander and his or her staff all of the actions taken on the battlefield by their forces and the opposing forces. Formal reviews are usually scheduled before the reviewed event takes place so everyone knows where to go after the event for the After Action Review. In commercial industry, the formal After Action Review may use performance charts or production charts as the training aids for the review.

▪ *Informal Reviews.* An informal review normally takes less time and is conducted by the chain of command of the unit. At the National Training Center these are commonly referred to as "Hummer top reviews." An informal review uses simple training aids (usually the map board). Informal reviews are conducted whenever the chain of command feels that they are necessary and are usually conducted at the site of the training event. This does not mean that they are any less useful or that they are conducted haphazardly. Leaders may use informal reviews as on-the-spot coaching tools while reviewing employee or section performances during an operation. Ideas and solutions a leader receives during informal reviews can be immediately put to use as the organization continues the operation. In addition, leaders often use teaching points and trends from informal reviews as discussion points when participating in higher headquarters' formal After Action Reviews.

Regardless of the type of review conducted, the preparation steps are the same. The amount and level of detail leaders need during the planning and preparation process depends on the type of After Action Review they will conduct and on the available resources. A lack of resources is no excuse for not conducting an After Action Review. The After Action Review may be as simple as a 3×5-inch note card with what went right and what went wrong and needs to improve. Lieutenant General Gus Pagonis used this technique throughout Operation Desert Storm. He had each of his key staffers and commanders provide him with a card every day with "three ups and three downs." The "three ups" were those things that went right and should be sustained. The "three downs" were things that did

202 ■ *Velocity Management in Logistics and Distribution*

not go as well as expected and needed attention to improve them. A key note here is that the After Action Review is not a substitute for getting problems and bad news to the boss. Bad news, unlike good wine, does not get better with time. Do not wait for the After Action Review to get the bad news to the boss.

According to the Army's *Training Circular*, the purposes of the After Action Review are as follows.[8]

- After-action reviews—
  - Are conducted during or immediately after each event.
  - Focus on intended training objectives.
  - Focus on workers, leaders, and group performance.
  - Involve all participants in the discussion.
  - Use open-ended questions.
  - Are related to specific standards.
  - Determine strengths and weaknesses.
  - Link performance to subsequent training. (This is a tie-in to the topics of Chapter 4, "Knowing Yourself," and Chapter 5, "Professional Development." The shortcomings identified in the After Action Review should help to focus the formal training and professional development plans for the organization.)

The conduct of the After Action Review follows the following format.[9]

- Introduction and rules.
- Review of training objectives, if used in conjunction with a training program.
- Leader's mission and intent. (What was supposed to happen? What was the assigned mission or operation?)
- Opposing force (OPFOR) commander's mission and intent (when appropriate). This may very well be the response of the customer or the competition. How did we expect the customer to respond to this product or service?
- Relevant doctrine and tactics, techniques, and procedures (TTPs) or standard operating procedures.
- Summary of recent events (what happened).
- Discussion of key issues (why it happened and how to improve).
- Discussion of optional issues.
- Closing comments (summary) and assigning responsibility for ensuring that areas needing improvement are actually improved.

The After Action Review process has four steps.

Step 1. Planning

"Leaders are responsible for planning, executing, evaluating, and assessing training. Each training event is evaluated during training execution. Evaluations can be informal or formal and internal or external."[10] Although every training event or class should have an After Action Review, this process is not limited to training events only. For training events, the After Action Review plan provides the foundation for a successfully conducted quality After Action Review.

When developing training plans, leaders should develop an After Action Review plan for each event, class, or course. A good review plan includes: (1) who will observe the training and who will actually lead the After Action Review; (2) what the observers should actually evaluate; (3) who should attend the After Action Review; and (4) the location and time for the review.

A good After Action Review plan will establish who will observe and control a particular event. An observer-controller not only observes the event or operation, but also is the leader for the formal After Action Review. At the Army's Combat Training Centers,[11] every leader is provided with an observer-controller to serve as a trainer and coach during the 28-day training exercise. These observer-controllers usually have performed the same jobs that they coach and are knowledgeable in the tactics, techniques, and procedures for that particular unit and job. Tactics, techniques, and procedures are analogous to blocking and tackling in football; they serve as the foundation for almost every activity that a unit or individual may encounter.

When planning for an After Action Review, it is important for leaders to establish scheduled times for the reviews. If used in conjunction with a training program, the plan should show planned After Action Reviews at the end of each critical phase of the training event. When used in conjunction with operations, a good time for scheduled After Action Reviews is at the completion of the operation or at critical stopping points in an operation, such as at the end of a picking cycle in the warehouse or at the end of a delivery run.

The After Action Review plan and overall calendar of events should allow for ample time to cover all of the necessary teaching points or comments on the operation or training event. Employees and leaders will remember the lessons and key teaching points or observations if the session is not rushed.

The plan should specify the desired attendees. Although only key players attend on a routine basis, there are times when the more participants there are in the After Action Review, the better the feedback and discussions for improvements.

Remember, the plan is designed to be a guide. You need to review the plan on a regular basis to ensure that new players are incorporated into the reviews and that the plan still meets your needs.

Step 2. Preparing

Preparation is important to execute any plan effectively. The preparation for an After Action Review starts long before the training event or operation. During the preparation time the observers and controllers need to brush up on their knowledge of the operations or plans. At the National Training Center, all observers must attend the "Observer/Controller Academy" to learn the latest tactics, techniques, and procedures, as well as how to conduct an effective After Action Review.

During the preparation phase, all of the assigned trainers and observers need to become familiar with the plans of the operation and the SOPs of the organization being evaluated. It is important to know what the organization plans to do during the operation or training event in order to later match the plan against reality. Failure to prepare at this stage of the process will result in a useless review and a loss of credibility for the leadership and the observers. Observers and controllers must focus their observations on the actions required to perform tasks to standard. As part of the preparation phase, the observer-controllers and leaders of all levels need to ensure that they are current and proficient on the standards for the operations or training event.

The observers need to take good notes during the conduct of the operation or event in order to be prepared to provide accurate and concise feedback during the After Action Review. The observer-controllers at the National Training Center prepare their notebooks prior to the training event so they know what the plan is for each day and then take notes comparing the plan to the actual event happening.

Table 8.1 shows an example of an observation technique (a full-page example is given in Appendix 7 for use in your operations).[12]

The final step in the preparation phase is the rehearsal. *Training Circular 25-20* states, "After thorough preparation, the leader reviews the After Action Review format, rehearses at the established site, and gets ready to conduct the After Action Review."[13]

Step 3. Conducting the After Action Review

The leader will provide the focus for the After Action Review by establishing the purpose and the ground rules for the review process. The opening remarks should include the following guidance to the group.

Table 8.1 Example of an Observation Technique

Training event/operation being observed:

Event:
Date/time:
Location of observation:
Observation (what did you see?):

Discussion (try to tie the discussion points to the task and the established standards for that event):

Conclusions:

Recommendations (what can be done better in the future to make this organization or section more effective? Be specific with your recommendations):

This is only an example of one way to capture the necessary observations and prepare for the After Action Review.

Remind the group that the After Action Review should be a candid and professional discussion of what happened compared to the stated plan and compared to established standards for such an operation or training event. The leader should encourage everyone to participate and offer observations in order to improve the overall organization.

The After Action Review is not a critique. There will always be time for that over a beer later. The goal of the review is to learn from each other, regardless of the position the person holds. Remind the group that no one has all the answers or all of the information, which is why you are conducting the After Action Review, to share the information and get answers to questions.

The outcome of the After Action Review should not be viewed as a mark of success or failure. Remember, the purpose is not to fix blame but to fix problems. The participation of all employees is important. The amount of participation is a direct result of the atmosphere established by the leader during the introduction. The leader should try to get as many employees involved as possible, especially those who appear to be a bit reluctant to participate. The more employees who participate in the discussions, the easier it is to get a buy-in for the fixes from the employees because they will feel that they are a part of the solution.

It is important to remember that the After Action Review is a process to solve problems and identify areas that are working according to the plan and must be sustained at the same level. The discussions during the review itself should be designed and structured to allow participants to discover their own strengths and weaknesses and participate in developing the plan for improvement.

Step 4. Following Up

Chapter 5 of *Training Circular 25-20* provides the following guidance on following up on the discussions and observations.

> BENEFITS: The real benefits of After Action Reviews come from taking the results and applying them to future training. Leaders can use the information to assess performance and to immediately retrain units in tasks where there is weakness. Leaders can also use After Action Reviews to help assess unit Mission Essential Task List proficiency.
>
> Leaders should not delay or reschedule retraining except when absolutely necessary. If the leader delays retraining, he must be sure the soldiers understand that they did not perform the task to standard and that retraining will occur later.
>
> After Action Reviews are the dynamic link between task performance and execution to standard. They provide commanders a critical assessment tool to use to plan soldier, leader, and unit training. Through the professional and candid discussion of events, soldiers can compare their performance against the standard and identify specific ways to improve proficiency.[14]

The After Action Review may reveal that the problem is outdated or inaccurate Standard Operating Procedures (SOPs). This is an easy fix but one that may have far-reaching impact on the performance of your organization. Changes to SOPs may mean a requirement for additional training to correct the old ways of doing business.

"The After Action Review sounds like a great tool in a training environment but I don't think it will work with my daily operations." This is a common statement about After Action Reviews. Take a look at what the Army's manual says about the use of After Action Reviews during combat.[15]

THE AFTER ACTION REVIEW IN COMBAT

Training does not stop when a unit goes into combat. Training is *always* an integral part of precombat and combat operations although limited time and proximity to the enemy may restrict the type and extent of training. Only training improves combat performance without imposing the stiff penalties combat inflicts on the untrained.

The After Action Review is one of the most effective techniques to use in a combat environment. An effective After Action Review takes little time, and leaders can conduct them almost anywhere consistent with unit security requirements. Conducting After Action Reviews helps overcome the steep learning curve that exists in a unit exposed to combat and helps the unit ensure that it does not repeat mistakes. It also helps them sustain strengths. By integrating training into combat operations and using tools such as After Action Reviews, leaders can dramatically increase their unit's chances for success on the battlefield.

If the After Action Review is such a valuable tool in combat operations, just imagine how effective and valuable it can be in improving your operations.

The Application of the After Action Review to Improving Supply Chain Operations

Now that we have seen how the Army applies the concept of the After Action Review, let's take a look at how this same concept will assist in improving your supply chain operations, or any operation for that matter. The best way to look at applications is by looking at the parts of an After Action Review. The Army's field manual on training, *Field Manual 7-1, Battle Focused Training,* states that the After Action Review consists of four parts. We use those four parts to establish how to use this process for assessing and improving supply chain operations.

The four parts of an effective After Action Review are the following.

- Review what was supposed to happen according to the plan.
- Establish what happened.
- Determine what was right or wrong with what happened.
- Determine how to accomplish the task differently the next time.

For this discussion, we use the warehousing inventory count as an example of applying the After Action Review to a supply chain issue (this is a factual example but the names will remain anonymous). The plan was to accomplish the financially mandated wall-to-wall inventory in less than four days with an inventory accuracy of 99 percent. That is what was supposed to happen according to the plan.

What really happened? The wall-to-wall inventory took six days to get to 85 percent accuracy. Although the number of SKUs that were within the set tolerance was met, the real accuracy of 85 percent was not acceptable. Moreover, the fact that it took 50 percent longer to accomplish the inventory was not acceptable. So, what would an After Action Review look like for this situation?

What was right? In this case very little. What was wrong? The inventory accuracy was not acceptable, especially for the amount of money being paid to the third-party provider to manage the warehouse. The time to conduct the inventory was excessively long. Furthermore, the number of SKUs that had to be "frozen" because of the numerous recounts was unacceptable, making these items unavailable for sale. What happened that produced such abysmal results? Were the standards and expectations too high?

By asking open-ended questions of the warehouse workers and the warehouse management staff, the following shortcomings were discovered. A quality location survey was not completed to ensure that the items in the warehouse were in the locations that the WMS and the tracking systems recorded for the items. In order to get the inventory started on time, a decision to do a smaller sample inventory location survey was made. This started the inventory process off badly. To improve this, the staff would have needed to implement cycle counting or do a complete 100 percent inventory location survey to ensure that the items are stored where the records say they are.

The lack of cycle counts coupled with the pressure to finish the inventory quickly produced inaccurate counts by some of the count teams. In addition, more questions revealed that some of the count teams did not receive a train-up before the start of the inventory. These problems can be fixed by ensuring that the teams are properly trained and supervised. If the staff does not announce a deadline for the completion of the count, less pressure is applied to the teams and a more thorough and accurate count may result. It seems that like so many other supply chain problems, in this case there was not enough time to do it right the first time, but lots of time to do the inventory over and over until a satisfactory count was achieved. Training the teams beforehand produces a better count the first time. This comes as a result of more confidence in the system because of the training and a more accurate count from knowing how to count unopened cases and knowing why every opened case should be carefully counted.

One further recommendation for improvement was to implement a cycle counting team for the third shift and give this team quality training and the responsibility for all inventories. The rationale was that there are fewer disruptions on the third shift. The fewer disruptions coupled with the dedicated team produced an increase in inventory accuracy from the 85 percent level to 99 percent in just over four months.

Conclusions and Final Thoughts

The After Action Review is a great tool for improving performance for individuals, teams, or entire companies. By using the steps outlined in this chapter, you will be able to get more from yourself, your employees, and your organization while improving customer support and maybe even adding velocity to your supply chain at the same time.

The parts of an After Action Review are as follows.

- Review what was supposed to happen. During this portion of an After Action Review, the reviewer, as well as the participants, reviews what was supposed to happen based on the guidance from the boss and his or her vision of success for the mission or operation.
- Establish what really happened. This is the critical part of the After Action Review and requires brutal honesty on the part of the participants in order to really gain value from the After Action Review. Failure to honestly assess what happened in the process or action will result in a waste of time. Furthermore, it will hamper the ability to successfully accomplish the goals of the next two steps.
- Determine what went right or what went wrong. During this step of the After Action Review, the participants, guided by the reviewer or evaluator, establish the strong and weak points of the process or operation. Lieutenant General Gus Pagonis prefers the points in this step to be bullets that will fit on a 3x5-inch index card, and he has told numerous audiences that he is always looking for what he calls "three ups and three downs" from any operation or process being reviewed.
- Determine how to do the task or operation differently to improve on the good points and eliminate the bad points. The discussion points during this stage of the After Action Review will determine the areas that a leader needs to focus on in developing training plans for the organization.

Figure 8.1 The U.S. cemetery in Hamm, Luxembourg.

Leaders must understand that sometimes tasks will not be accomplished according to their standards. Because of this, leaders need to plan time in their training plans to address retraining and the opportunity for junior leaders to apply the lessons identified in the After Action Review process.

It is important to reemphasize at this point in the discussion that nowhere in this process are you trying to place blame on an individual or section for the weaknesses. The goal is to find out what went wrong, identify weaknesses in the process, and prepare the training plans to prevent future recurrences of the same problem. In most operations, there is no shame in making mistakes; the key is to ensure that the same mistake is not made more than once and to learn from the mistakes.

In commercial supply chains it is important to learn from our mistakes to prevent losing customers. The loss of customers can and very well may lead to the death of the company. In the Army, making a mistake in a training event and learning from it can prevent the death of a soldier. Failure to learn from mistakes results in more sights such as the picture in Figure 8.1.

One of the side effects of not learning from training mistakes in the Army is the potential increase in the loss of lives for soldiers. One of the side effects of not learning from mistakes in the commercial world is the increased potential for the loss of the life of the company.

Is there a difference between an After Action Review and an historical account of an incident or operation? Yes, an historical account does not delve into why something happened and how to fix it. The Army recently published *On Point,* an historical account of the Army in Operation Iraqi Freedom. In late 2003, the Army conducted an After Action Review into the actions surrounding the ambush and tragedy of the 507th Maintenance Company's convoy, made famous by the rescue of Private First Class Jessica Lynch. The real difference between these two documents is that an historical account of the 507th Maintenance Company would have only told what happened during the convoy and the ambush. The After Action Review analyzed the actions that led to and contributed to the mishap, and made recommendations on improvements to equipment and training. These recommendations have since been incorporated into training exercises and Army schools to prevent future incidents of this nature.

Many companies have historical accounts of what happened in their operations. To reach world-class levels and identify ways to use the accounts to improve operations requires the use of the After Action Review. The After Action Review is not a cure-all for problems in your supply chain, but will assist you in reducing the problems and turning observations and historical accounts into lessons learned and applied to improve the operations.

Tips for a Successful After Action Review

1. Use open-ended questions.
2. Never use the After Action Review as a disciplinary tool.
3. Focus on the learning points and education.
4. Encourage maximum attendance and maximum participation from all in attendance.
5. Encourage differences of points of view.
6. Do not reprimand an attendee because of his or her actions or perceptions of the operation.
7. As the leader of the After Action Review, try to remain objective.
8. Capture all of the comments regardless of your perception of the value of the comments.

Questions for Thought

1. What areas of your operations would benefit from an After Action Review?

2. When should you conduct an After Action Review?
3. Why should you not focus on fixing blame during the After Action Review?
4. Does your company have the ability to gather the necessary information for conducting a good After Action Review?
5. Do you have personnel trained to act as observers and trainers?
6. Can you use the process map developed as described in Chapter 4 to drive your After Action Review process?

Book List for Chapter Eight

1. *Training Circular 25-20, The After Action Review,* U.S. Army Combined Arms Center, Fort Leavenworth, KS, available at www.rdtdl.army.mil.
2. *US Army Field Manual 7-1, Battle Focused Training,* U.S. Army Combined Arms Center, Fort Leavenworth, KS, 2003, available at www.rdtdl.army.mil.

Notes

1. *US Army Field Manual 7-1, Battle Focused Training,* U.S. Army Combined Arms Center, Fort Leavenworth, KS, 2003.
2. Cox, Bryan D., "After Action Reviews Are a Valuable Training Tool," NLETA Online Magazine, http://www.nleta.com/articles/afteractionreviews.htm.
3. *Training Circular 25-20, After Action Reviews,* U.S. Army Combined Arms Command, Fort Leavenworth, KS, Preface.
4. Center For Army Lessons Learned, http://call-search.leavenworth.army.mil/.
5. *Training Circular 25-20,* p. 1.
6. Ibid., p. 1.
7. Ibid., p. 2.
8. Adapted from *Training Circular 25-20,* figure 1-1, "Key After Action Review Points."
9. Ibid., Figure 1-2, "After Action Review Format."
10. Ibid., p. 6.
11. In addition to the National Training Center at Fort Irwin, California, the Army maintains combat training centers at Fort Polk, Louisiana, for lighter forces and the Combat Maneuver Training Center at Hohenfels, Germany, for use by European-based units.
12. This example is modified from *Training Circular 25-20,* Figure 3-1, "Example AAR Observation Worksheet."
13. *Training Circular 25-20,* p. 15.
14. Ibid., p. 5-1.
15. Ibid., p. 5-2.

Chapter 9

Lessons Learned from Military Operations and the Application for Commercial Supply Chains

> *"Logistics, the stuff that if you don't have enough of, the war will not be won as soon as." Supposedly this was the response of General Nathaniel Green to General George Washington when he was asked to be the Quartermaster General of the Continental Army.*[1]

The foreword to Alan Axelrod's book, *Patton on Leadership: Strategic Lessons for Corporate Warfare,* states, "Battle is a worst case condition in which the risks are high, the uncertainty great, and the hardships and 'workplace conditions' are unknown in any other field of human endeavor. If these weren't enough, battle is probably the only leadership environment in which both followers and leaders would rather be somewhere else."[2] However, the lessons that we can learn from these battles are enormous and have direct applications to 21st-century supply chains and other modern-day operations.

Just how big was the Army that Patton led in World War II that provides so many lessons on leadership? According to Axelrod, only modern-day companies such as General Motors, Wal-Mart, and PepsiCo exceed the size of Patton's Third Army today. Are there lessons in leadership and supply chains that we can learn from supporting such a large organization in a time before automation and in-transit visibility? Absolutely!

James Huston wrote in his book, *The Sinews of War,* "Rarely in Modern War has the side with logistical inferiority prevailed. However superior the generalship, or however brilliant the strategy, ultimate victory generally has gone to the side having the greater economic strength and thus the greater logistics potential."[3] Commercial industry is no different in the 21st century. The company with the most effective and efficient supply chain potential will be the victorious or successful company. Failures of many companies with seemingly strong leaders but poor supply chains dot the pages of *Fortune* and *Business Week* on a regular basis. This was the major reason for the downfall of some of the highly touted dot.coms in the late 1990s. Some of them had great leadership and good business plans on paper, but no supply chain potential. The Web site was fantastic and the business plans appeared sound until it came time to get the goods to the customer.

How long do lessons learned last and are they lessons learned or simply observations? An observation becomes a lesson learned only when the observation is applied to changing the way we do business. If all we do is make an observation about something that did not work as well as planned, then we have not learned any lessons from the observation.

We all know about the unprovoked, and apparently unnoticed, move by Japan to attack Pearl Harbor, Hawaii, on December 7, 1941. The Japanese accomplished this attack supposedly without any inkling or notice by the U.S. intelligence communities (sound familiar in the 21st century?). However, almost ten years earlier a young George Patton predicted with uncanny accuracy that Japan would indeed attack Hawaii in the fashion that they did and from the direction that they did indeed use. No one took Major Patton seriously.

On June 25, 1950, at 4:00 AM, the North Korean Peoples Army invaded South Korea with no warning notice or intelligence notice by the United States intelligence agencies. Just over 40 years later, on August 2, 1990, the Iraqi Army invaded Kuwait without any notice by the intelligence agencies or any warning. In March 2003, there was a lack of quality intelligence before the start of Operation Iraqi Freedom.

The lesson from these examples is if you are going to collect data make sure you have the ability to analyze the data and turn it into useful information. In commercial supply chain operations, the equivalents of military operational and intelligence data are sales and marketing data. If you are going to take the time and make the effort to collect this data, make sure you are able to use it. Otherwise, you may be surprised by the competition or by the customer.

Luckily, lessons in supply chain operations are usually easier to collect and apply than the lessons from the above incidents that all led to prolonged conflicts.

In 1991, Julian Thompson released his classic work, *The Lifeblood of War—Logistics in Armed Conflict*. It has long been an accepted fact that logistics is indeed the lifeblood of war. It is a recent revelation to many companies that logistics and supply chains are also the lifeblood of industry. In this chapter we look at lessons from armed conflicts from Sun Tzu up through Operation Iraqi Freedom and look at how these lessons can be applied to commercial supply chains.

In the human body, when the lifeblood becomes constricted, the flow of blood slows down, causing high blood pressure and related health problems. When excess materials and non-value-added processes constrict a supply chain, the flow of supplies, materials, goods, and services of the company slows down. This puts pressure on the company to produce results or suffer fiscal health problems. Fiscal fitness is just as important to a company as physical fitness is to an individual.

Just as a heart attack in the human body can prove fatal, supply chain pressures can and often do lead to corporate fatality. For that reason this chapter delves into the lessons that all supply chains can and should learn from the military to prevent corporate fatality or corporate fiscal health issues.

In this chapter we start with Sun Tzu. We could go all the way back to Moses in the Sinai, but his logistics provider has no competitors. Besides, Sun Tzu makes a good starting point because he was one of the earliest military writers to discuss the importance of logistics. From Sun Tzu we jump ahead in time to Alexander the Great. The planning and support for the Macedonian army showed that Alexander the Great had a good understanding of the importance of logistics.

We briefly look at the works of Karl von Clausewitz and Baron Henri Jomini because of their influence on modern military thought. The writings of these two Napoleonic War veterans have provided the basis for military instruction in the United States for over a century.

After a brief look at theory we then move into a detailed look at the impact of logistics on major conflicts in United States history and the lessons learned from these operations that can be applied to commercial supply chain operations of the 21st century.

The objective of logistics is to ensure that operations succeed.[4]

The predecessor to the Army's current capstone doctrinal manual, *Field Manual 3-0, Operations,* listed the following "Logistics Characteristics":

> Successful logistics must be both effective and efficient. Logistics operations are not successful unless they provide effective support. Scarce resources require logistics operations to be efficient. Effectiveness, however, cannot be handicapped by efficiency. These two aspects of logistics are balanced to provide the foundation for successful logistics operations.
>
> Five characteristics facilitate effective, efficient logistics operations. . . . These five characteristics—anticipation, integration, continuity, responsiveness, and improvisation—enable operational success. They apply to war and operations other than war.[5]

The key here is that for the Army these characteristics apply to all operations: "war and operations other than war." These same characteristics apply to the entire spectrum of commercial supply chain operations.

1. Anticipation

"Accurate anticipation of requirements can enhance both the agility of the force and its ability to seize and retain the initiative and synchronize activities in depth. . . . Anticipation means identifying, accumulating, and maintaining the assets and information necessary to support operations at the right times and places." Without anticipation there will be nothing to sell, no raw materials to convert into products, and if there happen to be products to sell, there will be no transportation assets immediately available to move the items. The need for anticipation has produced commercial supply chain initiatives such as Collaborative Planning and Forecasting of Requirements (CPFR) and the Supply Chain Operations Reference Model (SCOR).

In Chapter 7 we discussed vendor-managed inventory. For VMI to be successful, there has to be an anticipation or forecast of the needs of the retailer. For just-in-time to be successful, there has to be anticipation of the customer's needs. Failure to anticipate the customers' needs results in dissatisfied customers. Dissatisfied customers go to the competition for support when we let them down.

Food Lion anticipates the needs of their customers. During the winter, Food Lion can get by with delivering to stores on the Outer Banks of North Carolina once or twice a week. Based on anticipation of customer needs, Food Lion delivers daily to these same stores during the busy summer season. Why? Because Food Lion knows that if they do not have what the vacationers want, the customers will go to a competitor and may never return to Food Lion again.

2. Integration

"Integration during planning ensures support of operation during execution. Logistics capabilities often affect the feasibility of a concept of operations." *Field Manual 100-5* refers to logistics capabilities; because this manual appeared before the term "supply chain" came into vogue, it needs to be understood that these same principles apply to supply chains. The U.S. Army called everything that we currently call supply chains logistics in this manual. The truth is that very often supply chain capabilities affect the outcome of an operation.

Collaboration has become a very important aspect of supply chain operations and is the subject of numerous conferences and seminars on supply chains. If all of the supply chain partners are not integrating their plans, there is a potential for supply chain disruptions.

3. Continuity

"While both combat operations and logistics can vary in intensity, combat operations may enter periods of relative inactivity; logistics operations do not."[5a] This is one of the most accurate statements ever written. Think about this: how often is there a lull in manufacturing operations, retail operations, or even wholesale operations? None of these operations run full blast all of the time. How often is there a lull in supply chain operations? Very rarely, if ever!

During the buildup to Operation Iraqi Freedom, one soldier was quoted as saying, "They should call this Operation Enduring Boredom." This soldier was obviously not a logistician. Although the combat soldiers had little to do during the buildup, the logistics soldiers and civilians had to move the equivalent of over 150 Wal-Mart Super Centers to Kuwait. After the rapid move toward Baghdad, the combat soldiers stood down for an "operational pause." Did the logistics soldiers get a pause? No way; this was the perfect time to move supplies forward and resupply the soldiers and units that had been moving for the previous five days.

In commercial supply chains, failure to provide continuity of support results in stockouts. Granted the potential consequences of a stockout in a grocery store is not as potentially catastrophic as a stockout of ammunition in combat, but there are still consequences. How many times does it take a customer to go to a store that habitually is in a zero balance or stockout situation before the customer goes to the competition? How many lost customers before the company ceases to exist?

4. Responsiveness

"Responsive logistics, especially when time or other resources are constrained, relies greatly on worldwide, assured communications and automation networks."[5a] These words were written before enterprise systems and before the popularity of the Internet for passing information, but are as true today as they were in 1993.

In addition, what good is a supply chain that is not responsive to the needs of the customer? The whole reason for having a supply chain enterprise is to respond to the needs of the customers, both internal and external. The concept of adding velocity to a supply chain operation is to improve the responsiveness of the system to the needs of the customers. Responsiveness is often the aspect that serves as a contract award winner.

Responsiveness is simply providing the customers with what they want, in the quantity they want, at the location they want it, and when they want it.

5. Improvisation

"Improvisation is the talent to make, invent, arrange, or fabricate what is needed out of what is at hand. Successful logistics operations adapt to changing situations. . . . Improvised methods and supply sources can maintain logistics continuity when standard procedures fail." This supply chain characteristic depends on flexibility. A quality supply chain organization allows its personnel the flexibility to improvise to meet the needs of the customer.

In the U.S. Army, this is sometimes known as "make stuff up." The reason for this is that on numerous occasions decisions must be made on the fly to ensure that the other characteristics of integration and responsiveness are met. In several units that I have worked in we adopted the attitude of "Whatever it takes" to ensure that we had a responsive supply chain and that the soldiers we supported received what they needed when they needed it.

Now that we have looked at the general principles and lessons from the Army's doctrine, it is time to look at some specific examples from history and look at the lessons that we can apply to today's supply chains.

Sun Tzu

Sun-tzu ping-fa (Sun Tzu The Art of War) is one of those rare texts that transcends time. Though it was written more than 2,000 years ago, it is arguably still the most important work on the subject of strategy today.

Introduction to *The Art of War,* on the Sonshi.com Web site[6]

I always like to look at the teachings and writings of Sun Tzu because he was one of the first recorded military theorists to write about the criticality of supplies and supply lines to the success of operations. Little has changed over the past 2500 years since the days of Sun Tzu in this respect. Supply chains and supply lines are as important today to the success of military operations and commercial operations as they were in 500 BC.

It is important to set the stage by establishing who Sun Tzu was and how he came to prominence. This understanding is necessary to a study of *The Art of War,* Sun Tzu's treatise on military operations. Sun Tzu is believed to have written somewhere in the 500–300 BC period. One theory concerning Sun Tzu comes from the writings of Su-Ma Ch'ien from about 100 BC. According to Su-Ma, Sun Tzu's real name was Sun Wu, a general for the King of Wu, a province in China. According to this account, Sun Tzu (Wu) and the King of Wu were killed in battle around 473 BC. This would track with the defeat of the Armies of Wu in 473 BC and the Kingdom of Wu becoming extinct.

Another theory is that the writings may have actually come from Sun Pin, a descendant of Sun Tzu. Sun Pin's *Military Methods* was found in a Han dynasty tomb in the 1970s. Other theories suggest that Sun Tzu never existed at all and that *The Art of War* is a compilation of several writers of the period.

The most common theory is that Sun Tzu did indeed live in the 500 BC timeframe and was an advisor to the King of Wu. According to legend, when Sun Tzu was recommended to the king as an advisor, he boasted to the king that he could train anyone to do military maneuvers. The king agreed to provide a couple of platoons for the demonstration. What he provided was a couple of platoons of women to test Sun Tzu. Sun Tzu placed the king's favorite concubines in leadership positions. After careful training and drilling, Sun Tzu commanded the women to execute military drill moves and they laughed. He asked the concubines if they understood the instructions. They said yes. To the dismay of the king, Sun Tzu had the concubines beheaded because he said that if the instructions are clear and the army does not act, it is the fault of the leader. The next time Sun Tzu gave the instructions all of the women did the moves exactly as instructed. This demonstration showed the king the ability of Sun Tzu to train armies but did not make the king happy at the loss of his favorite concubines.

During the period of 500 BC in China, armies reached as many as one million soldiers and losses in battles reached as high as 100,000 to 240,000 soldiers. Because of the size of these armies, it sometimes took years to prepare them logistically. Usually the preparation produced what were a few days of battle that led to years of stalemates. Compare these years of buildup to the few months necessary to build up the logistics system to support the forces of Operation Iraqi Freedom. Although supply chains are faster and more efficient today than in Sun's time, the lessons are just as important.

It was this period that gave us the writings of Sun Tzu. It was not until Father Amiot, a Jesuit priest in France, translated *The Art of War* into French in 1782 that the Western world heard of Sun Tzu. French lore has it that this translation was "Napoleon's secret weapon" and that the deception he used at Austerlitz and Jena came straight from the pages of Sun Tzu. The first English translation was not until 1905 when P. F. Caltrop completed his translation.

The works of Sun Tzu were reportedly read and used by the Nazi High Command in preparing for World War II. *The Art of War* was obligatory reading for the political and military hierarchy of the Soviet Union and it served as the basis for Mao Tse Tung's *Little Red Book*, which should not be confused with the classic book by the same title written by the golf guru, Harvey Penick. Taiwan has novels and comic book versions of Sun Tzu's works and he is regularly quoted in contemporary media throughout Asia.

The most popular English translations are by Samuel Griffith, Kaufman, Lionel Giles, and James Clavell, the author of *Shogun*. Although all of these translations are similar, they have differing points of view. A quick look at some of the chapter titles provides an insight into the teachings:

- Laying Plans
- Preparations for War
- How to Think about War
- Tactics
- Weak Points and Strong
- Variations in Reality
- Control and Maintenance of Territory
- Fierceness in Combat

Sun Tzu mandates careful planning and analysis of terrain and the formulation of an overall strategy before starting an operation. This is just as important in today's supply chains as it was in warfare in 500 BC. Careful planning and collaboration in conjunction with an analysis of the business "terrain" will set a company up for success. It has been postulated by several students of Sun Tzu that if leaders, both political and military, would have read and understood *The Art of War*, perhaps the United States would not have gotten involved in Viet Nam, would not have tried the Bay of Pigs invasion in Cuba, may have never been in the middle of the hostage crisis in Iran in 1979, and could have possibly prevented or avoided World War II. Strong suggestions, but all tied to the basic premise of, "Supreme excellence consists of breaking the enemy's resistance without fighting."

In the introduction to his translation, James Clavell states,

> I would like to make *The Art of War* obligatory study for all our serving officers and men, as well as for all the politicians and all people in government. . . .
>
> If I were Commander-in-Chief, I would have written into law that all officers, particularly all generals, take a yearly oral and written exam on the thirteen chapters.[7]

Now that we have established who Sun Tzu was and the importance of his works that have stood the test of time for over 2500 years, let's look at some of his ideas as they pertain to 21st-century supply chain issues.

Sun Tzu introduced the concepts of the orthodox and the unorthodox methods. The orthodox method is a by-the-book, orderly, and deliberate approach to solving problems. The Army's Military Decision-Making Process discussed in Chapters 1 and 2 is a good example of an orthodox method. A company's standard operating procedures is a good example of the orthodox. Unfortunately, "We've always done it that way!" is an all-too-common example of the orthodox method.

Those that are comfortable with "We've always done it that way" sometimes frown upon the unorthodox method. Sun Tzu defined the unorthodox as imaginative, flexible, unconventional, or unexpected. Today we would probably call that "thinking outside the box." Perhaps Albert Einstein accurately described the need for the unorthodox when he said, "The significant problems we face cannot be solved at the same level of thinking we were at when we created them."

Many managers are comfortable with the orthodox way of doing business. All too often managers and line employees are content with the status quo. The status quo is a good example of the orthodox way.

Leaders have to be willing to move to the unorthodox methods to improve operations. Sun Tzu understood this; to be an innovator in your supply chain, you, too, must understand this. Being unorthodox does not necessarily mean breaking corporate culture and alienating your workers, but it does mean that a new way of thinking and acting is necessary in 21st-century supply chains. Remember, this is not "your Dad's supply chain." What worked ten years ago may not work today. For that matter what worked on September 10, 2001, in your supply chain may not work today.

Sun Tzu tells us that warfare is the greatest affair of the state. Some recent authors have linked warfare and business. Sometimes business may feel a little like warfare to the unprepared. Because the recent trend has been to apply the universal style of Sun Tzu to almost every endeavor in life, from business to investing to dating relationships, and because supply chain experts such as Dr. Eli Goldratt have stated that in the future the competition will be between supply chains, we substitute supply chains for warfare. This means that supply chain operations are the greatest affair of the company. (Those of us in the supply chain business already know this and our lives will be easier when we convince our senior leadership of this.)

Many in manufacturing could argue that manufacturing is the greatest affair of the company and the same argument could be made for sales and marketing. However, without supply chains, there would be no raw materials to manufacture from and there would be no way to get products to the customer. As my transportation friends say, "Nothing happens until something moves." If nothing moves we cannot support the customer. And without customers we are out of business.

That being the case, Sun Tzu tells us, "If the objective cannot be attained, do not employ the Army." Your army is your corporation. If analysis and research show that a product or service does not meet the needs of the customer, do not employ your "army." You will not be able to win and it only takes a few, maybe even one, defeat to crush an army or ruin a company. This is not to say do not take risks, but if you follow the guidelines of risk assessment and risk management in Chapters 1 and 2, you will not imperil your company. Just as "preparation for war should not be an intellectual exercise," the preparation for a commercial supply chain operation should not be just an intellectual exercise. It has to be well thought out and planned in excruciating detail. More than likely this plan will need an unorthodox approach to be successful and gain a competitive advantage.

Sun Tzu tells us, "Without logistics, the army is lost." Major General Larry Lust used to tell his soldiers, "An Army without logistics is just another parade." A company without logistics is just another failed dot.com. Sun Tzu was the first military theorist to recognize the importance of logistics to the success of an operation. The founders of many of the dot.com companies in the late 1990s and early 2000s would have benefited from listening to this advice. The goal of many failed dot.coms appeared to be to bring the customer in with the fancy Web site, take the orders for all kinds of goods, and then. . . . Well, there wasn't a then in their plans. They forgot that logistics was necessary to get the goods to the customer.

Sun Tzu understood that "supplies are essential for the proper management of a conflict and its resolution." Although many companies view inventory as an evil, supplies have to be somewhere and available for sale and delivery to the customer to make a profit and retain customers.

With the new interest in reverse logistics management over the past several years and the realization that inefficient reverse logistics management affects the forward supply chain and the bottom line, it is interesting that 2500 years ago, we were warned by Sun Tzu of the "hindrance of over supply." Sun tells us that oversupply presents problems of a different nature. Lieutenant Gus Pagonis wrote about the problems of "over supply" in his account of Operation Desert Storm logistics, *Moving Mountains.* Gus was referring to the mountains of supplies created by the "hindrance of over supply."

However, the U.S. Army continues to relearn this lesson with every major deployment or operation, as evidenced by the large amount of supplies at the end of every major operation (27,000 containers at the end of Operation Desert Storm and over 40 hectares (approximately 160 acres) of supplies awaiting retrograde to the United States in August of 2003 in Kuwait).

Almost 20 percent of what the Army orders is returned through the reverse supply chain. According to research by Reverse Logistics Trends, Inc., somewhere between three and six percent of companies' bottom lines are spent on reverse logistics management.[8] Sun Tzu warned of this two and a half millennia ago and yet it is still a problem.

This is not a problem unique to the military. Companies such as Big Lots! and e-Boomerang have come along to meet the corporate need created by the "hindrance of over supply." E-Bay and other online auction houses cater to the industry created by oversupply in commercial supply chains.

Sun also warned us about the criticality of securing our supply lines. His guidance was to "attack supply lines and rest areas." From the actions in Iraq, it is obvious that our opponents understand this concept. If you do not have secure supply lines, the merchandise will not make it to the customer.

Sun Tzu appeared to understand meeting the customers' needs. He tells us that it is bad policy to have to call for supplies when in maneuvers and even worse to need something only to discover that the item is not available. All too often we get to feeling that logistics and supply chain management is a relatively modern development, and yet, Sun Tzu appears to have grasped the situation a long time ago.

If you are in the middle of a battle, it is not a good thing to run out of food, fuel, water, or ammunition. If you are in the middle of an assembly line or other manufacturing process, it is not a good thing to run out of supplies. And the worst thing of all regardless of whether you are in combat, retail sales, or manufacturing is to need something only to find out that because of poor supply chain management the item is not available. This happened with some commodities during Operation Iraqi Freedom and is one of the shortfalls of a disruption in a just-in-time environment.

Before leaving Sun Tzu for more modern examples of military lessons for supply chains, let's take a look at some of the other advice that can be found in *The Art of War*.

- There are five factors for victory in military operations:
  1. Know when to fight and when not to. This equates to the old advice of "pick your battles." General Creighton Abrams told his staff, "He who defends everything, defends nothing." Be careful which battles you choose. This applies to new product introduction. Every new idea is not necessarily a good new product. Know when to take on the competition and when to adopt a new strategy. Look at Wal-Mart. Sam Walton knew when to take on the competition of Kmart and Target. He waited until the right time, when the Wal-Mart customer base was sufficient and the distribution processes were in place, and then took on the competition head on.
  2. Know how to employ large and small numbers of people. The leadership traits necessary for leading small organizations are the same as the leadership traits for leading large organizations. The tactics may be a little different but the basics are the same. Aspire to inspire your employees—regardless of the size of your operation.
  3. Upper and lower ranks must have the same desires. In the military, this is accomplished by providing clear and concise guidance in terms understandable by all levels of soldiers. The glue that binds this together is the corporate culture and the values of the organization. If the desires and goals are not the same across the corporation, tension will exist and workers may feel that management is only out to take care of themselves. It is this attitude that gave rise to the unions and keeps unions

alive and well. If the goal of your leadership is to get promoted at any cost, the goals of the workers may very well conflict with this and everybody suffers. I recently inquired how a new commander was doing only to be told, "He is focused on getting his promotion and getting out of here." Do you think his goals and the goals of his workers are the same? They could be if the workers want him gone as badly as he wants to be gone. But more than likely, their goals are different.

4. If you are fully prepared, you will prevail over the unprepared. This is the purpose of the risk assessment and risk management techniques discussed in Chapters 1 and 2. There is nothing more devastating than to roll out a new service only to find out that you were not prepared to fully meet the needs of the customer. I can guarantee the customer will be prepared; therefore, you must be prepared also. And you can safely bet that if you do not properly prepare for a new offering or service, your competition will take advantage of that lack of preparation to get a competitive advantage in the marketplace.

5. Generals who are capable should not be interfered with by the ruler. In modern business language, leaders who have proven themselves capable should be allowed to be a bit unorthodox as long as they continue to be successful and accomplish the mission of taking care of the customer profitably.

■ Carefully analyze actions that brought you victory. The purpose of the After Action Review discussed in the previous chapter is to analyze the actions that brought success in an operation and to prevent making the same mistakes again if the operation did not work. Sun Tzu also tells us that "failure to see new ways of doing things causes sloppiness and over confidence." Avoid the traps of "Been there, done that, didn't work" and "This is the way we have always done it." Look for new ways of improving your operations—always.

Remember, just because it worked the first time does not mean that the same tactic will work again in the future. In football, just because a team was victorious with the running game does not mean that a running play for every play from scrimmage against the same team in the future will be successful. Always look at how you are doing business and ensure that you know what still works and what needs to be improved to keep your competitive advantage or to gain one.

■ It is imperative to lead for the people and not just for personal glory. I can only assume that Sun Tzu observed what is still a problem today, not just in the military but also across many corporations. Sun must have witnessed the impact on the morale of the 500 BC soldiers when the leaders were self-serving and only out for the glory. As discussed earlier, if your attitude is, "Just make me look good," you will never be a true leader, but you will be a great example of how *not* to be a leader. Lead with the heart, not with the ego.

Alexander the Great

It has long been recognized that supply was the basis of Alexander's strategy and tactics.[9]

The next military leader that we look at is Alexander the Great. He is reputed to have once said, "If experience is all important, then I would have pack mules for Field Marshals." A man with that sense of humor deserves to be looked at for lessons in supply chains.

The U.S. Army has a concept known as a "tooth to tail analysis." This analysis of the logistics tail to the combat force ratio is used to determine what is really needed to support the situation and what is the ratio of the support force to supported force structure. In Alexander's day the supported force included not only the soldiers but in some cases the camp followers, the spouses, and the families of the soldiers. In Donald Engels' work on Alexander and his logistics structure and concepts, Engels did a "tooth to tail analysis" and determined that the support structure consisted of approximately one servant to every four combatants. This is a very robust support structure by any standards. What is the tooth to tail ratio in your company? Do you have too many folks supporting the effort or too few? This form of analysis may very well prove to your bosses that you really do not have enough personnel to do the job they are requesting in the timeframes allowed. However, this form of analysis may show you where you can streamline some processes.

A study of Alexander reveals an early need for an analysis of lift capability. How often have you found yourself with more items to ship than you had the capability to move in a given day? Or, how many times have you received a shipment that required a special piece of equipment to offload it? Alexander appears to have analyzed the mules, donkeys, oxen, and camels to determine the best method and the most efficient animal for transporting his supplies. Isn't this very similar to what less-than-truckload (LTL) carriers do every single day? Every day the LTL carriers, consolidators, and brokers do a very similar analysis to determine the most efficient and effective method of moving everything that the customers want moved. This form of analysis used by Alexander is the basis for most transportation management systems.

Conduct a thorough analysis of your needs before embarking on an operation. In 334 BC, Alexander's staff determined that approximately 30 days of supply were necessary to support the early part of the journey to Greece and Turkey. The standard of 30 days of supply on hand lasted well into the twentieth century. In the late 1990s, the Army in Germany still planned operations around a requirement of 30 days of supply on hand before starting a full-up operation. The application to today's supply chains is simple. Before starting any new venture or before bidding on a new contract for support, make sure you have completed a thorough analysis of your needs. The same is true if you are contracting out a function. Make sure your contract is awarded to a company that has done a careful analysis of your needs and has the proven capability to meet those needs. Just as you would not take off on a vacation without doing a complete analysis of what you will need on the vacation (beach towels, suntan lotion, swim trunks, clothes, etc.), you should not embark on a commercial project without doing a careful analysis of your needs.

There is a need to do periodic preventive maintenance on equipment. One of the aspects of total quality management is total productive maintenance. In the Army this is known as Preventive Maintenance Checks and Services (PMCS). The purpose of PMCS is to regularly check the belts, hoses, fittings, and other operational functions of every vehicle to ensure that it is ready to go on a moment's notice. Engels' work on Alexander states, "In addition to the time spent marching, the army would have to halt for at least one day in seven. These halts are necessary because cavalry horses and pack animals cannot withstand the pressure of loads on their backs for more than seven consecutive days without rest."[10] How long did it take us to realize that our current machines and vehicles cannot go 24/7 without some downtime for preventive maintenance? Just like Alexander's horses and pack mules, assembly equipment needs occasional "rest periods" and checks to ensure that they do not get out of tolerance. One area that is sometimes overlooked is that people need an occasional break for routine and "preventive maintenance." At the senior leader level, too many people think that they can go forever without taking a break. There is a reason why automobile manufacturers provide every vehicle owner with a suggested preventive maintenance schedule. The reason is to extend the life of your automobile. People need a similar schedule for "preventive maintenance" to keep workers fresh and prevent serious health problems.

Studying Alexander, we learn what some have known for years and some are relearning in today's economy. You need to place the warehouse/

distribution center close to where the customer will need the supplies. Wal-Mart and Target do a good job of placing regional distribution centers in close proximity to retail stores. During Alexander's journey to Greece and Turkey, he placed storage magazines along his planned routes to ensure that adequate supplies would be available when needed.

These supply points along the route of maneuver were probably the first regional distribution centers in history. This concept also gave birth to the logistics base concept employed by the U.S. Army in Operation Desert Storm. The dependence on prepositioned supplies along the routes was also an admission in 334 BC that a total reliance on just-in-time (JIT) may not always be feasible. For Alexander, JIT meant foraging and depending on the local populace for resupply. Alexander's concept of supply storage is one of the earliest examples of logistics and production planning. The "formulas" used by Alexander's staff to determine how much and where to place the supplies must have been pretty good because we will see the same supply requirements almost 2300 years later during the Korean War and in operational plans in Germany into the 1990s.

Although not acquainted with Sun Tzu, Alexander seemed to understand the importance of winning without fighting and employed this technique whenever possible. He was known to send his "spies" into villages and towns in advance of his armies. These "spies" would talk about how bad the village would be damaged or destroyed if they fought and how well they would be treated if they capitulated. Before too long the entire village was willing to give up without a fight. Some companies have used the same technique today to take over or merge with competitors.

Alexander shows us that there is a link between the intelligence preparation of the battlefield and supply chain security. "Alexander considered it essential to obtain advance intelligence of the roads, resources, terrain, and climate of the territory he was about to enter."[11] This is similar to Sun Tzu's writings on the impact of terrain and climate on operations. Knowing the impact of the operational terrain, gathering as much quality marketing and sales information as possible, and knowing the impact of these on your operations is as important today as it was in 334 BC. You have to know the business environment that you will be operating in and you must do your logistics preparation of the battlefield by knowing your distribution channels and road, rail, sea, and air networks in order to properly service your customers.

Alexander understood that the basis of a good operational strategy is logistics and supply chains. Look at some of the dot.com busts. They forgot the need to have logistics as part of their strategy and are now history. Wal-Mart, on the other hand, has built a competitive advantage around the importance of supply chain networks. In Alexander's time, just as today, successful companies must have a good supply chain management program as the basis of their strategy in order to be successful and competitive. According to Thompson in *The Lifeblood of War,* "Alexander's strategy depended on logistics, indeed his mastery of it allowed him to conduct the longest military campaign in history."[12] Shouldn't your company's strategy depend on logistics and supply chains to become one of the longest-lasting competitive companies?

Although there were a large number of wars and military operations between the time of Alexander and 1776, the lessons that could be learned from these battles and conflicts were more evolutionary in nature. For that reason we jump to 1776 and the American Revolution.

The American Revolutionary War

See Table 9.1.

General Mifflin was called the quartermaster general, however, it is important to note that although the term was still several hundred years from coming into vogue, he was in fact in charge of the entire supply chain for the Continental Army. But the real lesson learned from this passage is that you have to put the right person in the job. Just because a person has been in the company for a long time or has connections is no reason to put him or her in charge of your supply chain. This report shows that the well-documented problems at Valley Forge in the winter of 1776 were still plaguing the army two years later. Notice that this report states that General Mifflin was not well suited for the job. Although this is the opinion of Mr. Payson, the fact that a new quartermaster general was able to improve the situation shows the importance of putting the right person in the job.

Table 9.1   Nathaniel Greene and the Supply of the Continental Army

It was March 1778 and on the hills of Valley Forge, rising above the Schuylkill River, lay the winter quarters of George Washington 's Continental Army. But the greatest menace to the American cause during that long winter came not from Sir William Howe but from the breakdown of the American supply system. The Quartermaster General's Department, which was responsible for the procurement of tents, spades, shovels, and other camp equipage and of all transportation facilities, was in utter confusion. Quartermaster General Thomas Mifflin, a leading Pennsylvania patriot, was a politician, not a soldier; his talents were better to the hustings than to the administration of a complex supply service.

Source: Edward Payson, *The Quartermaster Review,* May–June 1950.

A committee appointed by the Continental Congress investigated the supply situation at Valley Forge. Their report revealed that truly alarming conditions prevailed in the quartermaster general's department. The committee recommended that these conditions be rapidly improved. The committee warned that not only "the future success" but also "the present existence" of the Army would be imperiled if no improvements were made.[13] How many companies today have alarming conditions in their supply chains that threaten the future success of their company or threaten its present existence? Is the leadership or lack thereof in the organization the problem? Or is it just the procedures that need to be fixed?

The committee's report revealed that there was a sufficient supply of pork in New Jersey to support the Continental Army's needs, but owing to the unavailability of wagons, not a single pound could be brought to Valley Forge. This is one of those cases where there should have been a lesson learned, but instead the committee's report is an observation or perhaps a lesson to be relearned. Over 226 years later we have almost an identical observation. During Operation Iraqi Freedom, there was no shortage of supplies in Kuwait to support the operations in Iraq, but there was a shortage of trucks to move the supplies.

In the seminal work, *The Sinews of War,* Huston wrote, "Systems of distribution and storage in the Revolutionary War depended upon customary ways of doing things, enemy threats, strategic plans, and procurement and transportation of supplies."[14] After September 11, 2001, the "customary ways of doing things" should have been thrown out the window. The "enemy threats" to the security of supply chains in the form of cyber-terrorism, bioterrorism, or other acts of terrorism can create delays to supply chains. This dictates a new level of security, which has an impact on the strategic plans of a company to procure and distribute supplies, commodities, and services. As much as everything appears to change, some things always remain the same. One of these constants over time is the need to adapt the "customary ways of doing things" to the environment and to adapt plans to meet the security needs of the supply chain.

Another critical lesson that should be learned from the logistics operations of the Continental Army is the considerations important to site selections and the locations of distribution centers. The Continental Army established their first ordnance depot at Carlisle, Pennsylvania. The Carlisle area is still a logistics and supply hub for the Navy and the Army. The thought process that led to selecting this location was to centrally locate the supplies to support as many customers as possible and to place the depot "sufficiently far inland to be reasonably safe from capture."[15] Placing a commercial distribution center to prevent capture is no longer a consideration, but placing a distribution center in a location centrally located to support as many customers as possible is still a primary consideration in location selection. A distribution center that is too far from the customer base reduces responsiveness or increases costs to become more responsive through the use of expedited services, and usually decreases the velocity of your supply chain due to increased support distances. The Army has discovered that increased support distances also increase the security requirements for the supply chain.

The Department of Defense consolidated from over 40 distribution centers to approximately 20 between 1992 and 1997. During this consolidation, the Department of Defense established two major centers, one on each coast. The purpose for this was to do the same thing as the Continental Army did in 1778. The goal was to have "mirror" distribution centers. The East Coast center focused on customers east of the Mississippi and Europe, and the West Coast center focused on west of the Mississippi and the Pacific region.

"Among the reforms which Steuben initiated after his appointment as the Inspector General in February 1778, was a policy of strict supply discipline."[16] Every leader at every level and the individual soldier was responsible for supply discipline. The implication for today's supply chains and operations is that everyone is responsible for serving as a steward of the resources of the company. How many times have you heard, "Hey, it's not my money." But it is their money. If everyone involved in the operations and the supply chain took a more possessive attitude, the savings and the increased velocity from the reduced waste would affect the overall bottom line and for those companies with stock options or profit sharing, it is the employees' money.

The outsourcing of logistics functions for the military is not a new phenomenon. Starting in 1776, the Continental Army hired civilian drivers for their wagons to free up soldiers to do soldiers' work. This precedent from 1776 set the stage for today's push for commercialization of some functions within the military. For commercial supply chains, this set the stage for today's third-party logistics providers (3PLs). The Continental Army realized that some functions were better performed by others in order to allow the Army to focus on its core competencies. "Congress discouraged the use of combat troops as drivers on the ground that it weakened the effectiveness of the line units."[17] What functions are you now doing that "weaken the effectiveness of your line units"? Do you need to outsource noncore competencies? Are you contracting functions that could be better accomplished by bringing the operations back in-house?

"To some extent American forces in the Revolution suffered a chronic shortage of supplies, but more often than not the real shortage was transportation."[18] This same problem surfaced again in Operation Iraqi

Freedom. Nevertheless, it is not limited to the military. Without the ability to effectively distribute goods, no amount of inventory will suffice. What is a bigger sin: to not have the items the customer wants (unstocked or a stockout) or to have the items but not the ability to get them to the customer? I will tell you having the item without the ability to distribute them to the customer is the bigger sin. This is what put a large number of online stores in trouble a few years ago during the Christmas season. They had the goods but could not deliver as promised. One prominent online and "bricks and mortar" retailer gave out more in service-related coupons after Christmas several years ago than they generated in online sales. The former Soviet Union realized the same transportation problem. They had potatoes rotting in the fields and corresponding empty shelves in the stores because of the inability to transport the produce from the fields to the stores.

During the American Revolution, "As a rule an Army tried to keep within two days" march from its advance depot. You never want your customers to wait for supplies. Several large companies promise delivery within five days, and more and more companies are establishing their distribution centers closer to the customer to ensure that customers have what they want when they want it without having to pay premium service charges to get the merchandise or materials. The purpose of the Revolutionary Army in having a two-day customer wait time was to improve responsiveness. Responsiveness is one of those characteristics that is very important in war. Responsiveness is also very important to set world-class companies apart from the also-rans and the merely good. What are you doing to improve your responsiveness? The techniques discussed in Chapter 7 on improving and supercharging velocity will also improve your responsiveness. Some of the ways that the Army and other large corporations have improved responsiveness include dedicated delivery trucks, time-definite deliveries, visibility, and regionally aligned distribution centers.

Napoleonic Warfare as Viewed through the Eyes of Karl von Clausewitz and Baron Henri Jomini

Napoleon's most prominent defeat, not counting Waterloo, is related to logistics. In his drive to Moscow, Napoleon outran his supply lines and did not plan sufficient lift to get his army back from Moscow. This coupled with the Russian winter caused more losses than the Russian army was able to inflict. One of the writers of what has become a military theory staple, Baron Henri Jomini, served as a staff officer in Napoleon's army under Field Marshal Ney. Jomini identified logistics as one of the six branches of the military. However, Jomini took a narrow view of logistics by defining it as "the art of moving armies . . . the quartering and supply of troops." What is important is that like Sun Tzu, Jomini recognized the importance of logistics in the success of an operation. Many companies are just now learning the link between operational success and logistics excellence. Jomini also discussed the importance of the lines of communication for moving supplies on and to the battlefield. Or in other words, Jomini realized the need to provide security to supply chains in order to be successful.

The most important lesson from Jomini's contemporary, Karl von Clausewitz, is one that we tend to learn and relearn. Clausewitz's book, *On War,* is one of the most quoted military works of the 18th century. The lesson that is important from Clausewitz for all operational planners and all supply chain planners is that all things change when you go from the abstract to the concrete. Simply put, just because it looks good in a plan does not mean that it will work well in reality.

Supply Chain Lessons from the American Civil War

> *The logistics lack of preparation for both sides probably prolonged the length of the war. . . . Lee and Jackson were the masters of the operational art. But the war was won by the logistic capability of the North, able to arm and sustain its armies, and eventually to maintain Grant in his strategy of relentless pressure on Lee.*[19]

All too often in the analysis of military and civilian operations, the impact of logistics on the operation are ignored when things go well. When logistics operations do not go well, everyone knows about it and wants to point fingers. Most analyses of military operations, the American Civil War being no exception, look at the tactics and operations without considering how the army and its equipment got to the battlefield or what actions were necessary to sustain the army, as long as the army won.

During the famous march to the sea, General Sherman realized that without the proper means of transportation, the ability to sustain his army was impossible. Similar to the problems facing the railroads in 2004, General Sherman found himself in a rail dilemma. He needed to move over 130 rail cars a day to support his forces and only had access to approximately 600 cars. At the same time that General Sherman was doing an analysis of his rail needs, he was also doing an analysis of the requirement to secure his supply chain to ensure timely delivery of needed supplies. To accomplish this mission, he established garrisons and supply depots along the route of the march. In addition to ensuring a continuous flow of supplies, this also provided a continuous communications link along the supply chain long before industry realized the need to have assured communications for supply chains.

Although not a supply chain manager by trade, General Sherman realized before the beginning of the campaign for Atlanta that the uninterrupted flow of supplies was critical to success or failure on the battlefield. Many companies are still learning this same lesson 140 years later.

General Sherman's exploits show the criticality of logistics in an operational environment. The ability of the U.S. Army to supply and replenish its forces became the difference between victory and defeat. History shows that the leadership abilities of the officers of the Confederate States of America were in most cases superior to those of their counterparts. The real lesson from the American Civil War is that superior supply chain operations can overcome average leadership and conversely, even great leadership cannot overcome inferior supply chains.

Logistics capabilities surface again in World War I as a critical difference between success and failure.

Lessons in Logistics and Supply Chains from World War I

World War I provides some great examples of the impact of logistics and supply chain operations on the eventual outcomes and results of operations. German logistics failures to plan for and get adequate ammunition led to their defeat at the Battle of the Marne, and the inadequate U.S. logistics system created difficulties that included running out of food during the Argonne campaign. Although the majority of the support for the Allied Expeditionary Force came from the French, there were still supply chain problems.

The lessons that modern-day supply chain operators should learn from these examples of logistics failure are that you have to develop a complete supply chain that is integrated with the operational plans of your company. There are still companies today that stovepipe supply chain operations as opposed to operating an integrated supply chain. The abysmal results from the German and U.S. logistics examples came from stovepipes coupled with information shortfalls.

World War I also provides an example of the need to secure your supply chains. The need for supply chain security is not as great as it is for military operations, but it is just as critical for supply chain success. Lawrence of Arabia (T. E. Lawrence) advised the Emir of Saudi Arabia to attack the supply lines of the railroads to bring about a quicker defeat. His advice led to the capture of Medina.

In preparing for World War II, British Field Marshal Montgomery supposedly said that during World War I, "eighty percent of our problems were logistical in nature." With that great disconnect and lack of faith in the system to meet the needs of the customer, it is hard to regain the confidence necessary in commercial supply chains to be successful. Just as one lie can ruin a reputation for integrity, one supply chain failure can ruin a reputation for reliability and responsiveness.

Supply Chain Lessons from World War II

Our cause would have been lost without the magnificent logistics support by our entire Nation. Logistics provided the tools with which our air, ground, and sea forces fashioned victory.[20]

Why look at World War II for supply chain lessons? The answer to this question comes from the U.S. Military History Center's account of logistics support for World War II. "World War II was the first war in our history in which there were no major failures in supply. . . . No battle, no campaign was lost nor substantially impeded by a logistics failure. The results attest to the wisdom of the decision to concentrate logistic activities in a single command."[21] There have been over 18,000 pages written on logistics in World War II, so there are a large number of lessons that can be learned from the logisticians of this period.

The first lesson from World War II logistics is that you have to do whatever it takes to support the customer. An example of doing whatever it takes to get supplies to the customer can be seen in the actions of the German Army in North Africa in early 1941. Because of the shortage of fuel, among other things, the German command requested Italian submarines to transport fuel through the Mediterranean Sea and offloaded the fuel using underwater hose lines to support the forward elements of Rommel's Afrika Korps.

The next lesson is a recurring theme: secure your supply chain. The early 1941 timeframe also gives us a good example of why it is important to provide security for supply chain operations.

> Thus, the point must be brought out that as a result of the gradually developing Anglo-American supremacy at sea and in the air in the Mediterranean, North Africa was cut off from Europe. The German-Italian forces operating in Africa, therefore, could not be adequately reinforced or supplied. This lack of any possibility of maintaining supply traffic was not due to any failure on the part of the German or Italian headquarters

responsible for the movement of supplies but solely to the fact that the German-Italian operational command did not succeed in keeping the supply routes to Africa open.[22]

Leadership is important. The German experiences in the desert of North Africa also provide us with a look at the importance of leadership in difficult situations. "Because of the close contact of the troops with each other, all officers had to give an example of soldierly bearing and good moral living. Any extravagance on the part of an officer is noticed by the men and scrutinized with a magnifying glass."[23] This is nothing different from today's supply chains and organizations. The workers on the shop floor and on the distribution center floor see what the leadership has and how they are treated.

When I was a young lieutenant, my battalion commander insisted on having a separate dining facility in Korea for the officers. While the soldiers were eating from paper plates, the officers were eating from china plates with real silverware instead of the plastic flatware the soldiers had. This caused a great bit of consternation with the soldiers who felt like the work they were doing 12 to 14 hours a day earned them the right to have meals served to them on real china as well. For me it created a bit of a problem; the meal time was when I had the opportunity to sit down with my noncommissioned officers and discuss the day's upcoming operations or review what needed to be fixed for the next day. It also gave me the chance to talk to soldiers about their perspectives on the quality of support that they were receiving. Many companies are moving away from the expense and aggravation of the executive dining room. The workers will not miss this passing and it will probably raise morale. In addition, how can you know what your workers are thinking if you do not spend time with them at the lunch table listening to what they have to say?

"Proper leadership, training, and welfare of the troops can lead to extraordinary successes." General Toppe said these words about Field Marshal Erwin Rommel's soldiers over 50 years ago. How true is this today? Leadership, training, and taking care of your workers are just as important today as in World War II. Compare the words of General Toppe from 1952 to these words from one of today's senior Army leaders: "Without leadership and discipline, bad things happen." Quality leadership never goes out of style!

A positive attitude is important: be straightforward but do not be a pessimist. According to Huston in *Guns and Butter, Powder and Rice,* "The story of logistics in support of the European Theater in World War II suggests that nothing is more embarrassing to the logistician than success in battle. At heart, he must be a pessimist."[24] There is a poem written by

Major General Moorman in 1947 while a student at the Army's Command and General Staff College known as the "Logistician's Lament." The moral of General Moorman's poem is that senior leaders hate logisticians because they are so pessimistic, telling the senior leaders that something cannot be accomplished because of the lack of support. If your boss wants to do a project that is not supportable, tell him or her. Instead of being pessimistic, offer alternatives that will succeed.

Do not be pessimistic as a logistician! All too often as logisticians and supply chain managers we present the worst-case scenario and refuse to move from that position. Although it is critical to the success of any operation or corporation to have personnel in the supply chain do a critical analysis of supportability, it is debilitating for the organization if the logisticians pass the point of analysis and become pessimistic. A classic example of this occurred with the Third Army and the First Army in France. The Armies of Lieutenant Generals Patton and Hodges reached the banks of the Seine River on August 24, 1944, a full 11 days ahead of a plan that logisticians said was impossible to support and accomplish. These logisticians continued to call the operation impossible even after the Armies had already accomplished it. Be realistic but do not harbor on the side of pessimism; you will start to lose credibility with your customers.[25]

How you organize your supply chain is important. According to the U.S. government's account of logistics in World War II, "At the time of Pearl Harbor, the internal organization of the War Department was antiquated and cumbersome. Its form was not suited for the waging of a major war. . . . Logistics activities were especially diffused and uncoordinated. They were spread through six Supply and eight Administrative Services."[26] If an activity is not needed in your supply chain, get rid of it. Organize your supply chain to be as efficient as possible without losing effectiveness and the ability to support your customer.

Understand your supply chain. "The task of insuring logistic success was enormous and almost beyond the comprehension even of many of those engaged in it."[27] Many companies experience a very similar situation. Corporate officers outside the supply chain have a tendency to underestimate supply chain requirements and overestimate the savings that can be harvested from supply chain operations.

The lesson here is that supply chain managers must ensure that operations management personnel understand the complexity of supporting their operations. Operation Iraqi Freedom demonstrated that this same attitude and lack of comprehension is still alive in today's military. How many times has your boss demanded that a new product be on the shelf by a certain time without knowing what was involved in getting the product to all the stores in the specified time? Or without considering the impact on the other products that have to move through the same pipeline?

Supply chain operations should influence strategic decisions. "World War II was a war of logistics."[28] Twenty-first century companies are in a "war of logistics," or more accurately a war of supply chains, with the company that possesses the best supply chain coming out on top. Wal-Mart is a classic example of this. Their supply chain operations allow them to sell products at a much lower price than their competitors. Today's battlefield for corporations is the responsiveness of the supply chain.

The Theory of Constraints is not a new concept even though it has become more popular over the past decade. Supply chain bottlenecks were decisive factors limiting the capabilities of combat forces during World War II. Long before Dr. Goldratt developed the Theory of Constraints, the Allied and Axis supply chain operators were aware of this concept. Just as Dr. Goldratt's theory focuses on eliminating bottlenecks in the manufacturing sector, the logistics community in World War II developed ways to eliminate the bottlenecks and identify ways to furnish the leadership with feasible solutions.

The distribution pipeline should be designed to provide continuous support and handle peaks and surges. The Afrika Korps outran its supply lines because the system was not robust enough to keep up with the move across Africa. In addition, the Afrika Korps moved faster than the ability to extend the rail and road networks necessary to support the forces. The same thing happened again in Operations Desert Storm and Iraqi Freedom. The decision to leave vehicles in the United States, because of a focus on occupation, produced an unfavorable reaction when these operations became campaigns of movement and distribution. Without the ability to distribute your product to the customer, the product is worthless.

Collaborate. You never know who will make a good supply chain partner until you start looking around for a collaboration partner. To get supplies to forces in Russia in World War II, the United States and the Soviet Union collaborated to use U.S. soldiers to operate a supply chain to move supplies and equipment through Iran into the Soviet Union. This collaboration allowed the Soviet Union to get supplies where they needed them and avoid using seas and oceans controlled at the time by the Germans.

To improve your supply chain, standardize your repair parts and supply chain processes. Over the past 20 years, there has been a growth in the use of materials resource planning, bills of materials, and interchangeable and substitution parts. This is nothing new. In November 1942, the War Production Board established a controlled materials plan. The purpose of this board was to standardize materials and provide suppliers with forecasts of needed materials and supplies.

Carefully analyze supply chain needs. Where should you place your distribution centers? When planning your distribution centers avoid sub-optimization of the system. The Department of Defense relearned this lesson in 1995 with the Defense Depot, San Joaquin, California and the Defense Depot, Susquehanna, Pennsylvania. The Defense Logistics Agency established a metric that rewarded purchasing managers for reducing first-destination transportation costs. This placed supplies in the Defense Depot closest to the suppliers/manufacturers to minimize transportation costs. The result was an increase in second-destination transportation costs. Should the distribution center be closer to the customer or closer to the supplier? In World War II, the distribution centers were placed close to the supplier, just as they were in 1995. The impact was on the ability to support forces in the Pacific Theater. The manufacturing centers were on the East Coast, so the majority of the supplies were stocked on the East Coast.

The need for uniform inspection and disposal procedures is important. Today, just as during World War II, the lack of standard procedures for inspecting and disposing of items in the reverse supply chain affect the ability to get serviceable (reusable) items back in the system in a timely manner and delay the ability to get repairable items back to the repair centers for eventual reissue or resale.

James Huston notes, "For the most part, Army schools and the War Department General Staff in peacetime planned, trained for, and studied Combat Operations. To a great extent the Army neglected the logistics problems of operations. This was a deficiency that proved to be costly."[29] The Department of Defense is still learning this lesson. The Department of Defense is not alone; finally, corporate America is waking up to the importance of supply chains to profitability and many companies are starting to offer employees classes in supply chain operations. Huston goes on to say, "Training in logistic planning and operations had been seriously neglected by the educational system of the Armed Forces. The Army War College and the Army Industrial College before the war gave some attention to certain phases of these subjects, but the overwhelming emphasis in officer education was upon tactics."[30] Corporate America is starting to wake up to the concept of linking operations and supply chain operations. The impact of logistics on victory in military operations and the emphasis on incorporating supply chain plans into operational plans was evident during World War II. This principle is still important 60 years later. Who wants to be the person in the supply chain that causes an operation to stop or a production line to stop because of a logistics failure? At the National Training Center, it was constantly emphasized that the logistics community would never be the reason why a training event was canceled.

Maintain good inventory accountability records. Although there were between 50 and 120 days of supplies on the ground in the World War II operational theaters, "Such stock levels were almost meaningless without accurate consumption and inventory records."[31] What good are your supplies if you do not know what you have and have not reconciled your sales and inventory data? The results are potential stockouts and excess or obsolete stocks. Not knowing what you have or where it is located in the supply chain is just as bad as having the items but not the ability to deliver them.

Supply chain security is important, just as Lawrence of Arabia emphasized in the "war to end all wars." This lesson was relearned in World War II. As Huston states, "The security of the United States presents a complex problem in logistics preparedness. . . . What should be the place of logistics in the organization? . . . Our future security depends upon the application of the logistic lessons of World War II."[32] Vietnam, Operation Desert Storm, and Operation Iraqi Freedom provide the same lessons. The need for supply chain security throughout the world is as important today as the need to secure supply chain operations was in World War II.

Communications security is another important factor. The use of the "purple code" and "magic code" during World War II is a good example of what the failure to secure communications can do to an operation. The Allied forces knew almost every move that the Axis was going to make because of the ability to "crack" the secret codes. Communications security and operational security proved to be invaluable to the Japanese Navy as they crossed the Pacific Ocean enroute to their attack on Pearl Harbor.

Improving morale is part of the mission of leaders everywhere. The U.S. Army used the Special Services to help improve the morale of the soldiers. Some of the initiatives used during this war—such as the G.I. Bill for education—led to some of today's programs to improve the quality of life and retain good employees by some of the Fortune 500.

World War II proved that wars cannot be won without supply chain superiority. Twenty-first-century businesses are starting to learn that they cannot be competitive and victorious without supply chain superiority. Logistics supportability is the first prerequisite for success. The Germans had logistics superiority at the beginning of the war but could not sustain it. In war and in business, you have to be there first, be the best, and be able to sustain against all competition.

A plan has to be flexible enough to allow subordinates the ability to make decisions and modify the plan based on the situation. The friction of war is just as applicable to the friction of business. The plan for supplies for supporting forces after D-Day did not take into account the user end of the supply chain and the constraints on that end. Because of the rigidity of the plan of support, which was designed to prevent excess, there was a buildup of excess supplies and a shortage of other supplies. It is important to analyze the capacity of the entire pipeline before setting plans in concrete. This is an example of needing to know yourself and your supply chain.

The importance of discipline and reverse logistics became apparent as the length of the supply chains became longer. During the move across Europe and the advent of the Red Ball Express, the largest commodity required was fuel. Because of the lack of supply discipline and the ordering of things that were not really needed, the critical transport assets were tied up moving items forward that were not really needed and then having to move them back again. In some cases in the Third Army these items were simply left behind in camps, not unlike in Operation Iraqi Freedom.

Another supply discipline problem resulted from the use of the five-gallon "jerrycans" for the transport of fuel. By August of 1944, more than one half of the 22,000,000 jerrycans had been lost or tossed. This provides another good example of the need for a quality reverse logistics system to maintain visibility of critical reusable items.[33]

Korean War Supply Chain Lessons

This section looks at lessons that can be learned from the Korean War from the North Korean People's Army and the Communist Chinese Army, as well as the lessons that can be learned from the United Nations logistics operations.

Lessons We Could Have Learned from the North Korean People's Army and the Communist Chinese Forces during the Korean War

- *Flexibility.* Both the North Korean Army (NKPA) and the Communist Chinese Forces (CCF) demonstrated flexibility and innovation in their logistics doctrine. This flexibility enabled them to counter the obvious superiority of the United Nations Command in resources and the ability to restrict movements. The NKPA/CCF logistics structure was based on the Soviet logistics structure and established a strict system of priorities for movement of supplies such as fuel and ammunition. This is not unlike the system used by U.S. forces worldwide. Although it is important to have a preplanned set of priorities to refer to, it is equally important to have the flexibility to alter these priorities to support the needs of the customers.
- *Logistics is a command responsibility.* The NKPA and the CCF made logistics a command responsibility. After the commander and chief of staff, the deputy commander for logistics (rear support) was the next in line in the command structure. Vince Lombardi tells us that

command and leadership are the same: this means that logistics is a leadership responsibility. How many corporations do not practice this philosophy or do not get leadership involved in logistics and supply chain operations until the company is on the brink of collapse or looking for new ways to improve the bottom line? Over 50 years ago the North Korean Army and the Chinese Army had this figured out. To be successful, you have to have leadership involvement in the supply chain operations and the chief logistics officer has to be part of the corporate leadership.

■ *Convoy/supply point security.* A critical lesson learned in Operation Iraqi Freedom was the need to provide convoy security for every convoy of supplies and personnel. During the Korean War, every Rear Service Section (equivalent of a battalion-sized element in the U.S. Army) had an organic Guard Platoon. This platoon provided security for supply convoys and for the storage locations. During Operation Iraqi Freedom, the majority of the convoy and supply point security was provided by infantry units. The use of infantry units to provide this mission took soldiers away from combat units. In addition, "Each Supply Base also had an attached security platoon of sixty to seventy-five men, who guarded the depots and supplies in transit."[34] Yet 50 years later we were not able to do that during Operation Iraqi Freedom because we had structured the U.S. Army to peacetime funding and personnel levels and were not structured to provide organic security platoons to the supply points and distribution centers. Any organic support came at the expense of the supply mission by diverting distribution center personnel to the guard mission. In addition, "Guides were posted at all important intersections, in villages, at bridges, and at other choke points."[35] If we had learned these lessons in the U.S. Army, perhaps the Operation Iraqi Freedom incident with the 507th Maintenance Company that produced the story of Jessica Lynch would not have happened.[36]

■ *Security and operations security.* The impact of the element of surprise can be seen in the 4:00 a.m. attack on June 25, 1950, that started the Korean War. The North Korean ability to maintain operations security can be compared to the operations security employed by the Japanese in their crossing of the Pacific Ocean enroute to their attack on Pearl Harbor.

■ *Standardization and reorganization.* The support structure for the Communist Chinese Forces in China differed from army to army and was different from the support structure for the forces in Korea. Standardizing the support structures in an organization can help to alleviate confusion. One of the benefits of shopping a Target or Wal-Mart is that almost every one of the stores for each chain is laid out the same way. So, if you are transferred around the country as most professionals are today, you can go into a store in a new location and be reasonably assured that the layout will be the same. The lack of standardization in the Communist Chinese Forces structure resulted in "several major revisions during the course of the Korean War."[37] Transforming a unit in operations is somewhat like trying to do open heart surgery. You are working on the support structure while continuing to function and have to be very careful not to overcompensate and kill the structure completely, thereby killing the organization. There is a difference between adapting the organization to become more efficient during an operation and completely transforming or reorganizing the organization during the busiest time of the year. Would you completely reorganize your operations during your busiest season? Of course not. But the CCF did and for a while they were successful in doing it.

- *Cross-docking.* The supply points at the railheads operated by the administrative branch units had a goal of receiving the supplies at the railhead or terminal and cross-docking the supplies within 24 hours of receipt. Cross-docking did not become a popular method of improving processing times in distribution centers in the United States until the 1990s. We are not talking about the miracle cross-dock where the merchandise just happens to arrive at the distribution center as a customer's truck is being loaded; we are talking about planned cross-docking.

- *Plan for all possible contingencies.* The North Korean People's Army understood the impacts of the terrain (the business climate), the constraints of transportation assets (Theory of Constraints), and the potential for interdiction of the supply chain (security) by the United Nations Command forces. This forced the NKPA/CCF to operate two supply chain branches to provide redundancy in the system. This is not unlike what we see in the U.S. support structure during Vietnam operations. The NKPA/CCF awareness of these threats to the supply chain enabled them to plan for such contingencies and develop a redundant backup system (an example of the importance of knowing yourself).

- *Use whatever means necessary to get the merchandise to the customer.* The limitations of motor transport in North Korea produced a distribution system that consisted of trucks, pack mules, and human porters to get the supplies forward. The amazing thing about this archaic distribution method is that the North Koreans were still able to maintain a six-day customer wait time.

■ *Know the capacity of your supply chain.* The North Koreans realized that there was a big difference between the peacetime capacities of the road and rail networks and their wartime capacities. Is this important? Consider the additional traffic that will be using the roads during a wartime scenario. Along with the additional military trucks, which are usually much heavier and loaded down than commercial trucks, the friction caused on the roads by refugees and displaced civilians makes the capacity significantly less in wartime than in peacetime. What is the impact of this on your supply chain? You have to know the capacity of your supply chain and any factors that may cause friction in your supply chain such as delayed shipments because of natural or technological disasters. This ties to the importance of knowing yourself and your processes. If you do not walk the process and know the constraints, you may be surprised when an action has an impact on your ability to support the customers. The North Koreans, acknowledging the aerial attacks could have an impact on the capacity of the road networks, established road repair battalions and placed them at regular intervals along the main supply routes to ensure that damaged roads did not create a new friction point or constraint on the system. Another excellent plan by the North Koreans was to establish assigned sections of the supply routes for the drivers. Not unlike the Pony Express in 19th-century America, these drivers only drove a certain part of the road or specified routes. This enabled the drivers to become familiar with the routes and enhanced their ability to operate in poor road or visibility conditions.

Lessons from United Nations Command (United States Forces) in the Korean War

Leadership

LTC Perry of the U.S. Army commanded an artillery battery in support of Task Force Smith, the infantry task force sent from Japan to Korea to stem the flow of the North Korean Army. The theory was that the North Koreans would see the United States Army and turn and run. They did see the U.S. task force and ran, but right through it not away from it. When the North Korean tanks started shooting at LTC Perry's position, most of his men started running. LTC Perry had to use exceptional leadership skills to get the soldiers back to their firing positions and back in the fight. When the infantry soldiers from Task Force Smith reached the firing position, some of them took off their boots to enable them to run faster.

More leadership skills were necessary to get these men back into an orderly defense of the area.

Here is another example of the impact of leadership. This provides a good instance of leading by example. General Dean, the commander of the 24th Infantry Division, personally led a team with 3.5-inch bazookas in disabling a North Korean tank. His rationale for leading the team was to boost morale and show his soldiers that a 3.5-inch bazooka could indeed disable a tank. By doing so, he also boosted their confidence in their equipment. Unfortunately, like Stonewall Jackson in the American Civil War, General Dean's insistence on leading from the front led to his demise.

Multiple Handling of Supplies Increases the Customer Wait Time and Decreases the Confidence in the Supply System

"Natural hoarding tendencies in understandable efforts by local supply officers to be prepared against any eventuality, the retention of what some officers considered to be unneeded items in tables of allowances, and the provision of too much in the way of luxury items contributed to heavy burdens on the supply and transportation systems."[38] This quote from Huston's book, *Guns and Butter, Powder and Rice,* brings visions of "Sergeant Zale" and other supply sergeants depicted as hoarders and traders in the television series, *M*A*S*H.* This mentality produced shortages of some items at the supply points and excess quantities of other items. This methodology persisted throughout the reports on logistics in Vietnam, Desert Storm, and Operation Iraqi Freedom. During Operation Iraqi Freedom, it was not uncommon to see items such as pallets of camp stoves, picture frames, document protectors, and electric pencil sharpeners come through the Theater Distribution Center.

Forecasting

Another problem identified during the Korean War was the depletion of peacetime forecasts for items and the lack of a new production line for the items. Sometimes we do not learn from the past. During Operation Iraqi Freedom, we saw the same thing with the new body armor vests. The peacetime forecasted production was quickly exhausted and the availability of the new body armor for all deployed soldiers was not met until well after the "end of hostilities" was declared. Forecasting supply requirements calls for the use of sound judgment and experience coupled with careful calculation of what is really needed based on the forecasted operations.

Supply Chain Discipline

"Cases of poor supply discipline, failure to take into account equipment returned to the depot stocks for reissue, and incomplete or faulty reports of materiel consumed had inflated the apparent loss of and consumption of many items substantially beyond actual or necessary loss and consumption."[39] Even in the Korean War there was a direct link between the forward and reverse supply chains that should have been an early lesson to commercial industry that is just now starting to get on board with the importance of reverse logistics.

Costs Should Not Drive the Logistics Train

During the Korean War forecasters were overly optimistic (a malady that appeared again in the planning for Operation Iraqi Freedom). This optimism fueled by the Department of Defense created a situation where the forecast was for all hostilities to cease by July 1951. Because of this set date, no supplies could be ordered if they would support operations after that date or if they would not arrive until after that date. Although logistics and supply chains are sources of great costs, the need to cut costs cannot drive the logistics train. In this situation, it created shortages and affected the ability to support the customer. We saw the same idea raise its head in Kuwait during the buildup for Operation Iraqi Freedom. In order to capture the costs of the operation, units were told to "sanitize" their supply and maintenance computers. This meant taking all demand and requisition data out of the computers prior to deploying. The impact? Loss of historical data for demands and loss of visibility of items still in the supply chain. The result? Additional items were ordered to "replace" the items with lost visibility, a generator of excess.

Everything Cannot Be a High Priority

When it was "discovered" that emergency requisitions received special treatment and handling, the majority of the requisitions leaving Korea became emergency requisitions. If everything is high priority, then nothing is high priority and everything gets handled the same. We saw this again in Kuwait. At one time almost 90 percent of all requisitions were high priority.

Some of the same lessons were learned again during the Vietnam War.

Supply Chain Lessons from Vietnam

The story of logistics in Vietnam is characterized by several distinct logistics influences. The first involved the French. The French did not possess the logistics to support the operations of occupation in Vietnam. The next logistics impact involved the U.S. forces. The United States and their allies in Vietnam possessed the logistics superiority that enabled them to counterbalance the political influence and flaws in the operational plans. However, after the Vietnamization efforts in the 1970s, the Army of the Republic of Vietnam did not have the logistics infrastructure to support its efforts to defeat the North Vietnamese Army.

General Joseph Heiser started his seminal work on the logistics in Vietnam with

> Although this assignment has officially ended, the U.S. Army must prepare for other challenges that may lie ahead. While cognizant that history never repeats itself exactly and that no Army ever profited from trying to meet a new challenge in terms of the old one, the Army nevertheless stands to benefit immensely from a study of its experience, its shortcomings no less than its achievements. . . . Knowing in general terms what logistics means is not enough.[40]

Twenty-first century supply chains fall into the same category in which General Heiser placed the U.S. Army after the war in Vietnam. Although supply chain history "never repeats itself exactly," the lessons of previous operations from within your industry and from the military operations discussed in this chapter provide a basis for gaining a better understanding of your shortcomings and achievements. The better you do in assessing shortcomings and achievements and determining the root cause for both, the better you will do in meeting the needs of the customer in the future.

Logistics and Operations

"Vietnam is a story of remarkable logistics achievement. At no time was logistical support a constraint on a major tactical operation."[41] This should always be the case in supply chain operations. The reason for failure of an operation should never be the failure of the supply chain to provide the necessary items to the customers. Your goal should be for the same words that General Heiser wrote about Vietnam to be true for your company's operations.

A Single Point of Contact for Customers

In March 1965, the First Logistical Command was established as a single point of contact for all but Air Force and Navy unique items of supply.

This provided every customer in the Vietnam theater one single point of contact for supply chain operations. We saw this again in Operation Desert Storm. The value of having one single point of contact for customers for all of your supply chain operations is a reduction of confusion. When there are multiple points of contact, one spokesperson may say something that is counter to what the customer heard from another point of contact. Not only does this create confusion, but it also has a tendency to give customers false impressions of what can and cannot be done to support them. Sometimes it allows customers to play the same game we all played as children. If Mom says no, ask Dad, and if Dad says no, ask Grandma. Some customers will do the same thing if there are multiple points of contact for your supply chain.

Customer Wait Times and Redundancy

There is always a requirement for some level of redundancy in your supply chain to prevent disruptions. It may come in the form of safety stock or multiple distribution centers. During the war in Vietnam, the United States military used two major depots to provide backup just in case of an attack on one of the depots. Too much redundancy has a tendency to slow down supply chain operations. Prior to establishing the First Logistical Command as the single point of contact for supply chain operations, the United States forces experienced a slowdown in the requisition flow. Before consolidation, there was a 40-percent loss of requisitions due to excess layers of bureaucracy and redundancy.

Plan Your Supply Chain Support Structure to Meet the Customers' Needs

You have to have a support structure in place before starting an operation. The inventory control team did not arrive in Vietnam until March 1966, roughly one year after the logistics operations started. Can you afford to go a full year with no inventory control in place and still remain profitable? Here is another example, one that will occur again in Operation Iraqi Freedom almost 40 years later. On May 15, 1965, the first supply ship was downloaded at Cam Ranh Bay. Because there was no personnel structure in place to do this mission it was accomplished by a Transportation Corps lieutenant and a group of "detail soldiers." During Operation Iraqi Freedom, the Theater Distribution Center was operated for two weeks using detail soldiers because the personnel structure was not there to operate the center with assigned personnel.

Know Yourself

One example of the benefits of knowing yourself is the improvements in Vietnam from using a crude form of the Theory of Constraints to analyze the flow of materials into the ports. This analysis revealed that the ports were the bottlenecks for supply chain operations. By December 1966, there were ten ports in use in South Vietnam, up from just one in 1965. This resulted in a reduction of berth wait time from just over 20 days in 1965 to less than 2 days by 1970.

Training

According to Heiser's account, "In many cases, support personnel assigned to Vietnam did not have the essential experience in such areas as depot operations, maintenance, and supply. . . . Logistics units that deployed to Vietnam were deficient in unit training."[42] We saw the same thing again in Operation Iraqi Freedom with some of the reserve units called to active duty and asked to serve in roles that they were not trained to perform. It was also evident in Operation Iraqi Freedom with the total lack of training on distribution supplies to the entire theater. The Army is fixing this now with the design and fielding of a new organization to handle such a mission in any environment.

Pushing Merchandise without Demand from the Customer Can Cause Problems

The support forces for U.S. forces in Vietnam tried to reduce customer wait times by pushing supplies to the units. This created problems such as confusion over to whom the supplies went or what quantities were actually in the supplies. The biggest problem that the lack of visibility of the push package contents created was that there were instances when there were supplies in-country but unavailable for issue. A lack of visibility still does this today to many companies when the supplies are on the receiving dock and the orders are in the warehouse. Another lesson from this experience is that the better the containers are labeled and packed, the quicker they can be delivered or identified: a great lesson on the impact of visibility and packing on velocity.

The Army implemented a program called Inventory in Motion to account for items that were in the in-country distribution pipeline. This concept is similar to the accounting of Dell Computers of items certified as inbound when doing their version of MRP at their plant in Austin, TX. This concept works well as long as you have world-class visibility of the items in motion and can divert the items to a critical operation or customer to fill a higher-priority need or order. Without the visibility, the items in motion are just that: they are in motion but not available to issue or sell.

The Use of a Closed Loop Support Concept

In the Army's closed loop system in support of Vietnam, all major end items and associated secondary items (engines, vehicles, transmissions, etc.) were intensively managed through the forward supply chain, the reverse supply chain, the rebuild/overhaul process, and back into the forward supply chain for reissue. The Army adopted this system to add control and to improve the logistics readiness within the theater of operations. The concept of a closed loop system is once again becoming popular for certain high-dollar items that can be sent back through the reverse supply chain, repaired/rebuilt, and put back in the supply system. Don Blumberg promotes this same idea for use in reverse logistics. To make a closed loop work you have to have real-time data and visibility throughout the entire supply chain.

Reverse Logistics Impact

Because of the amount of excess in Vietnam, the Army implemented a process of identifying and trying to redistribute excess items. Between April 1968 and January 1972, over $2.1 billion in excess items was screened for redistribution. This program had involvement from the secretary of defense, Robert McNamara.[43] During the Vietnam War, General Heiser observed that it took "three times as much effort" to process material for retrograde as it took to "receive incoming material" and issue the items to the customer.[44] This means that every item going into the reverse supply chain delayed the needed items coming into the country for customers.

Supply Chain Confidence

How much confidence do your customers have in the ability of your supply chain to meet their needs? Another lesson from Vietnam that should have carried over to the Operation Iraqi Freedom supply chain was a lack of confidence in the supply system. According to General Heiser, "Failures of the supply system to locate, identify, and provide a required item undoubtedly degraded supply discipline at the using unit level which in turn made a substantial contribution to further breakdown in control and to increasing excesses."[45] Because of the lack of confidence, a unit clerk would not waste time submitting a request for shipping status. Instead, items were requisitioned several times. This practice, seen in every military operation in modern times, served to constipate the supply chain and created more excess items while inflating the demand data at the other end of the supply chain. This inflation of demand created a bullwhip effect throughout the supply chain. As a result of the excess created by this practice and lack of confidence in the system, the Army implemented a program known as Project CLEAN. This project was very similar in nature to the Army's Velocity Management Program of the 1990s. The number of authorized lines or Stock Keeping Units (SKUs) was dramatically reduced from over 297,000 to under 75,000 within a four-year period while removing over $1.5 billion in excess supplies without degrading the quality of support to the forces. A fallout of this project was a decrease in the actual customer wait times and a reduction in the lost, damaged, and obsolete items feeding the reverse supply chain.

Although the concept of process mapping has only come into vogue in the past ten years, the Army in Vietnam implemented a program of process mapping and time mapping known as VERIFY. This program assisted in identifying what was actually happening at each link in the supply chain while providing a timestamp on how long each process was taking. The Army went as far as mapping the time necessary to fill out paperwork. This is not unlike the process used by General Electric in the 1990s to improve processing times for their service offices.

Supply chain security was addressed in Chapter 3; in Vietnam the need for supply chain security was never more evident than along the POL (Petroleum, Oils, and Lubricants) pipelines. During the course of the war over 5.7 million barrels of fuel were lost through pilferage, evaporation, or enemy action.[46]

Other supply chain lessons that we can learn from Vietnam include:

- Very few of the containers moved into Vietnam were ever returned to the supply system. This problem raised its ugly head again during Operation Iraqi Freedom. The shortage of containers during Iraqi Freedom meant having to take a risk with rations going forward on flatbeds and not in sealed containers.
- The logistics system depends on assured communications with the capacity to transmit all the necessary data. In Vietnam, the requirement for communications was not met. This resulted in lost requisitions and orders from customers. In commercial industry, we cannot afford to have lost orders. Lost orders usually lead to lost customers.

Lessons from Operation Desert Storm

The end of the Cold War saw the logistics system scaled back and a repositioning of the "Iron Mountains" of supplies and equipment from Europe to new potential hotspots. The defense industrial base shrank as demand declined. Nevertheless, much of the industrial age logistics system remained fundamentally intact. Desert Storm was fought with the industrial age logistics. It took six months to stage the forces and supplies needed for the operation and it took another thirteen months to withdraw the "Iron Mountains" of unneeded supplies pushed forward in the preparation phase.

However, there are some great lessons in logistics and supply chains— good and bad—from Operation Desert Storm. The most important lesson that can be learned from Desert Storm is that you have to have a single point of contact for logistics. This is a lesson learned from Vietnam that was applied with great success to Desert Storm.

The most important lesson that commercial industry should learn from Desert Storm is that shipments must be properly marked and tagged with a radio frequency tag to provide visibility and inventory control. At the end of Desert Storm there were over 27,000 containers sitting in Saudi Arabia with no one having any idea what was in them or to whom they really belonged. The use of radio frequency tags in the Department of Defense is a result of this lesson learned. The tags not only provide greater visibility but provide the customer with a feeling of confidence in the system.

The Most Recent Supply Chain Lessons from Operation Iraqi Freedom

> *The Theater Distribution Center was not the cancer or horror story you may have heard! The difference between Desert Storm and Operation Iraqi Freedom was the Theater Distribution Center. It made the difference and saved our butts.*

A senior Army logistics officer

In Operation Iraqi Freedom, the great distances covered in a short time by the combat forces placed a great strain on the transportation and the logistic communication systems. The combat forces often outran their supply lines in part because the logisticians used separate information and communications networks that were out of range of their higher headquarters. Just as in Korea 50 years earlier, the shortage of trucks was a serious problem and affected the ability to provide the quality of support that the soldiers were accustomed to at their home stations in the United States. Again like Korea, when a distribution failure occurred, it was usually at the local end and not at the strategic distribution system bringing items into the theater. Like Korea, the tactical situation changed rapidly, requiring constant attention to details and flexibility in the supply chain. The distance from the supply bases in Kuwait to the soldiers in Iraq created extremely long supply lines over road networks that were not always secure and safe. In Korea, one quartermaster officer said, "It has become axiomatic that if combat units want something done, they do it themselves, even to escorting supplies shipped by rail from deep in the rear, to prevent pilferage."[47] Ironically, this officer was in the 24th Infantry Division. This division was reflagged as the Third Infantry Division in 1996 and the soldiers of this division experienced the same conditions in Kuwait during the buildup for Operation Iraqi Freedom.

Overall, the more important lesson of Operation Enduring Freedom in Afghanistan and Operation Iraqi Freedom for logistics was the impact of hierarchical stovepipe systems. The lack of an integrated supply chain resulted in a system that was too slow and too inflexible to deal adequately with the new environments and types of operations.

One After Action Review pointed out that the success of Operation Iraqi Freedom "stemmed more from luck than design." These comments were in a Department of Defense white paper, "From Factory to Foxhole: The Transformation of Army Logistics." The purpose of this study was to set the direction of the transformation of the logistics, maintenance, transportation, and distribution systems into an integrated supply chain. The U.S. Army is not the only corporation in America that still has stovepipe systems that degrade the efficiency of the overall system (see Figures 9.1 through 9.4). Learn from the mistakes of the Army and move away from silos or stovepipe systems into an integrated, synthesized supply chain.

Conclusion and Final Thoughts

In an effort to improve efficiency, military logistics is attempting to apply logistics techniques developed in the commercial sector where just-in-time inventory management and improved methods for forecasting demand are well established. We should not hesitate to employ any technique that offers a means to increase our capabilities. However, in considering the adoption of these techniques for military purposes, logisticians can never forget that their objective and the environment in which they operate

Figure 9.1 Trucks lined up at the Theater Distribution Center, March 2003. The lack of an integrated supply chain reduced the efficiency of the overall distribution system.

Figure 9.2 Air Force 463L pallets awaiting processing, April 2003.

Figure 9.3 An example of the process to break down the Air Force pallets into smaller unit-configured containers (multipack boxes). The lack of an integrated supply chain produced delays in customer wait times as items sat on the ground awaiting processing.

Figure 9.4 April 2, 2003. Just a few days earlier a SCUD missile landed just north of the smoke stacks. Such attacks have a tendency to disrupt supply chain operations.

differ significantly from that of their business counterparts. Business is focused on the provision of a product or service in a safe and cooperative environment. Methods that prove efficient in peacetime will not necessarily succeed under the far more demanding conditions of war. For example, the ability of a parcel service to deliver a package anywhere in the world in a matter of hours is based on the assumption that no one is shooting at the aircraft carrying the package.

The essential lesson of this discussion is that we must balance effectiveness and efficiency in the conduct of logistics. "Efficiency contributes to effectiveness. . . . Furthermore, we must ensure that *efficiency does not become an end unto itself. Effectiveness should always be the defining feature of our logistics system.*"[48] Just as a military supply chain needs to balance efficiency and effectiveness without adversely affecting either one, so do commercial supply chains. During the periods between wars, the United States military has sought to organize logistics functions around efficiencies without focusing on the overall effectiveness of the supply chain. This always comes back to haunt the military. Do not try to organize your supply chain solely for efficiency at the cost of effectiveness. Your customers want an effective supply chain and if it is internally efficient, that is fine.

An army cannot conduct a deliberate war in an organized manner without logistics. Without logistics and supply chains, business as a deliberate organized activity is impossible. The effects of logistics operations go beyond the four walls of a company and can have a big impact not only on profitability but also on the view of the company by Wall Street. Your supply chain establishes what is operationally possible for your company.

Logistics by itself cannot win wars, but it has been the major contributing factor in losing many wars. Supply chain operations by themselves may not make your company profitable and successful, but a poor or average supply chain will almost guarantee an unprofitable company.

There are several themes throughout the military operations of the past 2500 years. These include the requirement to incorporate supply chain planning into operation planning. You should not think about production planning without first checking the availability of raw materials and components. This attitude should migrate to all operational procedures: incorporate supply chain factors into the operational plans.

The next common theme throughout history is the need for security and visibility of your supply chain to be successful. The lack of visibility of supply chains reduces the effectiveness of your supply chain and the need for supply chain security, so important in military operations, is more important today than at any time in history.

Two other common themes between military operations and commercial supply chain operations are the impact of leadership on the quality of supply chain operations and the need for a responsive, integrated supply chain to reduce the wait time for customers and the reduction of redundancy and cycle times. "Responsiveness is often the yardstick by which effective logistics is measured. Simply stated, responsiveness is the ability to provide the right support, at the right time, at the right place. *It is through responsiveness that we build confidence in our logistics system.*"[49]

Supply chain operations can shape the success of your operations. The use of supply chain operations to shape operations is evident in the island hopping during the Pacific Campaign to establish bases and distribution centers to be closer to the customer.

According to the final report on the logistics of World War II, "Overall performance of the oversea logistic mission was magnificent, despite the absence of adequate precedent. Lessons have been learned that are of great significance. To ignore these lessons would be perilous."[50] Lessons are only learned if they are institutionalized and applied, otherwise they are only observations. This is just as true for any commercial supply chain operation. The lessons of military operations provide examples and principles for supply chain operations that are applicable to your company. Adopting the lessons learned and applying corrective actions to prevent similar occurrences of the shortfalls and ensuring replication of the successes of the military may mean the difference between victory and defeat for your company.

> *My goal in peace or war is to succeed in any mission, therefore, I will not resort to guessing as I know that chance is a fool's god and that I as a logistician cannot depend on it. I will be sure— always!*

The Logistician's Creed for the U.S. Army

Questions for Thought and Discussion

1. Are the principles of logistics for the Army as presented from *Field Manual 100-5, Operations:* improvisation, anticipation, responsiveness, continuity of support, applicable to your supply chain? If not, why not?
2. Are the lessons from military history applicable to your supply chain?
3. Are you able to provide visibility and confidence in your system to your customers?

4. Is your supply chain a system of silos or stovepipes, or is your supply chain integrated?
5. Are supply chain operations integrated into your operational planning?
6. What can you apply from the lessons learned from military operations to your supply chains?

Book List for Chapter Nine

1. *Desert Warfare: German Experiences in World War II—Major General Alfred Toppe, 1952*, ed. The Combat Studies Institute at Command and General Staff College, Fort Leavenworth, *KS*, 1991.
2. Van Creveld, Martin, *Supplying War, Logistics from Wallenstein to Patton*, Cambridge University Press, London, 1977.
3. Thompson, Julian, *Lifeblood of War—Logistics in Armed Conflict*, Biddles, Guildford, UK, 1991.
4. *Field Manual 100-5, Operations*, U.S. Army, Washington, DC, 1995.
5. Axelrod, Alan, *Patton on Leadership, Strategic Lessons for Corporate Warfare*, Prentice Hall, Paramus, NJ, 1999.
6. Pagonis, William G., *Moving Mountains: Lessons in Leadership and Logistics from the Gulf War*, Harvard Business School Press, Boston, MA, 1992.
7. Huston, James A., *The Sinews of War: Army Logistics 1775–1953*, Center of Military History, U.S. Army, Washington, DC, 1966.
8. Huston, James A., *Guns and Butter, Powder and Rice*, Selinsgrove, London, 1989.
9. Walden, Joseph L., *The Forklifts Have Nothing to Do!*, iUniverse, New York, 2003.
10. Sun Tzu, *The Art of War*, trans. Ralph D. Sawyer, Barnes & Noble, New York, 1994.
11. Engels, Donald W., *Alexander the Great and the Logistics of the Macedonian Army*, University of California Press, Berkeley, 1978.
12. Clausewitz, Carl von, *On War*, Penguin, London, 1968.
13. *Logistics in World War II—Final Report of the Army Service Forces*, Center of Military History, U.S. Government Printing Office, Washington, DC, 1948.
14. Heiser, Joseph M., Jr., *Vietnam Studies, Logistic Support*, Department of the Army, Washington, DC, 1974.
15. *MCDP 4, Logistics*, U.S. Marine Corps Doctrinal Publication, HQ, U.S. Marine Corps, Washington, DC, 1997.

Notes

1. *Lifeblood of War—Logistics in Armed Conflict*, Julian Thompson, Biddles, Guildford, UK, 1991, p. 3.
2. Axelrod, Alan, *Patton on Leadership, Strategic Lessons for Corporate Warfare*, Prentice Hall, Paramus, NJ, 1999, p. x.

3. Huston, James A., *The Sinews of War: Army Logistics,* Center for Military History, U.S. Army, Washington, DC, 1966, p. 159.

4. *Field Manual 100-5, Operations,* U.S. Army, 1993, p. 12-2. Although *Field Manual 3-0, Operations,* superceded this manual in 2001, this statement is very true and accurate. Operators and logisticians, alike, often neglect the importance of logistics in making operations successful.

5. Ibid., pp. 12-3–12-5.

5a. Ibid.

6. Sonshi.com is a Web site dedicated to the study of Sun Tzu's *The Art of War.* The site can be found at http://www.sonshi.com. In addition to a fresh translation of Sun Tzu's work, the site also lists references to Sun Tzu in news articles. Recent articles include references to Sun Tzu in the *Christian Science Monitor* and the *Wharton Journal.* The *Wharton Journal* article by Hiranya Fernando, published on February 23, 2004, states, "We've all heard of Sun Tzu's *The Art of War* (well, you should have—it is required reading before joining any b-school program, much in the same vein as *Liar's Poker* or *Barbarians at the Gate*). Originally inscribed on bamboo strips around 500 BC, the Chinese military leader's advice in matters of war for emperors and generals has the strength of timeless wisdom. Today, subdue the enemy and win without fighting, know your battleground, maneuver to gain advantage, deceive your opponent, and always seek the high ground are part of the everyday vocabulary of corporate pop culture."

7. Sun Tzu is often quoted by leaders and *The Art of War* remains one of the most widely read theory books. Sun Tzu is taught in all upper echelon military schools.

8. Clavell, James, *The Art of War: The Essential Translations of the Classic Book of Life,* Bantam, New York, 1988.

9. Vick, Gailen, "Knowing the Difference Between SCM and RLM," Reverse Logistics Trends, Inc., 2003.

10. Donald W. Engels, *Alexander the Great and the Logistics of the Macedonian Army,* University of California Press, Berkeley, 1978, p. 12.

11. Ibid., p. 29.

12. Ibid., p. 71.

13. Thompson, Julian, *Lifeblood of War—Logistics in Armed Conflict,* Biddles, Guildford, U.K. 1991, p. 16.

14. Payson, Edward, "Nathaniel Greene and the Supply of the Continental Army," The Quartermaster Review, May–June 1950.

15. Huston, *Sinews of War,* p. 31.

16. Ibid., p. 31.

17. Ibid., p. 33.

18. Ibid., p. 35.

19. Ibid., p. 36.

20. Ibid., p. 28.

21. *Logistics in World War II—Final Report of the Army Service Forces,* Center of Military History, U.S. Government Printing Office, Washington, DC, 1948, p. viii.

22. Ibid., p. 24.

23. *Desert Warfare: German Experiences in World War II—Major General Alfred Toppe, 1952,* ed. The Combat Studies Institute at Command and General Staff College, Fort Leavenworth, KS, 1991, p. 16.
24. Ibid., p. 102.
25. Huston, James A., *Guns and Butter, Powder and Rice,* Selinsgrove, London, U.K. 1989, p. 130.
26. Van Creveld, Martin, *Supplying War, Logistics from Wallenstein to Patton,* Cambridge University Press, London, 1977, p. 214.
27. *Logistics in World War II—Final Report of the Army Service Forces,* p. 22.
28. Huston, *Sinews of War,* p. 24.
29. Ibid., p. 32.
30. Ibid., p. 158.
31. Ibid., p. 250.
32. Ibid., p. 169.
33. Ibid., p. 251.
34. Van Creveld, p. 221.
35. Schrader, Charles R., *Communist Logistics in the Korean War,* Greenwood Press, Westport, CT, 1995, p. 44.
36. Ibid., p. 134.
37. The Army conducted a thorough After Action Review of all of the actions that contributed to the horrible ambush of the 507th Maintenance Company in Nasariya to ensure that the same type of tragedy does not happen again.
38. Ibid., p. 40.
39. Huston, *Guns and Butter,* pp. 119–120.
40. Ibid., p. 128.
41. Heiser, Joseph M., Jr., *Vietnam Studies, Logistic Support,* Department of the Army, Washington, DC, 1974, p. iii.
42. Ibid., p. 4.
43. Ibid., p. 31.
44. Ibid., p. 59.
45. Ibid., p. 71.
46. Ibid., p. 60.
47. Ibid., p. 81.
48. Huston, *Guns and Butter,* p. 152.
49. *MCDP 4, Logistics,* U.S. Marine Corps Doctrinal Publication, HQ, U.S. Marine Corps, Washington, DC, 1997.
50. Ibid., p. 7.

Chapter 10

Conclusions

Regulation entails organizational effectiveness, a chain of command, and a structure for logistics support.

Chapter One, *The Art of War*, Sun Tzu

Over 2500 years ago, Sun Tzu wrote the words above. As we wrap up the topic of velocity management, think about the foresight of these words. To have organizational effectiveness, one must have a secure supply chain and know not only one's self, but the competition, the supply chain partners, and the needs of the customer. The chain of command is the leadership of an organization. In the military, the chain of command extends from the president of the United States down to the platoon leader and platoon sergeant. In commercial supply chains, the chain of command extends from the chief executive officer of the company all the way down to your first-line supervisors. Moreover, leadership is the key to organizational effectiveness. The great Vince Lombardi once told a crowd that the doctrine of command is leadership. Equating command and leadership makes it easier to understand the concept of the chain of command in a commercial supply chain.

Long before there was a chief logistics officer, long before anyone ever mentioned the word supply chain, Sun Tzu was writing about a structure for logistics support and the tie between logistics support and operational success. Today everyone knows the importance of logistics support for the success of an organization or an Army operation. Even your children understand the importance of supply chains and inventory levels. Let their favorite food item go to zero balance in the supply chain of your house and see how those customers react, especially if those customers are teenagers.

In April 2004, the U.S. Army published a pamphlet titled, "The New Paradigm: Bringing U.S. Army Logistics into the 21st Century." The pamphlet was republished as part of the Army's Torchbearer National Security Report. In the preface, retired General Gordon Sullivan stated, "Reactive logistics—the old logistics—will never be able to keep up with warfare as we know it." The same is true for commercial supply chains of the 21st century; if we are practicing reactive logistics we will not be able to meet the needs of the customer. And, if we don't meet the needs of the customer, someone else will. Reactive supply chains have long order cycle times and experience frequent stockouts, compounding the customers' frustrations. Velocity management supply chains rely on predictive support to have the right item in the right quantity at the exact time and place that the customer wants it.

"Connecting the logisticians is the linchpin of a distribution based logistics system coupled with an integrated supply chain that will have the speed and precision to support an expeditionary Army." This is just as true in your supply chain. The need to connect all the partners in your supply chain with speed and precision will provide the ability to support a demanding and educated customer. This need for speed and precision provides the impetus for the concept of velocity management.

Coupled with this concept is the need to secure those links, both the physical links and the informational links, to ensure an uninterrupted supply chain. Is security an issue for supply chains? Yes, and especially if you depend on products or materials coming in from overseas or have customers that are overseas waiting for your products. The 9/11 Commission Report states, "Opportunities to do harm are as great, or greater, in maritime or surface transportation. Initiatives to secure shipping containers have just begun."

An integrated, connected, end-to-end supply chain will enable you to see and determine the needs of the customer more quickly and thereby meet the needs in a shorter period, thus reducing customer wait times for products. To have an end-to-end supply chain, you have to have supply chain security.

In Section I, we looked at the need to assess the risks to your supply chain through a careful analysis of your operations. These risks are both internal to your supply chain and external to the supply chain, with the ability to disrupt your operations or at a minimum slow down your ability to meet the needs of your customers. Once the risks have been identified, a complete risk management program is necessary to eliminate or mitigate the impact of the risks. The risk assessment and risk management program provides the basis for establishing a security program for your supply chain.

When the World Trade Center was attacked on September 11, 2001, U.S. borders were closed and air travel shut down. With the help of the Internet and a worldwide network of suppliers, Dell Computers was able to identify where production would be disrupted for lack of supplies. It quickly ramped up production at its European and Asian plants and prioritized orders to fill the most important customers first. . . . Companies that lost thousands of computers in the attack were able to depend on Dell to deliver. In contrast, Compaq was unable to ship $300 million worth of orders due to supply chain disruptions.[1]

After September 11, 2001, securing your supply chain took on a whole new meaning. Country of Origin rules, the Customs–Trade Partnership Against Terrorism, and other programs from the Department of Homeland Security and the Customs and Border Patrol Agency make security a priority issue for everyone involved in supply chain operations. If you are doing business the same way you were on September 10, 2001, then you are way behind the power curve and may very well find that you have been left behind by your competitors.

Security is also a byproduct of supply chain visibility as demonstrated in the example of Dell Computers, above. Visibility provides the customer (internal and external) with a greater level of confidence in the system to provide the necessary goods and services. This increased confidence leads to fewer redundant orders and requests for order status, thus producing less excess in the supply chain and producing greater velocity in the entire supply chain. The lack of redundant orders placed in hopes that something comes in not only speeds up the forward supply chain but reduces the amount of stuff that enters the reverse supply chain, which also affects the velocity of the entire supply chain. The visibility system can be a very detailed system such as the FedEx online tracking system (examples of tracking are shown in Figures 10.1 and 10.2). Or the visibility system may be a simple e-mail stating that the item has shipped and providing the estimated delivery date. Visibility in the supply chain may come as a result of RFID tags that are read periodically as they pass through the supply system.

Just as visibility and security are related to the velocity with which an item moves through your supply chain, so is the quality of your training and professional development programs. The better trained your personnel are, the better they will be able to perform their jobs, and the better they perform their jobs, the faster the items will speed through your supply chain. It is not unlike a NASCAR pit crew. The faster the pit crew members perform their jobs, the faster the driver is able to return to the track and the faster the driver can finish the race—in front, we hope. What is trained should be a result of the processes detailed in Chapter 4, "Knowing

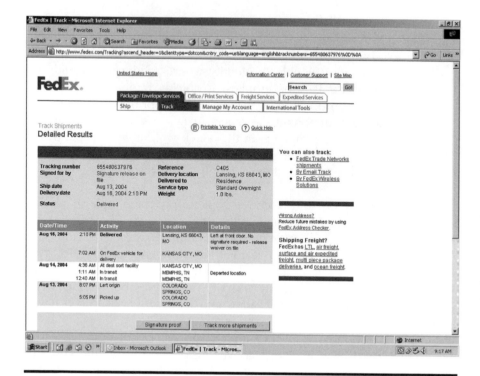

Figure 10.1   Example of tracking system report.

Yourself." The shortcomings identified by defining the problem, process mapping your supply chain, or as a result of the After Action Review process as discussed in Chapter 8, drive the topics and requirements of your professional development program.

Developing leaders with the attributes of world-class leadership as covered in the LEADERSHIP® discussion provides your organization with a pool of future leaders capable of providing direction and vision for your organization. In addition, this pool of future leaders provides for the long-term health of your company. The key to a successful company, regardless of its size, is the quality of the leadership. A great company can become an obsolete company as a result of poor leadership.

In addition to applications for the use of the After Action Review, there are some great lessons from past military operations that have applicability for today's supply chains. The most important lesson from past military operations is the criticality of including supply chain planning in the operational planning system. Other critical lessons that we can learn from military operations include the lessons from the North Korean Army to do whatever it takes to get the goods and services to the customer. Although you will probably never have to carry the supplies on your back

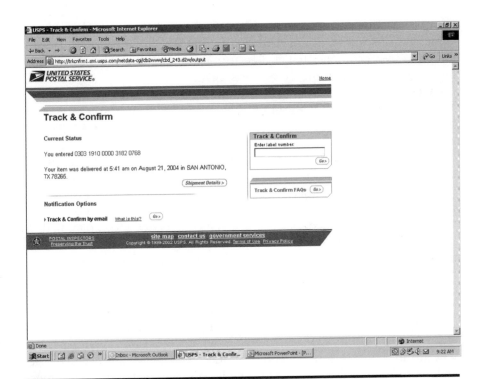

Figure 10.2   Another example of a tracking system report (from the U.S. Postal System Delivery Confirmation System).

over mountainous terrain in horrible climatic conditions, your business terrain and climate can be just as treacherous and the challenges to get the merchandise or materials to your customers can be just as great. The central themes in all of the military lessons are leadership, taking care of the employees, securing your supply chain, knowing what is in the inventory and what is in the entire supply chain, and providing the customer with that information to improve the customer's visibility and confidence in the system.

Regardless of where you are in the supply chain, reducing your supply chain cycle times is critical to the overall success of the chain. Increasing the velocity of the items moving through your supply chain will determine the overall success of your company and the success of your supply chain partners. To paraphrase Sun Tzu, supply chain operations are critical to the company. Moreover, velocity management is critical to your supply chain.

Reducing the supply chain cycle times contributes to reducing the total inventory in the supply chain. Reducing the inventory in the supply chain frees up capital for other projects or frees up capital to add different SKUs to your customer offerings. Other benefits of reducing inventory are the elimination of obsolete and damaged goods and the reduction of distribution center personnel travel time to pick orders. Reducing travel time increases velocity and the cycle starts again.

According to Thomas Craig in a webpronews.com article entitled "Cycle Time Reduction—Driver to Supply Chain Management Results," "Studies have shown that manufacturers and wholesalers have over 60 days of inventory and that retailers have over 90 days of inventory capital tied up. These times do not include the entire inbound inventory in the supply chain. Real supply chain inventory is likely 25% higher. This is a very significant amount of capital tied up in inventory."[2] Imagine how happy your boss will be when you apply the techniques of this book to your supply chain and reduce the excess inventory, reduce the capital tied up in inventory, and improve customer response times thereby improving customer satisfaction. A corollary benefit of reducing the response times is the corresponding reduction of the cash-to-cash cycle. You may not get to the negative 35 days that Dell enjoys, but a reduction in this cycle will put working capital back into the company faster.

The real key to improving the velocity and security of your supply chain is your people. Always remember, whatever business you may think you are in, you are in the people business and providing positive leadership and motivation for your employees will make the difference between a good and a great supply chain. Risk assessment, risk management, security, professional development, and velocity management all revolve around leadership and taking care of your employees.

If there are any questions, comments, or suggestions on the topics of this book, please feel free to contact me at joewalden@supplychainresearch.com.

Book List for Chapter Ten

1. Russell, Roberta S., and Taylor, Bernard W. III, *Operations Management,* Prentice Hall, Upper Saddle River, NJ, 2003.

Notes

1. Russell, Roberta S., and Taylor, Bernard W. III, *Operations Management,* Prentice-Hall, Upper Saddle River, NJ, 2003, p. 16.
2. Craig, Thomas, "Cycle Time Reduction—Driver to Supply Chain Management Results," webpronews.com, July 28, 2004.

Appendix 1

Bibliography

Aguayo, Rafael, *Dr. Deming—The American Who Taught the Japanese About Quality,* Simon & Schuster, New York, 1990.

APICS Dictionary, tenth edition, APICS—The Educational Society for Resource Management, Alexandria, VA, 2002.

Axelrod, Alan, *Nothing to Fear—Lessons in Leadership from FDR,* Penguin, New York, 2003.

Axelrod, Alan, *Patton on Leadership, Strategic Lessons for Corporate Warfare,* Prentice-Hall, Paramus, NJ, 1999.

Brauner, Marygail, et al., *Pricing Policies,* RAND, Santa Monica, CA, 2000.

Brown, H. Jackson, Jr., *The Complete Life's Little Instruction Book,* Rutledge Hill, Nashville, TN, 1997.

Clausewitz, Carl von, *On War,* Penguin, London, 1968.

Copeland, Thomas E. (ed.), *The Information Revolution and National Security,* Strategic Studies Institute, Carlisle Barracks, PA, 2000.

Desert Warfare: German Experiences in World War II—Major General Alfred Toppe, 1952, ed. The Combat Studies Institute at Command and General Staff College, Fort Leavenworth, KS, 1991.

D'Este, Carlo, *Eisenhower: A Soldier's Life,* Henry Holt, New York, 2002.

Dumond, John, Eden, Rick, and Folkeson, John R., *Velocity Management: An Approach for Improving the Responsiveness and Efficiency of Army Logistics Processes,* RAND, Santa Monica, CA, 1995.

Dumond, John, et al., *Velocity Management,* RAND Corporation, Santa Monica, CA, 2001.

Engels, Donald W., *Alexander the Great and the Logistics of the Macedonian Army,* University of California Press, Berkeley, 1978.

Field Manual 100-14, Risk Management, Department of the Army, Washington, DC, 2000.

Girardini, Kenneth, et al., *Establishing a Baseline and Reporting Performance for the Order and Ship Processes,* RAND, Santa Monica, CA, 1996.

Goldratt, Elihu, *The Theory of Constraints,* North River, Great Barrington, MA, 1990.

Heinrich, Claus, and Betts, Bob, *Adapt or Die,* Wiley, Hoboken, NJ, 2003.

Heiser, Joseph, *Logistic Support,* Department of the Army, Washington, DC, 1974.

Heiser, Joseph M., Jr., *Logistic Support Vietnam Series,* Center for Military History, U.S. Army, Washington, DC, 1974.

Huston, James A., *Guns and Butter, Powder and Rice,* Selinsgrove, London, 1989.

Huston, James A., *Guns and Butter, Powder and Rice: US Army Logistics in the Korean War,* Susquehanna University Press, Selinsgrove, PA, 1989.

Huston, James A., *The Sinews of War: Army Logistics 1775–1953,* Center for Military History, U.S. Army, Washington, DC, 1966.

Klein, Shelley, *The Most Evil Dictators in History,* Michael O'Mara, UK, 2004.

Kronenberg, Philip S., (ed.), *Planning U.S. Security: Defense Policy in the Eighties,* Pergamon, Elmsford, NY, 1981.

Logistics in World War II, Final Report of the Army Service Forces, Center for Military History, Washington, DC, 1948.

MCDP 4, Logistics, U.S. Marine Corps Doctrinal Publication, HQ, U.S. Marine Corps, Washington, DC, 1997.

Napolitano, Maida, *Making the Move to Crossdocking,* Warehousing Education and Research Council, Oak Brook, IL, 2000.

Pagonis, Gus, *Moving Mountains,* Harvard Business School Press, Boston, MA, 1992.

Pogue, Forrest C., *The Supreme Command,* Office of the Chief of Military History, Washington, DC, 1954.

Roberts, Harry V., and Sergesketter, Bernard R., *Quality Is Personal,* Free Press, New York, 1993.

Rogers, Dale, and Tibben-Lembke, Ronald, *Going Backwards,* University of Nevada, Reno, 1997.

Russell, Roberta S., and Taylor, Bernard W., *Operations Management,* 4th edition, Prentice Hall, Upper Saddle River, NJ, 2003.

Shrader, Charles, *Communist Logistics in the Korean War,* Greenwood Press, Westport, CT, 1995.

Sun Tzu, *The Art of War,* trans. Ralph D. Sawyer, Barnes & Noble, New York, 1994.

Thompson, Julian, *Lifeblood of War—Logistics in Armed Conflict,* Biddles, Guildford, UK, 1991.

Thorpe, George C., *Pure Logistics, The Science of War Preparation,* Franklin Hudson, Kansas City, MO, 1917.

Torre, Joe, *Ground Rules for Winners,* Hyperion, New York, 1999.

Training Circular 25-20, A Leader's Guide to After-Action Reviews, U.S. Army, Fort Leavenworth, KS, September 1993.

US Army Field Manual 3-19.30, Physical Security, U.S. Army, Washington, DC.

US Army Field Manual 3-0, Operations, U.S. Army, Fort Leavenworth, KS, 2001.

US Army Field Manual 3-90, Tactics, U.S. Army, Fort Leavenworth, KS, 2002.

US Army Field Manual 7-1, Battle Focused Training, U.S. Army Combined Arms Center, Fort Leavenworth, KS, 2003, available at www.rdtdl.army.mil.

US Army 2. Field Manual 7-1, Battle Focused Training, Department of the Army, Washington, DC, September 2003.

US Army Field Manual 22-100, Leadership, U.S. Army, Washington, DC, 1997.

US Army Field Manual 100-5, Operations, U.S. Army, Washington, DC, 1995.

US Army Field Manual 101-5-1, Operational Terms and Graphics, U.S. Army, Washington, DC, 1997.

US Army Regulation 530-1, Operations Security, Headquarters, Department of the Army, 1995.

US Army Training Circular 25-20, The After Action Review, U.S. Army Combined Arms Center, Fort Leavenworth, KS, available at www.rdtdl.army.mil.

United States Navy Supply Publication 529, Warehouse Modernization and Layout Planning Guide, U.S. Navy Supply Systems Command, 1985.

Utilizing the Six Steps to Six Sigma Participant Guide, Motorola University, 1997.

Van Creveld, Martin, *Supplying War, Logistics from Wallenstein to Patton,* Cambridge University Press, London, 1977.

Wademan, Daisy, *Remember Who You Are—Life Stories that Inspire the Heart and Mind,* Harvard Business School Press, Cambridge, MA, 2004.

Walden, Joseph L., *The Forklifts Have Nothing to Do! Lessons in Supply Chain Leadership,* iUniverse, Los Angeles, 2003.

Waltrip, Darrell, with Gurss, Jade, *DW—A Lifetime of Going around in Circles,* Putnam, New York, 2004.

Warfighting, U.S. Marine Corps, 1989.

Wavell, A.C.P, *Speaking Generally,* Cambridge Press, London, 1946.

WERCwatch, Warehousing Education and Research Council, Winter 2004. The Warehousing Education and Research Council puts out a monthly newsletter, *WERCsheet,* and a quarterly *WERCwatch.* Each of these publications contains valuable information on warehousing and distribution training topics.

Wooden, John, and Carty, Jay, *Coach Wooden One-on-One,* Regal, Ventura, CA, 2003.

Appendix 2

Warehouse Modernization and Layout Planning Guide

Department of the Navy
Naval Supply Systems Command
NAVSUP Publication 529
March 1985
0530-LP-529-0000

Warehouse Modernization and Layout Planning Guide

Applicable to functional concept planning for new facilities or modernization of existing facilities.

- Describes basic storage and material handling state-of-the-art system concepts.
- Provides modular layouts, system selection-design criteria, and comparative costs for self-help analysis of storage activities.
- Provides techniques for facility, inventory, product, and transaction data analysis to be used in developing preliminary alternative functional designs.
- Furnishes guidance for developing budgetary costs and final studies for which external assistance may be required.

A2.7 Facility Layout Requirements

A2.7.1 General

Facility layout determines the effectiveness with which the covered storage facility may be used. Included in the layout process is the arrangement of equipment, space, and activity within the facility. Although the location of the building on site and the effects of outside functions such as truck and employee parking areas are important, the primary effort is directed at the arrangement of departments within the building. The most important general consideration in facility layout involves the relationships of management and material flow.

Material flow relationships among receiving, storage, shipping, inspection, and other operations determine the relationship of these functions within the building.

The management relationship between functions is related to the operational control of functions and the grouping of operations to provide common management or supervisory control.

Other relationships also important in facility layout involve elements other than material flow. Typically, these relationships include employee health and safety, equipment, space, material, capital productivity, environmental protection, energy conservation, flexibility, employee morale, and labor relations. These other relationships, although not directly material or material-flow related, must be considered because they can have just as significant an impact on facility layout as any material-related operation.

A2.7.2 Material Flow

Analyzing material flow within a facility involves evaluating the relationships among the process functions, support service functions, and space. These relationships can be best analyzed by using an activity relationship chart (Figure A2.1). These charts are prepared by listing all the work areas involved in the facility. The chart is completed by filling in the intersecting rows with information describing the closeness relationship of the areas. The standard method of rating closeness uses the letters A, E, I, 0, U, and X to indicate the following characteristics.

- A—It is absolutely necessary that these areas be as close as possible to each other.
- E—It is especially important that these areas be as close as possible to each other. Areas rated with an E value may be separated if necessary to accommodate A areas.

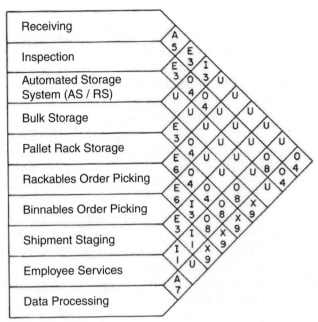

Reasons for Importance

1. Supervision
2. Safety
3. Material flow
4. Work flow
5. Material control
6. Equipment proximity
7. Shared space
8. Employee Health and Safety
9. Security

Proximity Importance

A. Absolutely necessary
E. Especially important
I. Important
O. Ordinary closeness
U. Unimportant
X. Undesirable

Figure A2.1 Typical activity relationship chart.

■ I—It is important that these areas be as close as possible to each other.
■ O—Ordinary closeness is satisfactory.
■ U—It is unimportant whether these areas are close or not.
■ X—It is undesirable that these areas be close to each other.

The closeness rating system is a priority structure in which each letter has priority over all letters below it. Therefore, areas sharing A values should be grouped before other letter combinations are considered. After

A values are grouped, then E value areas should be considered. When adjustments are necessary to area relationships, location changes are made based on the priority of closeness rating.

Supporting services can be handled in a similar manner and involve the same technique.

In addition to the letter closeness rating, priority values can also be included. These values can be in numerical ratings designating priority within a letter category and can be used in conjunction with the alphabetic closeness rating. Therefore, if two areas contending for space both have A values indicating an absolute necessity for closeness, but one area has an Al rating and the other has an A2 rating, the Al rating would be considered more important than the A2. It would receive priority for space assignment.

The determination of these relationships and the assignment of closeness ratings and closeness values is, in most cases, a subjective exercise subject to modification. The layout planner preparing such a relationship chart should consult with others involved in the project. This will ensure that everybody involved in the project will have input in determining the relative closeness range of each area.

A2.7.3 Material Movement

Material movement analysis involves the movement activity between areas and is related to, but independent of, the material flow and area relationships of operations. Material movement is generally evaluated using from–to charting, and proximity and flow density diagrams.

The process of from–to charting is similar to that used for preparation of area relationship diagrams. Instead of using closeness ratings, activity frequency figures are used to determine the relative activity rating between areas. This information may be similar to that developed in plotting area relationships but does not have to be related. This similarity is generally the case if two areas have a closeness rating of A (it is absolutely necessary that they be as close as possible). Usually these two areas will also have a high activity rate between them. This may not always be the case if other factors are responsible for the closeness rating. For example, it may be absolutely necessary that two areas be adjacent because they can share a common but very expensive environmental control system that would not be economically feasible to duplicate in two locations. These two areas may perform similar functions but on different materials and have absolutely no activity between them. Therefore, although they have an A rating for their area relationship, they would have no activity relationship in terms of material movement.

Activity From \ Activity To	Receiving	Inspection	AS / RS	Bulk Storage	Pallet Rack Storage	Rackables Order Picking	Binnables Order Picking	Shipment Staging	Employee Services	Data Processing	Total
Receiving	—	30	5	2	10						47
Inspection		—	15		8	3	4	3			33
AS / RS			—		7	4		9			20
Bulk Storage				—	1			1			2
Pallet Rack Storage					—		6	20			26
Rackables Order Picking						—	7	4	1	1	13
Binnables Order Picking							—	11			11
Shipment Staging	3							—			3
Employee Services									—		0
Data Processing										—	0
Total		33	20	2	26	13	11	48	1	1	155

Note:
Activity units expressed as frequency factor equal to units moved (pallets, pounds, cu. ft. etc.) times distance per move (usually feet).

Figure A2.2   Typical from–to activity table.

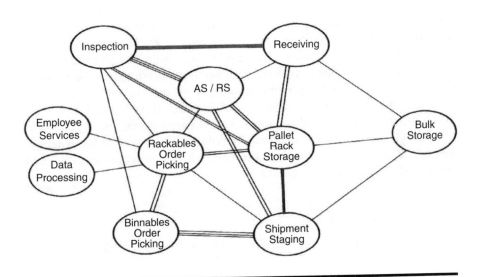

Figure A2.3   Typical activity/proximity flow diagram for warehouse design.

After a from–to activity chart is prepared that identifies the source and destination of transaction activity, a proximity diagram (Figure A2.2) and flow density diagram (Figure A2.3) can be prepared.

In a proximity diagram, designed to minimize travel distance, the emphasis is placed on minimizing the distance between areas having a high movement intensity. Once a satisfactory travel relationship is developed, the area relationship chart can be used to develop a space relationship.

A flow density diagram is used for identifying the high-activity material flow path. Its appearance and application are very similar to the proximity diagram.

A2.8 Manpower Requirements

Determination of the required staffing level for the facility is the last function to be performed in the analysis process. Staffing requirements are largely determined by the configuration of the facility, the functions to be performed, and a variety of management decisions that affect the nature and scope of work. All are necessarily related directly to adaptation of the materials handling system for physical inventory characteristics.

A2.8.1 Functions Performed

The quantity and nature of the work functions performed in day-to-day operations influence staffing levels. Estimates of required staffing levels can only be developed after a comprehensive listing of job functions is assembled. These consist of functions such as receiving check-in, truck unloading, inbound load accumulation, storage putaway, rewarehousing, order picking, order consolidation, truck loading, shipping order processing, information/paper work control, report preparation, and so forth. All functions important to the materials handling system should be evaluated and listed. A short description of the nature of the function and the work content should also be prepared.

A2.8.2 Activity Level

After job categories have been defined by function, projected activity levels based on basic data material handling requirements can be applied. Values of time needed to perform individual work functions at a given activity level must be assembled. These time values generally consist of composite standards that make allowances for unknowns and variables in work patterns. Detailed time and motion standards are generally not appropriate for the usual warehouse functions since work flow and activity levels are not consistent and introduce a variety of unknown or uncontrollable variations.

After assembling a list of required work functions and applying the expected activity level and time standards for each function, a preliminary estimate of man-hour staffing levels can be developed.

A2.8.3 Supervision

Worker supervision must also be considered when establishing staffing levels. The nature of the operation must be reviewed to determine the amount of supervision needed to perform the function properly. Some work functions may require high levels of supervision due to the critical or complex nature of the task. Other warehousing functions can be performed with a minimum of supervisory intervention. The number of supervisory personnel is determined by a combination of work function, activity, and facility operation requirement.

A2.8.4 Single Versus Multi-Shift Operations

Staffing and supervision levels can be affected by the choice of single-shift or multi-shift operations. Although the total man-hours required to perform specified job functions at a given activity level remain the same, the scheduling of these work functions and the amount of supervision required will vary, depending on whether the system is designed for single-shift or multi-shift operations. Multi-shift operations may require additional supervisory personnel, but in a single-shift operation additional workers can be added to the staff without necessarily increasing the number of supervisory personnel. When additional shifts are added to an operation, a full complement of supervisory people will be needed for each shift added, thus increasing the cost of supervision relative to the job functions performed. Multi-shift operations have an advantage in reducing the amount of materials handling equipment required to perform a given function since the same activity level is now spread over a longer time period. Therefore, the peak activity rates are reduced unless more equipment is required.

A2.8.5 Operational Variations

After additional staffing requirements are developed based on job function, activity rate, and supervisory allocation, operational variations must be considered. Operational variations include factors such as the frequent occurrence of peak loads requiring additional workers, the need to provide permanent additional capacity beyond projected requirements or service emergency needs, seasonal variations and work loads, and allowances for

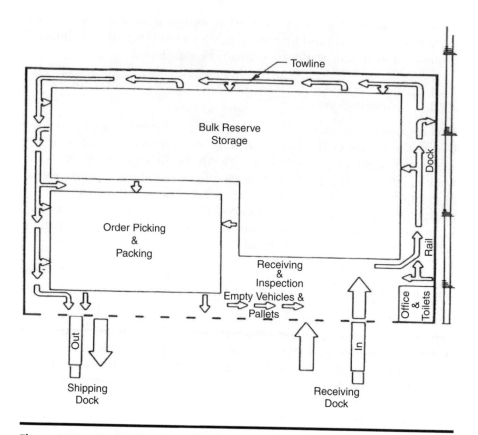

Figure A2.4 Conventional warehouse cyclic flow pattern.

sickness and vacation relief personnel. Operational variations must be considered on a case-by-case basis. Solutions depend on the mission of the facility and the characteristics of its work patterns.

Examples of Distribution Center/Warehouse Flows

The examples of warehouse/distribution center flows from Navy Supply Publication 529 (Figures A2.4 through A2.6) are shown as examples of how to establish logical flows in your warehouse/center.

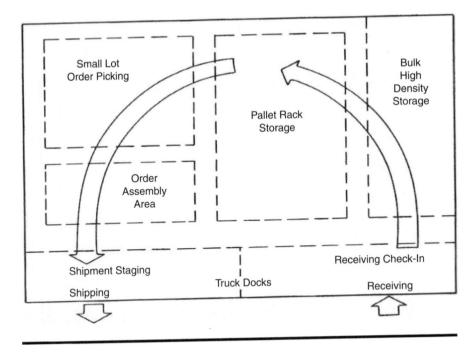

Figure A2.5 Typical cyclic flow pattern.

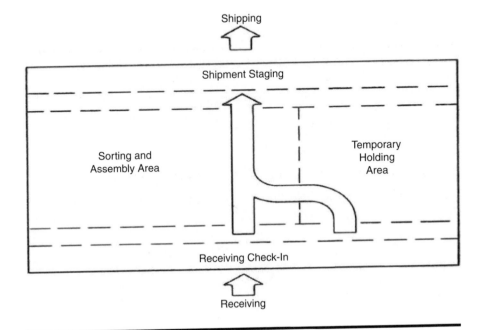

Figure A2.6 Typical straight line flow pattern.

Appendix 3

Forms and Checklists

The After Action Review Preparation Checklist

_____ Take notes during the operation or process

_____ What materials do I need? Are they organized in a logical manner to tell the story?

_____ Audio-visuals?

_____ Outline of After Action Review in logical sequence of events

     _____ What is the task being reviewed?

     _____ Materials needed to conduct the review

     _____ Purpose/ground rules/training objective

     _____ What went right and how to sustain

     _____ What did not go according to the plan, how to correct

     _____ How can we do things differently?

          (get all participants involved)

     _____ Summary

     _____ Actions based on the After Action Review

Keys to Success:

1. Participants do most of the talking.
2. Majority of participants are involved and participate.
3. Moderator uses pointed questions, not to put the participant on the spot but to stimulate thinking on how to do better the next time.

4. Use diagrams and visual aids to emphasize points.
5. Keep the discussion on track. Do not let the participants lose their focus on the issues at hand.
6. Ensure that the suggestions on what to do differently the next time are congruent with company standards and values.
7. *Do not fix blame;* find out what happened and how to fix it or how to sustain what went well. This is critical to the success of future After Action Reviews.

Checklist for Distribution Center Design

After using the Military Decision-Making Process model discussed in the previous appendix to determine if a new distribution center is actually needed, the following checklist and criteria can and should be used to design the new distribution center.

1. Where should the new center be located? Should the center be located closer to the customer, the manufacturing plant, or the suppliers? The purpose of a distribution center is to provide more responsive support to the customer. That being the case, determine where your customer base is or will be and that is where the distribution center needs to be. Select a location that will enable you to better serve the largest number of customers. Also important in the location selection is the proximity to a good road, rail, and air network. These three criteria explain the popularity of the Ontario/Fontana, California, location for major distribution centers. How many customers can you reach with same-day or next-day delivery?

2. Select a site that will provide the flexibility for expansion of operations in the future. If your center site does not provide this expansion flexibility, you may very well find yourself having to build a new facility again in the near future.

3. Do you need a consultant to assist with the design of the facility? Does the company you are working with have a good background in facility design? What is their experience in working in a distribution center? This is important because some companies are very good at coming up with concepts that look good on paper but do not actually work in practice. However, if they have experience in actually working in a distribution center, they will know what may not work in practice and be able to better assist you in designing a world-class facility. What is their background in applying best practices?

4. Assemble a project team to design, build, and equip the new facility. This team should have enough background and knowledge to analyze the automation requirements for the facility. Do you need a new warehouse management system to help manage the new facility? Does your project team have the knowledge of WMS to select the best system? Do you need any other technologies in your new facility?

5. What will be the flow in your new facility? This will drive the layout of the center and may very well have an impact on the necessary square footage for the new center.

6. What is your plan for moving into the new center? When Grainger moved to a new facility in Mira Loma, California, they stocked the new center and then carefully drew down the stocks at the old center until they were ready to go "live" at the new center. The best way to make the transition to the new center is a phased approach similar to the Grainger approach. This requires having to maintain two facilities for a period of time but prevents disruptions to customer support. If this approach is taken, you have to set a firm date for all customer support to come from the new facility.

7. You have to establish a good training and testing period to ensure that your employees and the systems are ready on opening day. You have to establish a viable training plan for your new employees.

8. What is your slotting plan? Are you going to slot according to size, similarity of product, or velocity of use? Slotting according to size is necessary with some large bulky items, liquids stored in drums, or items that are small in size. Are you slotting for pallet picks, case picks, or eaches? These decisions will have an impact on your design and layout.

9. What is your sortation plan? The large Defense Distribution Centers sort the items by military unit designators but then consolidate shipments for multiple customers if there are not enough supplies to fill a shipping container. How do you plan to sort your items?

10. What are your lift requirements? Do you need to plan aisles for wide forklift trucks or will you try to maximize space and use narrow sidelift trucks? How heavy are the loads that you need to lift and how high are the storage areas?

11. Are you planning on having a paperless distribution center based on your automation or will you need a large area for printing pick tickets and manifests?

12. What value-added services are you going to provide to your customers? What is the space requirement necessary to provide these services? What is the cost to add this space to your new center?

Checklist for Distribution Center Layout

1. *Cross-docking.* If you are planning on conducting real cross-docking, not as I have seen in so many distribution centers where cross-docking is by accident or miracle, you need to plan for an area convenient to the inbound/receiving docks and the outbound/shipping docks.

2. *Picking considerations.* The most efficient layout provides a logical flow for workers in the picking process and reduces the amount of travel time by the pickers.

3. *Receiving doors/docks.* How many will you need? You have to know what your maximum load will be at the receiving dock.

4. *Bulk storage.* Where do you put the bulk storage and how much do you need? It is recommended that the bulk storage be close to the picking area but not in such a location that it impedes the flow of supplies in the distribution center. If at all possible, place the bulk storage over the pick location. If this is not possible, place the bulk storage for all items in a separate part of the distribution center.

5. *Backup stocks/safety stocks.* Do you really need safety stocks for all items in your distribution center? Absolutely not, and you do not need the same level of safety stock for every critical item for which you decide to have safety stock.

6. *Shipping docks.* The shipping docks need to be close to the pick-and-pack areas and should have easy access to the cross-docking area. The flow through the center should be designed to allow for receiving and shipping in separate areas to reduce clutter but enable efficient operations. Ideally, the shipping docks are on the opposite side of the center from the receiving docks.

7. *Product flow.* This is one of the most critical aspects of distribution center layout and design. How will the product flow through your distribution center or warehouse? I have seen more than one distribution center that insisted on having the aisles run east–west and the receiving and shipping docks face north–south. This layout meant that the workers had to go to the far ends of the aisles to enter the aisles for stocking and picking activities. The design of the distribution center should consider a product flow that minimizes travel for the worker and minimizes the number of times that an item is touched after picking before loading on the outgoing truck.

8. *Use of conveyors.* In larger centers the use of conveyors is almost a necessity. Ensure that the conveyers do not create a safety hazard. One major distribution center in the Midwest continues to operate

a conveyer and trolley system, although no supplies are placed on these systems because of safety concerns. If you determine that a system is no longer needed, get rid of it. *Modern Materials Handling* magazine and the Materials Handling and Management Society (http://www.mhia.org) provide excellent insights into conveyor planning and operations.

9. *Consolidation of orders/staging areas.* The location of these functions depends on the decisions made on product flow. In order to minimize shipping costs and maximize transportation assets, orders for customers should be consolidated prior to moving them to the staging area. Once items are in a staging area awaiting loading, they should be considered in a "sterile area" and should not be touched again until loaded on the outgoing truck. I have found it beneficial to establish staging areas that coincide with the size of the vehicles being loaded.

10. *Vehicle flow pattern.* One of the biggest problems overlooked in many distribution center designs is the flow of the trucks into and out of the distribution center. When laying out the design for the distribution center, regardless of the size of the center, you have to consider traffic flow at the inbound docks and the outbound docks. The only time this is not a consideration is when the inbound and outbound docks are the same. In this case, the consideration turns to scheduling to ensure that you are not shipping and receiving at the same times.

Appendix 4

The Military Decision-Making Process— A User's Guide

This appendix contains an updated version of a previously published work on the use of the Military Decision-Making Process.

The military uses a set methodology for planning operations. Military planners used this methodology to plan for Desert Storm and more recently for Operation Enduring Freedom and Operation Iraqi Freedom. This appendix looks at uses for this methodology in solving supply chain problems.

There are many methods of solving problems and developing plans for improvements. One such method is the Military Decision-Making Process. This is a multi-step process that provides leaders at all levels the ability to carefully analyze the situation and come to a logical decision on a course of action or an alternative. Even within the military, there is confusion on the Decision-Making Process model. This model does not make the decision for you; it is a tool to guide the user in making the logical decision. In supply chains, the wrong decision can be the difference in profits or losses; in the military, the wrong decision can be the difference between life and death. In business, too many wrong decisions can lead to the death of the company.

This appendix provides the background of the Military Decision-Making Process and the steps involved in leading to a logical decision. Not only does this appendix show you some applications of this model to supply chain situations, but it also offers an example of how the model can be applied to personal situations, as well.

There are a number of problem-solving methods available to today's supply chain practitioner. Corporate employees use some of these on a daily basis in the performance of their jobs. Among the most popular techniques are the Theory of Constraints and Six Sigma[1] methodologies (for more on Six Sigma, please see Chapter 5). Another very popular problem-solving method in some organizations is to do nothing and hope the problem will go away. Most of the companies that adopt the do-nothing methodology end up doing nothing because the company goes out of business.

The Military Decision-Making Process model is an analytical model that assists the user in knowing if a decision is necessary. The model will then guide the user as to when and what the decision should be. The model uses a logical sequence of steps to guide the user through this process.

Before delving into the model itself, it is prudent to define decision making. *U.S. Army Field Manual 101-5, Staff Operations*, states, "Decisions are the means by which the commander translates his vision of the end state into action."[2] The *American Heritage Dictionary* defines a decision as: "The act of reaching a conclusion or making up one's mind."[3] The Military Decision-Making Process will not make up one's mind; it will assist in reaching a logical decision. The key to the success of applying the Military Decision-Making Process model is that it develops the leader in how to think and not what to think.

The Military Decision-Making Process helps leaders to examine a situation and reach logical decisions. It assists the leader by allowing the leader to apply thoroughness, clarity, sound judgment, logic, and professional knowledge to reach a decision. The model is a detailed, deliberate, and sequential process when time allows. When time is critical as it sometimes is in war, as well as in making supply chain decisions, an abbreviated version of the model can be used. Some of the advantages of this model over other methodologies for problem solving are:

- The model analyzes and compares multiple courses of action to identify the best possible action.
- The model produces integration, coordination, and synchronization for an operation.
- The model minimizes overlooking critical aspects by looking at multiple actions and reactions.
- When followed, the Military Decision-Making Process model results in a detailed plan and provides a common framework that enables parallel planning at multiple echelons.

The steps of the Military Decision-Making Process as applied to supply chain problem solving are:

- Receipt of the mission
- Mission analysis
- Course of action development
- Course of action analysis
- Course of action comparison
- Course of action approval
- Orders production

The first step in the process is the receipt of the mission or identification of the problem. This requires determining exactly what is expected or what is not going as planned if identifying a problem. This may come from corporate or from another source of information. Once the mission has been received or the problem identified, an initial assessment of the situation is necessary to determine the guidance that will be passed to subordinates for action and analysis. In the military, the initial assessment results in the commander's initial guidance. This may include additional tasks that must be performed in order to complete the mission or additional areas to look at to determine the true nature of the problem.

The second step in the process is the mission analysis. This is where the staff kicks into high gear. What does the boss really need to know? What is the intent of the higher headquarters and what do they really expect of us in this situation? How does this problem or mission influence my area of responsibility? Each area of the staff should be working both independently on their area of expertise and jointly with the other staff to ensure that any impact in one area is fully understood by the other staff members. The steps in the mission analysis phase are:

- Analyze the higher headquarters' order or the problem identified. Determine the specified, implied, and essential tasks. What was specifically in the higher headquarters' order for us to do? What is implied that needs to be done in order to meet the mission requirements or solve the problem that has been identified? Which tasks are essential to completion of the mission or solving the problem?
- Review available assets to accomplish the mission or solve the problem. Here is where the "troop-to-task" analysis is important. Are there sufficient workers? Is there enough equipment and supplies?
- Determine the constraints that limit the ability to successfully solve the problem or complete the mission.

■ Identify the critical facts and assumptions. For this discussion, facts are statements of known data and assets available for the mission. Assumptions replace necessary but missing or unknown facts.

Assumptions must pass two tests. The first is the validity test. Will this situation still exist when the plan becomes an order? The second is the necessity test. Is this assumption essential to the solution of the problem? Moreover, will the results of the plan change if we do not make this assumption?

The next step in the decision-making model is the course-of-action development. What are the options for action? Always keep in mind that one potential course of action is to do nothing and hope the problem will go away. This is not usually a viable course of action and could very well be the reason the problem existed to begin with.

During this phase, the following actions take place: analysis of your capabilities, the generation of options, the development of the scheme of operations, and assigning responsibility for actions. The courses of action that are developed in this phase must meet the following criteria to be considered in subsequent phases of the decision-making model.

■ *Suitability*—does the course of action accomplish the mission and comply with the commander's guidance?
■ *Feasibility*—does the unit or firm have the capability to accomplish the mission in terms of time, space, and resources?
■ *Acceptability*—does the cost justify the gain?
■ *Distinguishability*—does this course of action significantly differ from other courses of action?
■ *Completeness*—does this course of action answer the questions of who, what, when, where, how, and why?

The next step in the model is the course-of-action analysis. During this phase of the model is where the concept of "war-gaming" is applied. Staff officers must anticipate events and what the reactions may be to each action taken. During this war-gaming it is imperative that the participants remain objective and not become attached to a particular action or course of action. During the analysis if any of the courses of action do not pass the feasibility, acceptability, or suitability tests, reject that course of action. You do not make comparisons between courses of action during this phase. The purpose of this phase is to record all strengths and weaknesses for each course of action.

After analyzing each course of action, it is time to start the course-of-action comparisons. During this phase of the decision-making model the following actions take place.

- Analyze and evaluate each course of action.
- Highlight the advantages and disadvantages for each course of action.
- Determine which action has the highest probability of success.
- Determine which action poses the minimum risk.
- Ascertain which action best positions the force for future operations.

After analyzing and comparing all of the courses of action, the commander (boss/leader) has the necessary information before him or her to make a logical decision and issue the orders for implementation.

As with any methodology, there are criticisms and benefits. The criticisms of the Military Decision-Making Process include that it is too rigid, and that it is time-consuming, too deliberate, and too resource intensive. This process tends to err on the side of caution—the primary reason being that if a course of action does not work for the military, there will be undue loss of lives. Although the Army does not really consider the financial impacts to the bottom line, the unnecessary loss of lives is too important to risk with faulty analysis and course-of-action development. In business, the lack of careful analysis and comparison of courses of action may well result in the loss of a business.

This same model used constantly by the military to plan operations can be applied to various supply chain problems such as deciding on the location of a new distribution center, or even if a new distribution center is necessary. The model can be used to determine if a new warehousing management system is necessary and if so, which one. Another potential use of this model for supply chains is the selection of a third-party provider or keeping the function in-house.

Whatever the application, the Military Decision-Making Process model provides the user with a simple-to-use, easy-to-understand model that has multiple applications to supply chain management. The Military Decision-Making Process is also useful to solve personal problems such as where to go on vacation this year to meet the needs of everyone in the family. The model will not make the decision for you, but it will guide you to making a logical decision if you follow the steps and answer the questions for each step in an unbiased manner.

Let us look at how to use the model to determine the location or need for a new distribution center.

- *Receipt of the mission*—This is determined to be guidance from the boss to look at the capability of the current distribution center to meet the needs of growth and customer support.

- *Mission analysis*—What is the implied mission and the stated mission? Does the boss want a new distribution center, a larger distribution center, or does he or she want us to look at outsourcing the operations altogether?
- *Course-of-action development*—What are the feasible, suitable, and acceptable courses of action? The possible courses of action based on what we have from the boss could include:
  - Do nothing—This is the status quo, tell the boss that the current center will work and drive on. This may not meet the intent of what the boss is looking for and will take a good deal of data to back it up.
  - Build a new distribution center—Grainger chose this option in Mira Loma, California. Their rationale was that by building a new facility, they could design it to meet their needs and growth plans. This is the same decision that Target reached in their plan to increase the number of distribution centers rather than expand the old ones.
  - Take over an old/abandoned distribution center—Amazon.com chose this option for their Kansas distribution center. Amazingly, this option is not always the preferred one. This is evident by the "new" state-of-the-art facility in Hesperia, California. In 1997, Heilig-Myers built a new facility in Hesperia, only to go bankrupt and out of business within two years. This left the new facility vacant in close proximity to several major transportation corridors. As of this writing, that facility is still vacant.
  - Outsource to a third-party logistics provider (3PL)—This is a popular option when companies realize that storage and distribution are not among their core competencies.
  - Expand the current distribution center in size and/or in technology—This option could include actual construction to the facility, implementing new technologies to expedite the flow of material through the center, or adding a mezzanine to increase the storage capability.
- *Course-of-action analysis*—What is the most feasible, suitable, and acceptable solution? This analysis could be as simple as constructing a matrix of the important criteria to meet the intent of the boss.
- *Course-of-action comparison*—Determine which of the courses of action meet the boss's intent and meet the majority (preferably all) of the identified success criteria.
- *Course-of-action approval*—This step involves your marketing plan to the boss to get his or her approval and decision on the best course of action.

Some Additional Decision-Making Checks and Balances

Decision-Making Checks:

1. Sanity check—Does this decision make sense?
2. Dignity check—Will the decision enhance the reputation and dignity of the organization and leadership or undermine it?
3. Systems check—Is the decision internally coherent and consistent with the goals of the organization?
4. 60 Minutes/CNN/Washington Post check—How will the decision appear when written up by a media critic. This is why the Army spends a great amount of time teaching soldiers and leaders how to respond to the media. This training is not about what to say when talking to the media but how to say it and how to respond to the questions of the press.
5. Safety check—What is the impact on the physical or psychological safety of employees and customers?
6. Strategy check—Conduct objective strategy check of competition and customers.
7. Integrity check—The means and ends of decision goals, this check can be a very effective deterrent against employee dishonest behavior.

Notes

1. Six Sigma is a methodology first used by Motorola to improve their quality. The literal application of Six Sigma is striving toward no more than 3.2 errors per one million transactions or items produced.
2. *US Army Field Manual 101-5, Staff Operations.*
3. *American Heritage College Dictionary*, Houghton Mifflin, Boston, 1997, p. 359.

Appendix 5

World-Class Distribution Center Qualities and Attributes

In this appendix, we look at those qualities that make a distribution center world class. We look at 18 qualities or attributes. Your distribution center or warehouse does not need to meet every one of these attributes. However, the more of them that you do meet, the better the service you can provide to your customer. The better you meet the needs of the customer, the better your chances of increasing your customer base.

The first attribute is *inventory accuracy*. The Army used to have a standard of 90-percent accuracy as the measure of a quality warehouse. Why is this not a good measure of efficiency in a warehouse? In the private sector, 90-percent inventory accuracy means at least a 10-percent unplanned stockout. Unless you are stocking to 100 percent of your customers' demands, this 10-percent unplanned stockout is probably the little extra frustration that will lead your customers to your competition. In the military, such low inventory accuracy could be the difference between the life and death of a soldier. In addition to the customer frustration, you need to calculate the financial shortfall from not having 10 percent of your valuable inventory on the shelf. *The inventory accuracy standard for world class is 100 percent.*

The next attribute is *perfect order fulfillment*. This relates to inventory accuracy and to stocking the right items on the shelf. Perfect order fulfillment is a combination of having the right items in the distribution center and picking and packing the right quantity to meet the customer demand. Again, just like inventory accuracy the standard is 100 percent.

Value-added services. What services beyond just picking and packing are you providing your customers? Are they asking for custom shipping labels, or custom packaging? Are you providing it for them? If you are not, I can assure you that someone else will and your customer will walk.

Distribution center cleanliness. Every world-class distribution center and warehouse that I have been in was a clean distribution center. You can tell the centers in which the employees have pride. In these distribution centers when a worker sees trash on the floor, he or she goes out of the way to pick it up. Cleanliness also includes the location maintenance. How well are the storage locations maintained? Is there a worker responsible for each location?

Cleanliness and location maintenance ties to location accuracy. Location accuracy ties to inventory accuracy, which ties to customer fill rates and customer satisfaction. One tip for improving location cleanliness and maintenance is to assign a worker or team of workers to each aisle and put their name(s) on the end of the aisle along with the location and inventory accuracy for the aisle. Not only will this build worker esteem and pride, but it will also build a little internal competition for the best accuracy rates.

Time-definite delivery. Do you provide this to your customers? Do your suppliers provide it to you? Knowing when the deliveries will arrive (this may even be linked to advanced shipping notification) allows the distribution center manager to plan the workforce around the delivery schedules. This planning ensures that the maximum workforce is available to unload incoming deliveries and load outgoing deliveries. One center in Virginia that works with a major tobacco company not only knows exactly when to expect a delivery, it also knows if the truck is late based on its tracking systems and time-definite delivery schedule.

On-time deliveries. This one ties to time-definite deliveries but focuses on our deliveries to our customers. Are the trucks leaving our docks arriving to the customer as promised? Are we providing our customers with time-definite deliveries? If our trucks are not arriving as promised, do we know why? We had this problem at the National Training Center for a while. When we walked the process, we found that the times we expected the trucks and the delivery times provided to the drivers were different.

Logical warehouse/distribution center flow. Do the supplies flow through your center in a logical manner? Most warehouses do not have a logical flow from receiving to storage locations or from receiving to customer staging locations or customer bins (if the customer picks up from the warehouse). Not having a logical flow of material through the warehouse results in additional "touches" or handling of the material more times than necessary. Additional handling can lead to lost or damaged items and contributes to additional waste of movement within the warehouse itself. The less an item moves in the warehouse, the quicker it is where it is supposed to be and ready for issue.

Employee education systems. Toyota spent over $50 million to develop the University of Toyota to educate its employees. Employees in their Ontario, California, distribution center are required to have 80 hours of training a year. That is a strong commitment to employee education. Technology in supply chain management has advanced rapidly over the past decade. If we do not keep our employees trained and up to date, how can we expect to compete with the companies that do, such as Toyota? Employee education is not optional in today's business environment.

Safety. This is critical to retaining quality employees. If you do not provide your employees with a safe work environment, they will leave or worse, suffer a serious injury. If the employees do not feel safe, their productivity will suffer, leading to a decrease in customer support and responsiveness. This will lead to a decrease in customers. A decrease in customers will eventually lead to the death of the company. This is the responsibility of leaders at all levels to ensure that workers feel safe in the workplace.

Layout. The majority of a warehouse worker's time is spent in traveling to a location to pick an order. Many of the warehouses and distribution centers that I have visited have the workers walking past locations of obsolete stocks to get to the locations of the active stocks. Fast-moving stocks are scattered throughout the warehouse, resulting in additional wasted movement for the workers. A good layout will place like ordered items close together, and fast-moving items closest to the customer locations or staging lanes and in the ergonomic reach of the workers. Just as most warehouses use a form of A-B-C analysis for inventory frequency, warehouses and distribution centers could benefit from using an A-B-C analysis to identify fast-moving items for locating closer to traffic areas.

Obsolete stocks. While you are rewarehousing to get the fast-movers closer to the customer area or traffic areas, move the obsolete items out of the warehouse. What value do they add to your operation? More than a few managers have expressed concern over this comment because they "may need the item someday." If the item has not moved in a year, the chances are good that the item is of no value to you. If the item is of no value to you or your customer, it is costing you money to maintain it on your shelves.

Turns. When the Army started looking at inventory turns as part of the velocity management program, the average number of turns for repair parts was less than three per year. Three turns per year is obviously not even close to world class. Dell, on the other hand, has at last report more than 60 turns per year. That may be a bit too far to reach but anything less than 12 to 15 turns per year may be an indicator that you are stocking either the wrong stuff or in the wrong quantity. You do not make money if the parts are not moving.

Processing times. One major operation that I visited a couple of years ago was proud of the fact that they met their goals for dock-to-stock times. Our questioning of their goals revealed that their standards included three days to clear the dock and move the stocks to the functional areas of the warehouse and then three more days to have the stocks in the proper locations. This totals six days from truck to dock to stock. That is a lot of inventory that is not available for sale, not to mention that if the items are receipted but not on the shelf, you will never have good inventory accuracy. The standard for world class has to be to clear the floor of today's work *today* regardless if this means processing the material or processing today's pick tickets today. Depending on the time buckets that your system measures, you should be able to apply a pit crew mentality to unloading a shipment and have it in the proper location in a matter of hours. World-class distribution centers establish goals for orders picked per day per worker or per picking team.

Cross-docking by design—not by miracle. For most distribution centers cross-docking occurs as a miracle or because of a late shipment arriving just as the truck is ready to leave the dock. For world-class centers cross-docking is by design and areas are set aside for cross-docking of important orders and critical materials. During the first two weeks of operations of the Theater Distribution Center in Kuwait, the few cross-docking operations were indeed a miracle, even though the center was designed as a cross-docking operation. After a few weeks of operations, the frequencies of cross-docking improved because of careful attention to detail and leadership. Cross-docking enables the distribution center personnel to handle items once as opposed to multiple times.

Process flow charts. World-class distribution centers have detailed process flow charts of the operations and post the charts for employee reference and guides. One of the requirements of ISO 9000 certification and competing for the Malcolm Baldrige Quality Award is a detailed process flow chart. Just as important as developing the chart is following and applying diagrams on the charts. Process flow charts serve multiple purposes. They enable workers to quickly refer to the charts if in doubt as to what is the next action in the process, and the charts serve as a great tool for educating new employees on the processes of the distribution center.

Employee involvement. Getting employees involved in streamlining processes and solving problems is usually the best method of identifying problems and solutions. This is because the person doing the job is usually the subject matter expert in that particular process. Moreover, getting the employee involved in the solution gets the buy-in of the employee as part of the solution and gets a stronger commitment to improving the process.

Performance-based standards. The measures of effectiveness of a world-class distribution center are performance based. More important, the standards have to be perceived as achievable by the person being measured. Performance-based measurements include orders picked per hour/day, shipments per worker per day, on-time delivery, and the previously discussed perfect order fulfillment.

Warehouse-in-a-warehouse concept. This attribute of world-class distribution centers is a method of organizing the warehouse to reduce transit time in the distribution center or warehouse. The warehouse in a warehouse could be as simple as stocking all the parts for one particular model of equipment in one general area. The tool section at Lowe's and The Home Depot is an example of a warehouse in a warehouse. All of the tools are stored in one central location to control and consolidate the tools in the store. Stocking all of the service items in one location is another example of a warehouse in a warehouse. Using this concept improves response times to customers, reduces transit times in the warehouse, and contributes to improved inventory accuracy.

Appendix 6

Counseling Checklist

The Army has an established doctrine and guidelines for the counseling of subordinates. The success of any professional development program for new employees or employees that we want to promote up the ladder is dependent on the quality of the counseling we provide those employees to assist them with their personal professional development. Figure A6.1 is from a presentation that I make on a regular basis to future commanders on how to better counsel and develop their young officers and noncommissioned officers. Before we take a closer look at each one of the points in the figure, we need to establish the types of counseling necessary to develop employees and leaders.

The form of counseling that most people associate with the term counseling is adverse. Unfortunately, as we mentioned, the only time an employee gets counseled is when something goes wrong: this is commonly

---

Counseling

- When
- How often
- Where
- Formal vs. Informal
- Action Plans/Improvement

Figure A6.1

known as "getting written up." There are other forms of counseling. Professional development counseling is a requirement in the Army for all young officers to make sure that they are learning the areas of leadership and their chosen skill necessary for promotion and success. Another form of counseling is more teaching and discussing than counseling and is lacking in many organizations. In this form of counseling you are really conducting one-on-one teaching with the employee. The other common form of counseling is performance appraisal counseling. If you are doing the other forms of counseling on a regular basis, there should be no surprises at the performance appraisal counseling.

Having established the types of counseling necessary to develop employees, now we need to look at the specifics of counseling.

1. When and how often should you counsel your employees? Unfortunately for most employees, the only times that the boss or supervisor talks to them is either when they screw up or right before their annual performance appraisal. The Army's policy is that every soldier will be counseled by his or her immediate supervisor at a minimum at the start of a performance period or the start of a new job, every quarter after the initial counseling, and then again at the time of the performance appraisal. For civilian Department of the Army employees the counseling requirements are a little looser. A Department of the Army civilian employee has to be counseled on his or her performance plan at the start of a new job or the start of the annual appraisal period, at the midpoint of the year, and then again before receiving a performance appraisal. Is every three to six months often enough to develop employees? If the employee is a senior employee or long-time employee of the firm, every three months may be enough. For newer employees once a month may not be often enough to prevent them from forming bad habits on the job. Every counseling plan has to be individual in nature; there is no one-size-fits-all method or timeline for counseling and developing employees.

2. Where should the counseling sessions take place? If you are conducting performance appraisal counseling or counseling to correct an adverse situation, the counseling session needs to be conducted behind closed doors without any interruptions or distractions. Counseling of this nature needs to be in writing and documented. This is especially important if the condition continues and you need to take action against the employee. However, if the counseling is educational in nature or professional development counseling, the counseling session can be almost anywhere. As a

brigade commander at the National Training Center I would frequently take an officer on a walk around the Rotational Unit Field Maintenance Area (RUFMA). The RUFMA is a ten-acre concrete maintenance pad that can accommodate over 3000 combat vehicles and trucks needing maintenance or services to prepare the equipment for future use. The walks around the RUFMA could have easily been a walk around the production floor or a walk around the distribution center floor. The purpose of these walks was to have a one-on-one session with that officer and discuss different situations we came across and how the officer would improve on the action or operation. If this type of counseling is effective, the individual being counseled may not even realize that he or she was receiving a counseling session.

3. At this point it is necessary to differentiate between a formal counseling session and an informal session. A formal counseling session is the type that needs to be documented. This includes regulatory counseling sessions such as the quarterly sessions required by the Army. Formal counseling also includes any adverse counseling necessary to correct inappropriate or substandard performance. Informal counseling sessions are those one-on-one sessions designed to impart wisdom or build confidence on the part of the employee. Both forms of counseling are necessary to be a successful leader.

4. Action Plans/Improvement Plans. Perform and Counseling should result in a plan of improvement, actions to improve performance, or an agreed upon training plan.

Counseling Form (reproducible) PERFORMANCE COUNSELING CHECKLIST/RECORD

EMPLOYEE	FIRST-LINE SUPERVISOR
DIVISION/SECTION	
PAY PLAN, SERIES/GRADE RATING PERIOD	
PURPOSE. The primary purpose of counseling is to define organizational mission and values, discuss individual job expectations and performance, reinforce good performance/work-related behavior, correct problem performance/work-related behavior, and enhance the employee's ability to set and reach career goals. The best counseling is forward looking, concentrating on the future and what needs to be done better. Counseling should be timely. Counseling only at the end of the rating is too late since misunderstandings that impact performance and work-related behavior cannot be resolved in time for improvement before the next annual rating. RULES FOR COUNSELING. 1. Face-to-face counseling is highly recommended. 2. Initial counseling should be conducted within the first 30 days of a rating period and again at the midpoint of the rating period.	AFTER COUNSELING 1. Summarize key points of the counseling on the back of this form and initial in the block provided. You may attach additional pages. 2. Give the Employee the form to review/initial. 3. If the Employee provided written input, attach it to this form for future counseling sessions. 4. Give the Employee a copy and keep the original to use for the next counseling session.

INITIAL COUNSELING

PREPARATION

1. Schedule the counseling session and notify the Employee; suggest the Employee write down or be ready to discuss ideas about expectations and requirements.
2. Get a copy of the Employee's position description, rating chain, the counseling checklist, and a blank evaluation form.
3. Think how each Value and each Responsibility in Part V of the evaluation form applies.
4. Decide what you consider necessary for success in each Value/Responsibility. Be specific.
5. Make notes to help you with counseling.

COUNSELING

1. Discuss the position description. If the Employee has worked in the job before, ask if he/she believes the description is accurate.
2. Review the Employee's written input if he/she provides it.
3. Discuss what tasks and level of performance you expect for Success.
4. If you and the Employee have different views, discuss them until you both are clear on requirements. Even if the Employee disagrees, he/she must understand what you expect.
5. Ask the Employee about career goals and training needs.

SUBSEQUENT COUNSELING

PREPARATION

1. Schedule the counseling session with the Employee. Tell him/her to come prepared to discuss accomplishments and review requirements and effectiveness of any completed training.
2. Review notes from the last session.
3. Make notes to help focus when counseling.

COUNSELING

1. Discuss job requirements and areas of special emphasis and priorities that have changed or that are new. Ask the Employee if he/she is having problems and needs your help.
2. If the Employee gives written input, review it.
3. Tell how the Employee is doing. Give specific examples of observed actions/results. Discuss differences in your views. Offer assistance if needed. The goal is to help the Employee succeed.
4. Give examples of Excellence that occurred or could have occurred.

AFTER COUNSELING

1. Follow the same procedures for documenting, initialing, and dating as you did for the initial session.

Employee's Signature/Date _____

Supervisor's Signature/Date _____

Appendix 7

After Action Review Format

Training event/operation being observed:

Event:
Date/time:
Location of observation:
Observation (what did you see?):

Discussion (try to tie the discussion points to the task and the established standards for that event):

Conclusions:

Recommendations (what can be done better in the future to make this organization or section more effective? Be specific with your recommendations):

Index

Note: Italicized page numbers refer to tables and illustrations; italicized *n* refers to notes.